Reasoning with Democratic Values

ETHICAL PROBLEMS IN UNITED STATES HISTORY

Volume 2: 1877 to the Present

Reasoning
with Democratic Values

ETHICAL PROBLEMS
IN UNITED STATES HISTORY

Volume 2: 1877 to Present

Alan L. Lockwood
University of Wisconsin
Madison, Wisconsin

David E. Harris
Oakland Schools
Pontiac, Michigan

**TEACHERS
COLLEGE
PRESS**

Teachers College, Columbia University
New York and London

Published by Teachers College Press, 1234 Amsterdam Avenue, New York, N.Y. 10027

Library of Congress Cataloging in Publication Data

Lockwood, Alan L., 1941–
    Reasoning with democratic values.

    Includes bibliographies.
    Contents: v. 1. 1607–1876   —   v. 2. 1877 to the present.
    1. United States—History. 2. Decision-making (Ethics) [1. United States—History.
2. Decision making] 1. Harris, David E., 1945–   . II. Title.
E178.1.L82   1985   973   84-8597
ISBN 0-8077-6094-3 (v. 1)
ISBN 0-8077-6095-1 (v. 2)

Grateful acknowledgment is made for permission to reprint, in the selection "Stealing North", excerpts from pp. 128–129, 142–143, 159–160, 177–180, and p. 181 of BLACK BOY by Richard Wright (New York: Harper & Row, 1966). Copyright 1937, 1942, 1944, 1945 by Richard Wright.

Cover photo credits: Top left, middle, and bottom right courtesy of the Library of Congress ; top right courtesy of the Herbert Hoover Presidential Library ; bottom left courtesy of the Carter White House Photo Office Collection, Carter Presidential Materials Project, National Archives and Records Service .

Manufactured in the United States of America

21 20 19 18 17 16 15 14 13   19 18 17 16 15 14 13 12 11

Contents

Dear Students,

This book is to accompany your study of United States history. We have written true stories showing people making difficult decisions. These decisions involved such basic values as authority, equality, liberty, life, loyalty, promise-keeping, property, and truth. We invite you to follow the stories of these decisions and make judgments about them.

In this volume there are 28 stories. Each story brings you in contact with an ethical problem from our history. For example, you will observe as Illinois Governor John Peter Altgeld struggles with the case of the Haymarket anarchists. You will witness William Jennings Bryan take a stand on American entry into World War I. You will be a bystander as Michigan Governor Frank Murphy grapples with the General Motors sit-down strike. You will accompany Jewish refugees from Nazi Germany seeking admission into the United States. You will face President Dwight D. Eisenhower's dilemma about spying during the cold war. You will follow Marie Ragghianti as she decides whether or not to expose government corruption in Tennessee. You will trace President Jimmy Carter's long ordeal over American hostages in Iran. You will watch officials of the University of California defend their affirmative action plan for minority medical students.

Although many of these events took place long ago and all are now history, the values involved continue to influence our lives. We believe that citizens of today must often make decisions involving these values. That is why we have written this book.

Rational, intelligent citizens need to recognize value problems and think carefully about them. Therefore, we have presented you with questions and activities that, with your teacher's help, will allow you to do such thinking. We also think the stories will help you gain a deeper understanding of our nation's remarkable history.

We hope you find the stories interesting and our questions thought-provoking.

Alan L. Lockwood and David E. Harris

PART 1

Expansion and Reform
(1877-1918)

Reservations Not Accepted

CHIEF JOSEPH

(Courtesy of the Library of Congress)

Chief Joseph, Nez Perce

(Courtesy of the Library of Congress)

General Oliver O. Howard

Centuries before the arrival of whites, American Indian tribes roamed freely throughout what is now the northwestern part of the United States. Animals were hunted for meat. Other foods, such as roots and berries, were gathered from the land. Among the tribes in the area were the Palouse, the Yakima, the Spokan, the Wallawalla, and the Nez Perce.

When Lewis and Clark explored the area in 1805–1806, the Nez Perce was one of the largest tribes. According to one estimate, there were four to six thousand Nez Perce living in bands in the area where the borders of present-day Oregon, Washington, and Idaho meet.

Lewis and Clark, as well as other whites, reported that the Nez Perce were friendly and helpful. As more and more whites came to the area, however, conflicts developed. There were significant differences between white and American Indian ideas about religion, property, and law.

Christian missionaries came to the Northwest in the early 1800s. They believed it was their duty to convert the various tribes to Christianity. Often the missionaries failed to understand the importance of Indian religious beliefs, or looked upon them as being of little worth.

The Nez Perce, and other tribes, held strong religious views. In general their religions were related to nature and the spirits they believed influenced human and animal behavior, as well as the climate and the weather. The Indians' respect for the natural environment was partly a result of their religious beliefs. For example, each Nez Perce might have a personal guardian spirit or *Wyakim*. Each Wyakim was connected with some feature of the natural world.

Whites and Indians also differed in their ideas about property. For example, the whites believed that individuals could own a portion of land and buy or sell that property. Each Indian tribe lived and traveled on territories that traditionally were associated with that tribe. They did not believe, however, that the land was owned in the sense that it could be bought or sold.

Whites and Indians also held different ideas about what laws to obey. The whites followed the laws of the United States; the Indians were bound by traditional tribal authority.

The conflicts between whites and Indians often erupted into bloody battles. The Nez Perce were generally successful in avoiding violence. At times members of the tribe served as scouts for U.S. soldiers. Unfortunately, the Nez Perce's time of war was to come.

As the United States moved westward, it was its policy to place Indians on *reservations* (tracts of land on which Indians were required to live) in an effort to control the Native American population. When Isaac Stevens became governor of the Washington Territory, he set out to establish reservations for the various tribes in the Territory.

In 1855 Stevens met with the leaders of many tribes, and, after much debate, a treaty was established. According to the treaty, large areas of land were set aside for reservations. The government promised to provide money and make certain improvements on the land, and no whites were to be allowed on the reservations without permission of the tribes.

The treaty provisions were soon violated. White settlers often moved onto tribal lands. Gold was discovered in the area, and miners began to enter the reservation areas. There were occasional outbreaks of violence.

Because of the treaty violations, a new treaty meeting was held in 1863. The chiefs of the Nez Perce bands had a major disagreement. Some were willing to draw boundaries for a new reservation, others were unwilling. As a result, some Nez Perce tribes signed a new treaty establishing reservations and others refused to sign. Those who refused to sign returned to the lands they had inhabited after the treaty of 1855.

One group of Nez Perce, which had refused to sign the treaty, returned to their lands in the Wallowa Valley. When the chief of the band died in 1871, he told his son Joseph: "When I am gone, think of our country. . . . Always remember that your father never sold his country. You must stop your ears whenever you are asked to sign a treaty selling your home. . . . Never sell the bones of your father and mother." Joseph, holding his dying father's hand, said that he would protect the land with his life.

Young Chief Joseph, now in his early thirties, tried to live in peace with the white settlers in the area. He occasionally ate dinner with the settlers and played with their children. He would explain why the land traditionally belonged to the Nez Perce. As more and more white settlers came into the area, however, tension increased.

Government policy did not reduce the tension. In 1873, President Grant issued an order prohibiting whites from settling on the Nez Perce land in the Wallowa Valley. The order was ineffective partly because the boundaries of the Nez Perce land were not clearly established. Then, in 1875, the president revoked the 1873 order, opening the valley to white settlers. The president's decision was based on an incorrect report stating that Joseph and his group were willing to move onto the Nez Perce reservation.

Pressure to move tribes onto reservations continued. In some parts of the Northwest, nonreservation Indians fought battles with whites. Throughout the area, a fear and distrust of nonreservation tribes grew among whites.

Efforts were made to persuade the nonreservation Nez Perce to move onto the reservation. General Oliver O. Howard was military commander of the area. At first he opposed moving Chief Joseph's group. In 1875 he wrote to the War Department: "I think it is a great mistake to take from Joseph and his band of Nez Perce Indians that valley . . . possibly Congress can be induced to let these really peaceable Indians have this poor valley for their own." Howard's advice was not followed.

Relations between Joseph's band and neighboring whites reached a dangerous point. Two whites killed a friend of Chief Joseph's whom they accused of horse stealing. Joseph was particularly outraged when it seemed that the two whites were not going to be brought to trial. At one point he threatened to drive the white settlers out of the valley, and he demanded that the killers be turned over to the Nez Perce. Eventually the killers were brought to trial by white authorities, but they were not convicted.

Soon after this crisis, Howard and other government officials were ordered to place the Nez Perce on the reservation. A meeting was arranged in November 1876.

At the meeting, Chief Joseph made his position clear:

> The earth was my mother. . . . I could not consent to sever my affections from the land which bore me. I ask nothing of the President. I am able to take care of myself. I do not desire the Wallowa Valley as a reservation, for that would subject me to the will of another and make me dependent on him and subject to laws not of our own making. I am disposed to live peaceably.

General Howard and others argued that the U.S. government made the laws and that all people must follow them. According to Howard, the Nez Perce were denying the proper authority of the government. Joseph and the other chiefs were not persuaded, and the meeting ended.

The time for discussion was over. The government ordered Howard to move the Nez Perce onto the reservation. Violence was to be avoided, but force was to be used if necessary. As Howard later wrote, "In fact the time for loving persuasion had now gone by. Positive *instruction* had come, and *obedience* was required."

In May 1877, Howard again met with the nonreservation Nez Perce. It was an angry meeting. One chief challenged the general: "The Great Spirit made the world as it is and as He wanted it. . . . I do not see where you get your authority to say that we shall not live here as He placed us."

The argument continued and finally Howard announced: "I stand here for the President, and there is no spirit good or bad that will hinder me. My orders are plain, and will be executed. I hoped that the

Indians had good sense enough to make me their friend, and not their enemy."

Many of the Nez Perce were furious and wanted to begin a war. Chief Joseph was angry also, but he opposed war. He believed a war could be disastrous for his people. The U.S. Army had too many soldiers and weapons. After much discussion, the Nez Perce reluctantly agreed to move onto reservations.

General Howard wanted to be sure that the tribe would move as quickly as possible. He said the Nez Perce would have 30 days to move to the reservation. Then, it is reported, he gave a warning: "If you let the time run over one day, the soldiers will be there to drive you on the reservation, and all your cattle and horses outside of the reservation at that time will fall into the hands of the white men."

It would be difficult for the Nez Perce to reach the reservation lands within 30 days. They owned thousands of horses and many heads of cattle, and they would have to cross flooded rivers and rocky terrain. Nonetheless, Howard insisted upon the 30-day time limit. Frustrated, sad, and angry, the Nez Perce began their move to the reservation.

As they moved, a warlike spirit grew in some of the Nez Perce. Young warriors of Chief White Bird's band were especially agitated. Whites had made their lives difficult. One white had killed the father of Wahlitits, a young man of White Bird's band, two years earlier. The memory of his father's death fueled the flames of resentment in Wahlitits. One day a Nez Perce taunted Wahlitits: "If you are so brave, why don't you go kill the white man who killed your father?" Before he died, Wahlitits' father had told him not to seek revenge, but now Wahlitits could no longer restrain himself.

Wahlitits and two other young men rode out to seek revenge. They were unable to find the man believed to have killed Wahlitits' father, but they knew other whites in the area who had mistreated the Nez Perce. The young warriors attacked and killed a number of white settlers. The next day more whites were killed.

Although the killings had taken place without the consent of the tribal leaders, Chief Joseph and others were certain the entire tribe would be blamed. Hopes for peace faded, and the Nez Perce prepared for war.

On June 14, the 30-day deadline for reaching the reservation had passed, and General Howard heard about the killings of the whites. He ordered troops to pursue the Nez Perce. Howard was convinced that Chief Joseph was the war leader of the tribe. He was incorrect. Joseph's main responsibility was to oversee the protection of the women, children, and elderly. Other chiefs directed the war efforts.

The first battle was fought on June 17, 1877, and the Nez Perce were able to beat back the soldiers. The tribe then began a long series of maneuvers to avoid the troops. The plan that developed was to leave Idaho by crossing the mountains into Montana. Once in Montana, the Nez Perce hoped they could live in peace in the buffalo country. If not, they would cross the border into Canada as the Sioux had done after the defeat of Custer the previous year.

Peace did not await them. U.S. troops from the Montana side of the mountains surprised the Nez Perce at Big Hole on August 9. The Nez Perce suffered heavy losses including the death of many women and children. The troops were unable to capture the tribe, however, and the surviving Nez Perce moved on.

In the meantime, General Howard and his troops had made the difficult trek across the mountains and were about two days behind the Nez Perce. Public opinion began to turn against the former Union hero of the Civil War. Newspaper articles explained that Howard was moving too slowly; that he should have captured the Nez Perce by now. There were many fears that the Nez Perce would bring war against white settlers in Montana. General William Sherman, Howard's superior officer, heard the criticisms and fears. He ordered Howard to pursue the Nez Perce more vigorously: "That force of yours should pursue the Nez Perce to the death, lead where they may. . . . If you are tired, give the command to some young energetic officer."

Howard sent a reply to Sherman saying that the delay had been caused by the difficult march and the need to wait for supplies. He said that he and his troops would continue to chase the Nez Perce.

Grief-stricken from the casualties suffered at Big Hole, the Nez Perce continued to maneuver away from the troops. They moved through Yellowstone Park. On the way they encountered some tourists and killed them. The Nez Perce feared that the tourists would report their movements to Howard.

The tribe then turned northward toward Canada. Howard's forces were still two days behind, so the Nez Perce stopped to rest in a section near Bear Paw Mountains. For many of them it would be their final resting place.

General Howard had sent a message ahead to Colonel Nelson Miles. Miles commanded a group of soldiers who were in a position to head off the Nez Perce. In late September, Miles and his men discovered the location of the tribe.

A battle began on September 30. Miles was eager to capture the Nez Perce. If he could defeat them before Howard arrived, he would get all the credit for the victory and probably a promotion to general. If Howard arrived before the defeat, Howard, as the superior officer, would receive credit for capturing the Nez Perce.

On October 1, Miles sent out a flag of truce and said he wanted to meet with Chief Joseph. Miles told Joseph he was in an impossible situation and that he should surrender at once. Joseph disagreed and refused to surrender.

Fighting continued, and it began to look hopeless for the Nez Perce. Joseph and other leaders held a meeting. Chief White Bird wanted to attempt an escape to Canada; Joseph believed surrender would be best. They decided that each band could do as it chose.

When Howard and his troops arrived on October 4, Miles gave them a chilly reception. Howard assured Miles that he would receive full credit for the victory, and Miles quickly warmed up. Some of Howard's men were angry because they had suffered during the long march and believed they deserved credit. Nonetheless, the general had his way.

On October 5, Joseph was invited to surrender. Miles and Howard told the chief that if he surrendered, his people and their remaining horses and cattle would be returned to the reservation in Idaho. Joseph accepted the terms of surrender and said: "I am tired of fighting . . . little children are freezing to death. . . . Hear me, my chiefs, I am tired; my heart is sick and sad. From where the sun now stands, I will fight no more forever."

After Joseph's surrender, a number of Nez Perce led by White Bird escaped to Canada. Of the group that surrendered with Joseph, there were approximately four hundred of the over eight hundred Nez Perce that had started out together in June. During the course of their 1,700 mile trek, approximately one hundred and twenty men, women, and children had been killed. About one hundred and eighty whites had died.

The surrender terms promised by Miles and Howard were rejected by General Sherman and other higher authorities. Howard agreed with their decision. He said that because White Bird and his group had escaped after Joseph's surrender, the terms of agreement had been violated, and the promise no longer counted.

Miles pleaded with his superiors to honor the surrender promise. Sherman and others would not agree. They said it would be too dangerous to send the Nez Perce to the Northwest. Violence might begin again. Miles apologized to Chief Joseph: "You must not blame me. I have endeavored to keep my word, but the chief who is over me has given the order and I must obey it or resign. That would do you no good. Some officer would carry out the order."

The Nez Perce were taken to Kansas and then to Oklahoma. The climate and other conditions were different from the cool, dry mountain air to which the Nez Perce were accustomed. Many of them died of malaria and other diseases.

Chief Joseph continued to apply for better treatment, and finally public opinion began to shift in favor of the Nez Perce. In 1885, the government returned the Nez Perce to reservations in the Northwest. Some were settled in Idaho; others, including Chief Joseph, were sent to a reservation in Washington.

Joseph made repeated efforts to persuade the government to return his group to their homeland. His appeals were rejected. In 1904, the sad, old chief died on the reservation in Washington.

The major sources for this story were:

Beal, Merrill D. *I Will Fight No More Forever: Chief Joseph and the Nez Perce War.* New York: Ballantine Books, 1971.

Chalmers, Harvey, II. *The Last Stand of the Nez Perce: Destruction of a People.* New York: Twayne Publishers, 1962.

Howard, Oliver O. *Nez Perce Joseph.* Boston: Lee and Shepard Publishers, 1881.

Josephy, Alvin M., Jr. *The Nez Perce Indians and the Opening of the Northwest.* New Haven: Yale University Press, 1965.

Place, Marion T. *Retreat to the Bear Paw: The Story of the Nez Perce.* New York: Four Winds Press, 1969.

ACTIVITIES FOR "RESERVATIONS NOT ACCEPTED"

Write all answers on a separate sheet of paper.

Historical Understanding

Answer briefly:

1. Name three tribes that whites encountered when exploring the Northwest.

2. Identify the differences between white and Nez Perce ideas about religion, property, and authority.

3. Why did the United States government pursue a policy of placing American Indians on reservations?

4. What were the differences between President Grant's orders of 1873 and 1875?

Reviewing the Facts of the Case

Answer briefly:

1. What were the provisions of the 1855 treaty?

2. What was the major disagreement among Nez Perce during the 1863 treaty talks?

3. What did Joseph promise his dying father?

4. In what way did General Howard's opinion about placing the Nez Perce on reservations change from 1875 to 1877?

5. What orders did General Sherman send to General Howard as he pursued the Nez Perce?

6. To what surrender terms did Joseph agree? Why did General Sherman and other authorities refuse to honor the surrender terms?

7. What was the difference between Miles' and Howard's opinion about honoring the surrender promise?

Analyzing Ethical Issues

There are a number of incidents in this story in which people made decisions involving values. Among the values involved are the following:

LIBERTY: a value concerning what freedoms people should have and the limits that may be justifiably placed upon them

LIFE: a value concerning when, if ever, it is justifiable to threaten or take the life of another

PROPERTY: a value concerning what people should be allowed to own and how they should be allowed to use it

AUTHORITY: a value concerning what rules or people should be obeyed and the consequences for disobedience

PROMISE-KEEPING: a value concerning the nature of duties that arise when promises are made

For each of the incidents listed below, identify what value or values are involved and explain how they are involved. Use the example that follows as a guide.

President Grant's decision to open the Wallowa Valley to white settlers.

This involved the values of liberty and property. Liberty was involved because he was allowing whites the freedom to move into the area. Property was involved because he was deciding the Nez Perce did not have the right to own land there.

1. Wahlitits' decision to seek revenge for his father's death.

2. Howard's decision to follow orders in moving the Nez Perce onto a reservation.

3. Joseph's decision to surrender at Bear Paw.

4. The Nez Perce killing of tourists in Yellowstone Park.

5. General Sherman's decision to oppose moving the Nez Perce to the Northwest.

Expressing Your Reasoning

1. The Nez Perce disagreed with the white settlers over who had the right to the Wallowa lands. What is the best argument supporting the Nez Perce rights to the land? What is the best argument supporting the whites' right to the land? Which group should have had these rights? Explain the reasoning for your decision.

2. At the meeting in November 1876, Chief Joseph refused to move to a reservation. Should he have agreed to move to a reservation? Why or why not?

3. General Sherman overruled the surrender promise to Chief Joseph. Colonel Miles told Chief Joseph that he disagreed with Sherman's decision. Should Miles have resigned? Why or why not? Write a paragraph expressing your opinion.

4. *Seeking Additional Information.* In making decisions about such questions as those above, we often feel we need more information before we are satisfied with our judgments. Choose one of the above questions about which you would want more information than is presented in the story. What additional information would you like? Why would that information help you make a more satisfactory decision?

A Rare Medium

VICTORIA WOODHULL

(Engraving from a Matthew Brady Photograph. Courtesy of the Library of Congress)

Victoria Woodhull

In 1868 Victoria Claflin Woodhull, her parents, and the rest of her family moved to New York City. At the age of 30, Victoria had already led an exciting, though often strange and frustrating life. The coming years would hold more adventure than even she could imagine.

Victoria had a lively imagination, and, from as early as the age of three, seemed to possess unusual powers. She had visions and claimed to be able to speak with the spirits of the dead. People who claimed such powers were called mediums. Both Victoria and her younger sister Tennessee appeared to have such powers. It seemed they also had the ability to predict the future and perform miraculous healings. With their parents, the girls traveled throughout the midwest performing for amazed audiences.

Audiences were often amazed, but other people were often outraged. At one point it was claimed that cancer could be healed by the family's medicines and other treatments. Such claims by the girls' parents proved incorrect, and they were threatened with lawsuits or worse. It was necessary for the family to keep moving.

While still a little girl, Victoria said the vision of an ancient Greek told her: "You will know wealth and fame one day. You will live in a mansion . . . and you will become ruler of your people." In many ways that prediction would come true. There would be suffering as well.

At her parents' request, Victoria married Dr. Channing Woodhull. She was 15 at the time. A year later a son was born, and later a daughter. Sadly, the son was severely brain damaged. To make matters worse, her husband turned out to be an alcoholic. He and Victoria were soon divorced.

In St. Louis, soon after the Civil War, Victoria met Colonel James Blood. He was a respected, well-to-do man in the community. He also was a *spiritualist* (a person who believes mediums have special powers). Because of this, he was instantly attracted to Victoria. It is likely that he was attracted for other reasons as well, for Victoria was extraordinarily beautiful. The attraction was mutual and in a short time they were married. Colonel Blood began traveling with the family.

Victoria was an intelligent woman but had little formal education. James, on the other hand, was well educated and familiar with many social issues of the time. Through her discussions with him, Victoria learned much and was able to formulate her ideas more clearly.

During the nineteenth century many people wished to improve

society in various ways. Discussions of how to reform society were common. There were those who campaigned against alcohol. There were those who worked to improve the condition of newly freed slaves. There were those, often called "Utopians," who created model communities in which people attempted to create ideal societies. There were also those who struggled to gain equality for women—especially to obtain voting rights for women. Victoria supported the movement for woman's rights.

She also believed society would be improved if it followed what she considered to be two principles: telling the truth and permitting greater personal freedom.

It was her belief that too many people were untruthful. She was offended by those who would say things they did not believe just to gain public approval. In their private lives such people failed to "practice what they preached."

The second of what Woodhull called her principles was that of freedom. She believed that law and social custom placed too many restrictions on people—especially women. For Victoria, the tradition that men could do one thing and women another, in their personal behavior and in their careers, was an unnatural limitation on freedom.

Victoria's most controversial application of her ideas of freedom was to the relationship between men and women. She said the laws on marriage and divorce created "the slavery of the poor wife." Perhaps her most shocking proclamation occurred in an 1871 speech in which she said: "I have an inalienable, constitutional, and natural right to love whom I may, to love as long or as short a period as I can, to change that love every day if I please! And with that right neither you nor any law you can frame have any right to interfere." The wedding vow of "till death do us part" was not for her.

At the time of her arrival in New York, however, few people knew who she was or what she stood for. It was not long before Victoria and Tennessee were in the news.

Living in New York was Commodore Cornelius Vanderbilt, one of the richest men in the world. Vanderbilt had made his millions in the steamship business and in the New York Central Railroad. In his seventies, he was a spiritualist as well as a businessman. At that time, he meet the sisters and was struck by their beauty and their work as mediums.

Vanderbilt and the sisters became close friends. Tennessee seemed able to cure him of various ailments, and Victoria was the most ravishing medium he had ever met.

With Vanderbilt's financial aid and advice, the sisters decided to open a brokerage house on Wall Street. As brokers, Victoria and Tennessee gave advice on money matters and arranged for the purchase and sale of stocks and other financial instruments. When they opened their office in early 1870, there was widespread publicity. It was unheard of for women to be in such a business. The first female brokers fascinated some and offended others.

Vanderbilt's advice and the publicity soon made the business successful. Now that money was rolling in, Woodhull moved her large family into a huge, attractive house in one of the better neighborhoods in the city. The Greek spirit's prediction of wealth and fame was coming true.

With increasing publicity, the public began to hear about Victoria's ideas about freedom. Rumors of scandalous personal behavior began to circulate. Gossip increased after an incident at Delmonico's, one of the most prestigious restaurants in New York. One evening Victoria and Tennessee decided to dine at the restaurant. As the sisters knew, it was a policy of the finer eating places that women could not dine in the evening unless they were accompanied by men. The manager politely reminded the sisters of the policy. Instead of leaving, they called in the carriage driver who had brought them to the restaurant. The embarrassed cab man obeyed. It was reported that the three ordered tomato soup and then left.

Victoria was interested in more serious matters than tweaking the nose of respectability as she had done at Delmonico's. Her house became a meeting place for people with ideas about social reform. Virtually every night there were discussions with her husband and others about ways to change society for the better. All ideas were welcome, but Victoria became most interested in those dealing with woman's rights.

For years, leaders of the women's movement had fought for female equality with men. Victoria decided to enter politics. She announced herself a candidate for president of the United States!

The first woman broker would now be the first woman to run for president. James, Victoria, Tennessee, and others decided to publicize Victoria's candidacy by publishing a newspaper. Called *Woodhull and Claflin's Weekly*, the paper would print Victoria's ideas as well as articles by the social reform thinkers in her circle. The first issue appeared in May 1870. It was sent throughout the United States and had especially good circulation in New York City.

Victoria now considered herself a leader of the women's movement. More established leaders of the movement were not all pleased with Victoria, however. Many, such as Susan B. Anthony, feared that Woodhull's extreme ideas about freedom, and the scandalous gossip about her did more harm than good for woman's rights. Many of those who were initially cool toward Victoria were won over after she achieved another first.

Massachusetts Congressman Benjamin Butler had met Woodhull in New York and was impressed with her ability. He helped arrange for her to give testimony before the House Judiciary Committee early in 1871. She was the first woman ever to testify before a congressional committee. On the day she was to speak, the meeting room in Washington was crowded with men and women eager to hear and see the famed Victoria Woodhull.

Many feminist leaders, including Susan B. Anthony, were in the crowd. Tension was high as Victoria began her argument in favor of women's right to vote. She began speaking softly, but soon powerfully. The central point of her position was that the Fourteenth and Fifteenth Amendments had extended rights to blacks that should also be extended to women.

Woodhull had presented the argument with dignity and intelligence. The committee did not follow her recommendations, although that was no surprise; permitting a woman to address the committee was a breakthrough in itself. The feminist leaders in the audience were impressed. Soon thereafter, Victoria received a hero's welcome at a women's convention meeting in Washington. She was invited to address the convention and again made a strong impression. The woman of many firsts was now becoming famous as a leader of women.

Victoria had reached the peak of her popularity. She was invited to speak in many places and always attracted a large audience. Her reputation was still clouded by her convictions about complete personal freedom. Channing Woodhull, now addicted to morphine as well as alcohol, had appeared at her house seeking help. Victoria and James took him in and allowed him to live there. The news that Victoria's first and second husband lived in the same house with her added to the gossip about Victoria's free life-style.

In spite of her accomplishments, many people did not think highly of Woodhull. Some claimed she had used her rare beauty and charm to get men like Blood, Vanderbilt, and Butler to advance her career. These men had been of help to Woodhull, of course, but she was distressed by the attempts to discredit her own ability and integrity.

One of those intent upon demeaning Victoria was the famous novelist Harriet Beecher Stowe. Her book, *Uncle Tom's Cabin*, had been an international best-seller, and now she began publishing chapters of a new novel. One of the characters in the novel apparently was intended to represent Victoria Woodhull. Stowe made the character appear silly and frivolous. A newspaper published the chapters as a serial, and Woodhull was hurt at the thought of people throughout the nation laughing at her as each new chapter appeared.

Harriet's brother, Reverend Henry Ward Beecher, lived in Brooklyn. He was one of the most distinguished and respected men in the United States. Years before he had been a leader in the antislavery movement, and now he was a supporter of woman's rights. He was a minister at the Plymouth Church, and thousands of people attended his services. His sermons were published and sold throughout the nation. Many regarded him as an advocate for what was right and good.

Reverend Beecher believed women should have the right to vote, but he did not share the more revolutionary ideas of freedom and equality held by Woodhull and her group. He did not argue with her publicly, but he considered the unsavory parts of her reputation to be a hindrance to the women's movement. His sermons about women expressed the common belief that women should observe the highest moral code and strive to maintain good reputations. There were rumors, however, that his private life did not always conform to the high standards he preached.

Woodhull heard rumors that Beecher had been romantically involved with another man's wife. Prominent leaders of the women's movement also heard the rumors. If the rumors became public, they feared their cause would suffer, because Beecher was a respected spokesman for woman's rights.

In the meantime, Victoria's newspaper had been continuing with her efforts to tell the truth and fight hypocrisy. If the great minister had failed to practice what he preached, it would be a most startling episode of hypocrisy. Victoria did not publish the story at that time, however, for she had other things on her mind.

The brokerage business was failing; the family was becoming financially hard-pressed. In addition, attacks on her ideas and behavior continued. One editorial said that she was vain and immodest, a person "with whom respectable people should have as little to do as possible."

Some of the people attacking Woodhull were friends of Reverend Beecher. That they would attack her and cover up Beecher's supposed misdoings disgusted Woodhull. In one edition of the newspaper, Victoria said that she knew the names and circumstances of a scandal involving some respectable people. She said she might soon print the details. She had printed the names of lesser-known people, she argued, so why not print the names of the famous?

Woodhull sent a message to Beecher requesting that he introduce her at a meeting where she was going to give an important speech. She believed that if Beecher were on the same stage with her, her ideas would gain added respectability. Beecher did not wish to support her ideas. If he failed to appear with her, however, he feared she might print the scandalous rumors about him. Nonetheless, he refused her request.

In her speech, Victoria made one of her most dramatic arguments in favor of personal freedom and against the restraints of marriage. Victoria had never been more unpopular. She had been evicted from her large house, and other landlords refused to rent to her. They said other tenants would leave if the notorious Victoria Woodhull and family were in the same building. The brokerage business had failed, the newspaper had stopped publishing, and Victoria was virtually broke.

She decided to print the Beecher story. Somehow enough money was raised for a special edition of the *Weekly*. The story was published in the autumn of 1872. Victoria claimed her personal integrity required publication: "Was I not, in withholding the facts, and conniving at a putrid mass of seething falsehood and hypocrisy, in some sense a partaker in those crimes?" She apologized to Beecher as a private citizen, saying he had the right to privacy and freedom to do what he pleased as an individual. But, she said, she was printing the accusations because Beecher was a "representative man . . . a power in the world," and one who stood in the way of what she was trying to accomplish.

Word of the publication brought a rush to the newsstands, and the issues sold out quickly. Demand was so intense that one man said he sold his copy for forty dollars; others rented their copy for one dollar.

In 1875, the husband who believed he had been wronged by Beecher brought a lawsuit against him. The best lawyers were hired by both sides. Many people considered it one of the most sensational trials in the history of the United States, and daily reports were printed throughout the nation. The trial dragged on, and eventually the jury voted 9 to 3 in favor of Beecher. Although he had won the lawsuit, his reputation was permanently tainted.

A change had come over Victoria by this time. Apparently the only way she could raise money to support herself and those who depended on her was to give public lectures. She traveled through many parts of the nation giving lectures but was less successful than in the past. The crowds that once had flocked to hear her dramatic speeches were no longer interested in what she had to say.

Victoria Woodhull eventually left the United States and settled in England. She died there in 1927.

The major sources for this story were:

Johnston, Johanna. *Mrs. Satan: The Incredible Saga of Victoria C. Woodhull.* New York: G. P. Putnam's Sons, 1967.
Marberry, M. M. *Vicky: A Biography of Victoria C. Woodhull.* New York: Funk & Wagnalls, 1967.

ACTIVITIES FOR "A RARE MEDIUM"

Write all answers on a separate sheet of paper.

Historical Understanding

Answer briefly:

1. Identify three social reform movements during the nineteenth century.

2. What was guaranteed by the Fifteenth Amendment?

3. How did Cornelius Vanderbilt make his fortune?

Reviewing the Facts of the Case

Answer briefly:

1. What were Victoria's two general principles?

2. Victoria was the first woman to do a number of things. What were three of her firsts?

3. Why were some leaders of the women's movement opposed to Victoria?

4. How did both Harriet Beecher Stowe and Henry Ward Beecher show their disdain for Victoria Woodhull's ideas?

5. What reason did Woodhull give for printing the story about Beecher?

Analyzing Ethical Issues

There are a number of incidents in this story involving the following values:

EQUALITY: a value concerning whether people should be treated in the same way

LIBERTY: a value concerning what freedoms people should have and the limits that may be justifiably placed upon them

PROPERTY: a value concerning what people should be allowed to own and how they should be allowed to use it

TRUTH: a value concerning the expression, distortion, or withholding of accurate information

For each of the values above, write a sentence describing an incident from the story involving that value. For example:

Woodhull's decision to print the story about Beecher involved the value of truth.

Expressing Your Reasoning

1. Woodhull decided to print the story about Henry Ward Beecher. Should she have printed the story? Why or why not?

2. There are many arguments that could be made for or against printing the story. Evaluate each of the following arguments and decide whether you think it is a strong or weak point of view. Explain the reasons for your judgments.

   a. It was right to print the story because Woodhull's reputation had been attacked by many people, including Beecher's sister and his friends. By printing the story, she would be getting even.

b. It was wrong to print the story because Beecher was a respected leader and supporter of women's right to vote.

c. It was right to print the story because Victoria believed in truth-telling and exposing hypocrisy.

d. It was wrong to print the story because the charges against Beecher had not been proven.

e. It was right to print the story because Victoria was in financial trouble and needed to support her family.

f. It was wrong to print the story because it would embarrass the woman and her husband.

g. It was right to print the story because in a democracy people should be allowed to print whatever they believe is true.

h. It was wrong to print the story because Woodhull was criticizing Beecher for exercising the kind of personal freedom for which she had argued.

3. It was the policy of Delmonico's restaurant not to allow women to dine during the evening without a male escort. Should the owner of the restaurant have the right to make such a policy? Write a paragraph expressing your position.

4. *Seeking Additional Information.* In making decisions about such questions as those above, we often feel we need more information before we are satisfied with our judgments. Choose one of the above questions about which you would want more information than is presented in the story. What additional information would you like? Why would that information help you make a more satisfactory decision?

The Maine Magnetic Man

JAMES G. BLAINE

(State Historical Society of Wisconsin)

James G. Blaine

The decades following the Civil War were a turbulent time for the United States. Economically, there was rapid industrial growth, including expansion of railroads. Socially, increasing numbers of immigrants settled in U.S. cities. Politically, the Republican party, in power since Lincoln's election, tried to maintain its strength. Internal divisions and the reviving Democratic party threatened the Republicans.

James G. Blaine had a major involvement in these and other contemporary events. Although little known today, he was one of the most famous and controversial men of his time. He had a powerful impact on the nation.

Blaine was born in 1830. After spending time as a teacher, he turned to politics. At the age of 24, he became editor and part owner of a newspaper in Augusta, Maine. That same year the Republican party was founded and Blaine was attracted to its policies. In his editorials, Blaine gave constant support to Lincoln and firmly opposed the actions of the Southern states. It was said that Blaine grew up with the Republican party. He was a loyal Republican throughout his life.

In 1858, the young editor was elected to the Maine legislature. At the outbreak of the Civil War, he wrote articles urging young men to volunteer for the Union army. For himself, however, James chose not to carry a musket. He was selected to fight with Augusta's quota of Union soldiers, but hired another man as his substitute, which, at that time, was a legal procedure. Later in his life some critics questioned Blaine's patriotism. They asked why he had not joined the army after urging others to do so.

Although he was not a soldier, Blaine worked hard for the Union cause. As a popular and leading politician in the state, he used his influence to see that the troops received proper supplies, and he helped raise money to support the war. He also visited hospitals and made efforts to see that proper medical attention and treatment were given the wounded.

James G. Blaine was a man of great personal charm and ability. He was a loving husband and father. His intelligence was impressive. People were amazed by his ability to remember names and faces as well as by his knowledge of history and politics. He was one of the finest public speakers of his time. James was so attractive a personality that a friend called him "the magnetic man." He said: "I defy anyone,

Republican or Democrat, to be in his company half-an-hour and go away from him anything less than a personal friend."

There were people, however, who found it easy to resist Blaine's magnetic attraction. One was the powerful New York Republican, Roscoe Conkling. Conkling was a leading force in the Republican party and had many devoted followers. He was elected to Congress in 1858. Five years later, Maine sent Blaine to Washington as a representative.

Blaine and Conkling had different personalities and could not get along with one another. A seemingly minor incident made the two congressmen enemies for life.

In 1866, Blaine was supporting a bill to make permanent a military office known as the Provost Marshal's Bureau. Conkling opposed the bill because he did not think the office was necessary, and because he despised the man who was likely to head the bureau. Debate between the two men became nasty, and personal insults were exchanged. Blaine said Conkling strutted like a "turkey-gobbler." Their personal feud became increasingly bittter and, although they were both Republicans, they were never able to work together. Years later, when Conkling was asked to support Blaine in the 1884 presidential election, he replied sharply: "No, thank you, I don't engage in criminal practice."

In 1869, Blaine was elected Speaker of the House of Representatives, one of the most important positions in the Congress. He was regarded by most as a very effective leader of the House. Many people began talking of him as an ideal candidate for president.

The presidential election year of 1876 was an important one for the Republican party. President Grant was finishing his second term in office and would not run again. During his time as president, there had been a number of scandals associated with the Republican party. Men had been accused of taking bribes and stealing tax money. The Republicans needed a candidate with a reputation for honesty if they were to defeat the strengthened Democratic party. Perhaps James G. Blaine could carry the day.

Blaine's chances for the presidential nomination were damaged when he was accused of corruption. According to the charges, Blaine was said to have used his power as Speaker of the House to help the Little Rock and Fort Smith Railroad obtain land in Arkansas. He was also accused of using his influence to sell bonds of the railroad, for which he supposedly received a generous amount of money. James denied all of the charges, but a congressional committee began an investigation.

As the investigation began, it was learned that a man named Mulligan had letters written by Blaine concerning his dealings with the railroad. Mulligan had been the aide of businessmen to whom Blaine had been writing and thus had been able to obtain the letters. Mulligan did not like Blaine and believed that, if published, the letters would establish Blaine's guilt.

In the spring of 1876, Mulligan came to Washington to testify before the investigating committee. He brought the letters with him. When Blaine learned that Mulligan was in the city, he arranged a meeting with him. At the meeting, Blaine persuaded Mulligan to hand over the letters. He said he wanted to look them over. According to Mulligan, Blaine promised to return the letters. They were never returned.

The investigating committee wanted to see the letters, but Blaine would not permit it. He said the letters were his own private correspondence, and no one had a right to see them except himself and the man to whom he had written them. Blaine argued that protecting his privacy did not mean he was guilty. To the committee he said:

> Would any gentleman stand up here and tell me that he is willing and ready to have his private correspondence scanned over and made public for the last eight or ten years? Does it imply guilt? Does it imply wrong-doing? Does it imply any sense of weakness that a man will protect his private correspondence? No, sir; it is the first instinct to do it, and it is the last outrage upon any man to violate it.

Blaine would not permit the letters to be made public, but he said he would read them to the committee, and he did just that early in June. It is difficult to tell if he read entire letters or selected parts of them that he was willing to make public. The reading indicated that he had some involvement with the railroad but not that it was illegal or improper. The investigation was eventually dropped. To this day historians are uncertain as to the exact nature of Blaine's involvement with the railroad.

One Sunday soon after the investigation, James collapsed after returning from church. His friends said the pressures of defending himself had weakened him and he had suffered from a sunstroke.

Critics said he was faking in order to get public sympathy. Either way, Blaine was back on his feet in two days and paying careful attention to the Republican convention in Cincinnati.

Blaine clearly was a leading candidate for the 1876 presidential nomination. The man who nominated Blaine at the convention called him a hero, "a plumed knight," and a man of honesty and ability. After the speech, the convention erupted with cheers for Blaine. There were many other candidates. On the first ballot Blaine had a large lead, but not a majority. In later ballots, Rutherford B. Hayes gained strength and defeated Blaine, 384 to 351.

Blaine had failed to win the presidential nomination, but the Maine legislature unanimously elected him to the U.S. Senate. His senatorial career began in 1877.

Senator Blaine became concerned about racial conflict between whites and Chinese in California. A treaty with China in 1868 permitted Chinese immigration to the United States. Tens of thousands of Chinese were brought into the country by employers to build railroads. White workers often resented the Chinese, because they were willing to work for low wages and their manners and customs seemed strange to whites.

In 1877 California was suffering from an economic depression. Jobs were scarce, and white hostility toward the Chinese was peaking. Violent confrontations were frequent. Whites began to demand that Chinese immigration be stopped. A white labor leader in San Francisco ended his speeches with the phrase: "And whatever happens, the Chinese must go."

James was sympathetic to the problems of the white workers. He actively supported a Chinese Exclusion Act that would prohibit further Chinese immigration. Cheap Chinese labor, he said, was leading to too much unemployment among whites. He also said that an end to Chinese immigration would help restore law and order in California. The House and Senate passed the act, but it was vetoed by President Hayes.

The president argued that the treaty with China should not be broken by the United States. New negotiations with China would have to be opened up if the treaty were to be changed. Hayes' veto stood.

As the presidential election of 1880 approached, the Republican party was divided. One group was called the *Stalwarts*. Led by

Roscoe Conkling, Blaine's old enemy, the Stalwarts supported Grant for a third term as president. Another group, called the *Half-Breeds*, believed that a man should not be president for three terms. The Half-Breeds opposed Grant and supported Blaine. A third group was called the *Mugwumps*. This group favored civil reform. Mugwumps argued that people should receive government jobs on the basis of their ability and not as rewards from the politicians they supported. Winning politicians typically gave jobs to their supporters. This practice is known as patronage, and it helped politicians maintain their power. Both Grant and Blaine did not favor big changes in the patronage system. The Mugwumps opposed both men.

Neither Grant nor Blaine could get a majority of votes at the nominating convention. To break the deadlock, delegates began switching their votes to James A. Garfield. During the convention, some delegates urged Conkling to support Blaine. Conkling did not like Garfield, but he despised Blaine and refused to support him. Blaine probably would have won the nomination if Conkling had given his support.

Conkling was politically powerful and a stirring public speaker. Garfield was convinced that he would need Conkling's support to win the election. Conkling seemed reluctant to help, but the two men met in New York City in August 1880. Garfield reportedly promised that Conkling would have major control over patronage in New York State, and that he would appoint Conkling's friend Morton as secretary of the treasury.

Conkling agreed to support Garfield. He gave up thousands of dollars that he would have earned practicing law, and went out to campaign for Garfield. Conkling worked hard in Ohio, Indiana, and New York. In the election, Garfield carried those states and won the presidency.

Garfield's first appointment angered Conkling. Garfield appointed his friend James G. Blaine as the Secretary of State. Garfield often sought Blaine's advice, and Blaine was happy to give it. He urged Garfield not to reward the Conkling branch of the party. He told Garfield to avoid open war with the Conkling group, but to be clever and sly. He said the Conkling group would never be loyal to Garfield and "they must have their throats cut with a feather."

The way to cut Conkling's throat was to deny him patronage. Garfield decided not to appoint Morton to the treasury, and appointed one of Conkling's political enemies to head the New York Customs-house. The Customshouse provided thousands of jobs, and Conkling would not be able to determine who would be rewarded with them.

Conkling was outraged. He met with Garfield and screamed at him for failing to live up to their agreement. Garfield denied there had been any agreement. Conkling resigned from the Senate and returned to his New York law practice. He may have hoped that New York would show its support of him by re-electing him to the Senate, but it was not to be. He was not returned and his power was broken.

President Garfield's life ended in tragedy. On July 2, 1881, he was shot by an assassin. He held on to life for a number of months, but finally died in September.

James's career was not over. In 1884, he finally received the Republican nomination for president but lost the election to Grover Cleveland. During the campaign, Blaine's enemies found more Mulligan letters and published them in a newspaper. Some believed that Roscoe Conkling had some role in getting the letters published. Whether he did or not, he was probably pleased to see Blaine in trouble again. The letters did not reveal much of Blaine's railroad involvement, but they reminded the public of possible involvement in shady dealings. Their publication contributed to Blaine's election defeat.

James G. Blaine did not run for the presidency again, but he continued his involvement in politics. He served as secretary of state again under Harrison, and devoted much of his time to writing history. He died in January 1893.

The major sources for this story were:

Jordan, David M. *Roscoe Conkling of New York*. Ithaca, N.Y.: Cornell University Press, 1971.
Muzzey, David S. *James G. Blaine: A Political Idol of Other Days*. New York: Dodd, Mead & Company, 1934.
Peskin, Allan. *Garfield*. Kent, Ohio: Kent State University Press, 1978.
Stanwood, Edward. *James Gillespie Blaine*. Reprint of 1905 edition of *American Statesmen*, vol. 34. New York: AMS Press, 1972.

ACTIVITIES FOR "THE MAINE MAGNETIC MAN"

Write all answers on a separate sheet of paper.

Historical Understanding

Answer briefly:

1. Identify one economic, social, and political characteristic of the United States during the period 1865–1885.

2. Why was the Republican party expecting difficulty in winning the election of 1876?

3. Why did the presence of Chinese immigrants in California lead to tensions during the 1870s?

4. Identify three competing groups in the Republican party in 1880. How did the groups differ from one another?

Reviewing the Facts of the Case

Answer briefly:

1. Why was James G. Blaine called "the magnetic man"?

2. Who was Roscoe Conkling? Why did he and Blaine become enemies?

3. What were the Mulligan letters? How did they affect Blaine's political career?

4. What was Blaine's opinion about Chinese immigration?

5. It is believed Garfield made a promise to Conkling. What was the promise?

Analyzing Ethical Issues

There is agreement about the answer to some questions. For other questions there is disagreement or uncertainty about the answers. We call these questions issues. Issues can be categorized as factual or ethical. A factual issue asks whether something is true or false, accurate or inaccurate. An ethical issue asks whether something is right or wrong, fair or unfair. Factual issues ask what *is*; ethical issues ask what *ought to be*. For example:

Did Garfield promise patronage to Conkling? *Factual.*

Should winning politicians be allowed to reward their supporters with government jobs? *Ethical.*

For each of the following questions, decide whether the issue is factual or ethical.

1. Should James G. Blaine have fought with the Union Army?

2. Was Blaine wrong in helping the railroad?

3. Did the Mulligan letters prove Blaine had done something wrong?

4. Did the Mulligan letters keep Blaine from winning the presidency?

5. What caused Blaine to faint in 1876?

6. Would passage of the Chinese Exclusion Act have restored law and order in California?

7. Was it wrong for Conkling to refuse to help Blaine in the 1884 election?

8. Should Garfield have rewarded Conkling for his help in the 1880 election?

Expressing Your Reasoning

1. After receiving the letters from Mulligan, Blaine refused to return them or to make their contents public. Was Blaine justified in withholding the letters? Why or why not?

2. In the 1870s some people wanted to stop Chinese immigration. What would have been the best argument for stopping immigration? What would be the best argument for allowing it to continue? Should it have been stopped? Why or why not?

3. When he was a newspaper editor, Blaine urged men to join the Union Army. When he was selected to fight, he hired a man to be his substitute. Should Blaine have joined the Union Army? Write a paragraph expressing your position.

4. *Seeking Additional Information.* In making decisions about questions such as those above, we often feel we need more information before we are satisfied with our judgments. Choose one of the above questions about which you would want more information than is presented in the story. What additional information would you like? Why would that information help you make a more satisfactory decision?

A Simple Act of Justice

JOHN PETER ALTGELD

(Courtesy of Chicago Historical Society [ICHi 09402])

John Peter Altgeld

In the spring of 1848, a young couple named Altgeld came to Ohio from a tiny province in Germany. With them they brought their infant son, John Peter. After a series of crop failures in Germany, the Altgelds had joined a stream of impoverished German peasants who made the voyage to the United States in search of a better life.

Poverty followed the Altgelds to Ohio. Their farm had a huge mortgage. The land was poor. Eight more children were born to the couple in rapid succession. Young Pete, the eldest child and the only one not born in the United States, toiled from dawn to dark in the fields. After dark he did chores. When there was no work for him on the family farm, he was hired out to the neighbors. The boy became work-weary and dulled. By age 12 he had spent only three terms in school.

Childhood for Pete was harsh in many ways. He had a slight harelip, which impaired his speech. His nose was large, his legs short, and his jaw heavy. His hair was awkward and grew straight up in a stubble. These features, combined with a heavy German accent, made Pete the object of scorn and ridicule from the other children.

To make matters worse, Pete's father was extremely strict. The father believed that "to spare the rod spoiled the child." Often he beat Pete with a harness strap in the barn. The abuse left a lasting impression on the boy. He remembered what it meant to be mistreated.

Pete grew up during a time when many Americans began to resent foreigners. The *Know-Nothings*, a secret political organization hostile to immigrants, gained strength. This group wanted those of foreign birth, especially Catholics, to have no part in government. When Pete was nine, in nearby Louisville and Cincinnati, the Know-Nothings brought violence against foreigners. When asked about attacks on foreigners, a member of the secret society would reply, "I know nothing," hence the name of their group.

The conditions of his childhood left Pete Altgeld with a strong desire to rise in the world. What seemed to be his first opportunity came with the Civil War. During his teens, Pete watched as Union troops drilled in Mansfield, Ohio. Inspired by the uniforms, drums, and flags, Pete marched off with an Ohio volunteer infantry unit in 1864. He gave all but $10 of his $100 enlistment bonus to his father. One lasting effect of his war experience was a case of "Chicahominy fever," which was to plague him all through his life.

When Altgeld was released from the army, he returned to Ohio. But life on the farm would not be the same for him. He had seen something of the world beyond rural Ohio, and new ambitions had been awakened. He announced that he was going to enroll in high school at Mansfield. His father objected strongly. He wanted his son working in the fields to help pay the mortgage, not wasting time with books. If the boy insisted on going to school, he would receive no money, food, or clothes from his father.

That fall Altgeld spurned his father and took a room with two other students above a carpenter shop in town. He scraped rent and some food money together by running errands and clearing outhouses after school. His mother managed once in a while to secretly bring him baskets containing potatoes, cabbages, meat, butter, and eggs. Clothing, however, remained a problem.

One evening a neighboring farmer found Altgeld walking about Mansfield in a dejected mood. His clothes were ragged and he needed new ones. The neighbor took Altgeld to a store and fitted him with a suit and overcoat. That night Altgeld sneaked into his father's barn and transferred to the neighbor's barn enough wheat to pay for the clothes.

During the period that Altgeld went to school, teachers were not required to be college educated. Altgeld's immediate ambition was to become a schoolteacher. It seemed the best way to get away from the drudgery of the farm. At age 19, he applied for and received a teaching certificate. He was hired to teach in a small Ohio town called Woodville.

At the Woodville school there was a pretty teacher named Emma Ford who caught Altgeld's eye. Emma was a rich girl. Her family lived in a large brick home on a fine farm. Pete fell in love with her. Emma responded with interest, but her family looked down upon Pete. They thought him an odd-looking boy and called him "that little Dutchman from down in the hills." When the romance became serious, Emma's father put his foot down. The girl was told to stop seeing Pete. His feelings were deeply hurt.

Rejection by the Ford family, his father's bitterness, and the narrowness of small town life led Altgeld to strike out in search of a new place. In the spring of 1869, now 21 years old, he quit his teaching job and headed west.

By moving westward, Altgeld joined the flow of an American tide.

From thousands of villages and farms, youths like Altgeld were making the same journey. Some were lured by the Homestead Act passed under Lincoln. It promised free government land in the West to those who would settle it. Others were drawn west to build the way for the "iron horse," just then chugging its way across the continent.

Altgeld was among those who wielded picks and shovels as a section hand on the railroad. Laying track in Arkansas and Kansas, he was paid $3.50 a day, an enormous wage for the time. Under the broiling southwestern sun, however, the fever came back to him. He collapsed on the job and was hospitalized. It was doubtful whether he would ever recover. By the time he did, his savings had all been spent for hospital bills. Too weak to work, he drifted north. He walked a hundred miles, through open prairies, on bare feet, the sickness coming and going. His tramping came to an end in the little town of Savannah, Missouri. There a kind farmer took him in.

In Savannah, Pete first worked as a farm hand; then he taught school. He made friends with the leading lawyer of the district, read law at night, and began his own practice in 1871. The next year Altgeld was appointed city attorney. Gone was the awkward immigrant youth called Altgeld. There had now arrived an attorney at law, a public official—J. P. Altgeld, Esq. More confident now, Altgeld became interested in politics.

By this time, the Granger movement was popular in the rural areas of the United States. Farmers of the West were suffering from the financial collapse of 1873. Credit tightened and mortgages were foreclosed. Western farmers blamed politicians and financiers from "the East" for their plight. Reaching for a weapon, the farmers transformed their old social associations called *granges* into political groups. Their slogans were: "Drive out the rascals in both parties! Down with the railroads! Down with monopolists!" Altgeld watched this movement very closely.

Missouri was one of the strongest Granger states in the country. The Granger farmers near Savannah organized a political party, the People's party, and nominated Altgeld for county prosecutor. During the campaign he dazzled farmers with his speeches against huge corporations. He said that farmers had been "ground down under the heel of monopoly." Altgeld proved himself as a campaigner for public office. At the age of 26, he was elected by county farmers to be their public prosecutor.

Ohio now seemed far behind him, but still he was not satisfied. The scope of his dreams was expanding. In 1875 he suddenly resigned as prosecuting attorney, sold his office furnishings and library, and took a train to Chicago.

Four years had passed since its "Great Fire," and Chicago was an impatient city. It squirmed restlessly on the shore of Lake Michigan. Perhaps the most American city of the time, it reflected the strains of industrial growth. The commercial East and the agricultural West met there and clashed. Major industries were mushrooming in Chicago: railroad cars, farm machines, meat packing plants, lumber yards, and granaries. The captains of industry were in Chicago, but so were throngs of laborers just beginning to organize against them. Both native Americans and a flood of immigrants inhabited the booming city. Chicago was a place attuned to the ambitions of the young lawyer from Missouri. He was fired by the same quest for success that drove the feverish metropolis.

It was hard work for a young unknown lawyer to build up a practice in the big city. Because he could not afford to pay rent for an apartment, he slept in his small office downtown. Within a year, however, Altgeld was making a good living.

That summer he felt confident enough to visit Ohio and claim his old flame, Emma Ford, as his bride. This time he was not rebuffed and the two were married. Theirs was a happy marriage. Emma, cultured and dignified, could have had a career of her own in music or literature. She chose instead to devote herself to her husband's ambitions. Being Emma's husband helped Pete to feel even less like a country bumpkin and more like a gentleman.

It was in real estate that Altgeld figured out a way to win a share of Chicago's growing wealth for himself. With $500 saved, he made his first real estate investment. In an amazingly few years he became a well-to-do builder. In one year alone he erected five blocks of buildings costing over one-half of a million dollars.

During these years there was a tragedy in the life of the Altgelds. A son was born to the couple, but he died immediately afterward. Childless, Altgeld invested himself in a political career more keenly than he might have otherwise.

He ran for Congress as a Democrat in 1884 but lost. Despite his defeat, he made a strong showing at the polls. At the next election he ran for judge of the Cook County Superior Court. With the backing of the Democratic party and the support of the laboring immigrants of the city, he won the election.

About this time, Judge Altgeld wrote a little book entitled *Our Penal Machinery and Its Victims.* The main theme of the book was Altgeld's belief that society ought to get at the causes of crime rather than simply punish the wrongdoers. In the book he pointed out that most of those arrested were poor young people without much opportunity. Once arrested, their circumstances became even worse. Altgeld deplored brutal treatment of prisoners. "Remember," he wrote, "brutal treatment brutalizes and thus prepares for crime."

The judge's book recommended several reforms. For example, it suggested that prison inmates be allowed to work for wages outside the prison. After reading the book, officials of the National Prison Reform Association invited Judge Altgeld to address their 1885 convention in Detroit. His speech was well received. The book also made a profound impression on a young Ohio lawyer named Clarence Darrow. After reading it, he moved to Chicago, became Altgeld's friend, and soared to the top of his profession.

While Judge Altgeld was rising to prominence, other foreigners in Chicago did not fare so well. Many had flocked to the "Windy City" for jobs in its meat packing plants, railroad yards, and factories. For every job available, however, there were two workers waiting to take it.

Those who were hired became dissatisfied with their low wages and long hours. Many bonded together to form unions. The unions demanded that employers bargain with them. On behalf of their members they demanded higher pay, safer working conditions, and a workday reduced from twelve or ten hours to eight.

Employers, including George Pullman, Cyrus McCormick, Marshall Field, Phillip Armour, and others, refused to recognize the unions or comply with their demands. Strikers were fired and replaced by *scabs* (workers who take strikers' jobs). Union organizers were put on *blacklists* (a list of people not to hire, circulated among employers). During strikes, Chicago police often overstepped the law by clubbing or shooting protesting strikers. Because of an epidemic of strikes and street violence, Chicago became known in the 1870s as the nation's most radical city.

During the next decade, storm clouds of labor trouble continued to gather over the city. Labor leaders were branded "foreign agitators," "European scum," "extremists," and worse by Chicago newspapers.

Some labor organizers, especially those who called themselves anarchists, made wild statements. For example, in 1885 the anarchist Lucy Parsons said: "Let every dirty, lousy tramp arm himself with a revolver or knife and lay in wait on the steps of the palaces of the rich and stab or shoot the owners as they come out. Let us kill them without mercy, and let it be a war of extermination and without pity."

The anarchists were the most extreme of the labor groups. Anarchy held that all forms of government were evil and unnecessary. They sought liberty unrestricted by laws. Business and social affairs could be handled by free agreement and cooperation among voluntary groups. Farms and factories could be owned in common. The anarchists hated wealthy *capitalists* (those who owned big businesses). Influenced by those trying to overthrow the czar in Russia, some anarchists urged violence and terrorism to destroy the power of the state.

The hatred and violence in Chicago made the city an overheated pressure cooker. An explosion threatened. The spark that set one off was an incident at McCormick's reaper works where a strike was in progress. On May 3, 1886, a clash occurred between union followers and McCormick scabs. Police riot squads rushed to the scene and were taunted by the crowd. The officers responded with nightsticks and bullets. Two rioters were shot to death.

To protest the incident at McCormick's, August Spies, editor of an anarchist paper, called a mass meeting at Haymarket Square for the following night. A small crowd showed up and peacefully listened to speeches by anarchist leaders. The crowd dwindled as a thunderstorm started.

Suddenly, armed police appeared and ordered the crowd to disperse. At that moment, from somewhere on the edge of the crowd, a round sputtering object hurtled through the air and landed near the first rank of police. It exploded with a flash, instantly killing one officer and fatally wounding six others. The police, first stunned and then enraged, closed ranks and charged. They fired their revolvers into the fleeing crowd. Scores of civilians and police were injured by bullets.

Hysteria followed the bombing at Haymarket Square. It was widely believed that the anarchists had launched their long threatened revolution. Other acts of violence were expected to follow. In a frantic search for the bomb-thrower, Chicago police jailed more than two hundred known radicals, most of whom had not been at the Haymarket meeting. The bomb-thrower was never found.

Eight of the men arrested were charged with murder. Only two of the men, August Spies and Samuel Fielden, were at the scene when the bomb exploded. Following a sensational trial, all eight men were found guilty. Joseph E. Gary, the judge in the case, sentenced seven to death by hanging. The eighth, Oscar Neebe, was sentenced to fifteen years in prison.

Most Americans believed that justice had been done. Even though none of the accused had thrown the bomb, they were all outspoken anarchists. The Illinois Supreme Court upheld the convictions. The U.S. Supreme Court voted not to review the case.

During the months after the trial, two men begged for mercy. Their death sentences were reduced to life imprisonment. The others refused to ask for mercy. One killed himself in his cell with a dynamite charge. After speaking last words of defiance, four of the anarchists were hanged from the gallows built for them in the courtyard of the county jail. Three men remained in the Illinois State Penitentiary.

All during the Haymarket drama, Judge Altgeld kept silent. His eyes were set on his political future. His highest ambition was to become a U.S. senator from Illinois. If the Constitution had not barred those born outside the country from becoming president, Altgeld would have made the presidency his goal.

After the Haymarket convictions, a labor leader and close friend of the judge asked him to speak out against the executions. Altgeld refused. He said, "If I talked now as radical as I feel, I could not be where I am. I want to do something, not just make a speech. . . . I want power, to get hold of the handle that controls things. When I do I will give it a twist."

Power was soon to be his. In 1891 the Democrats of Illinois nominated Altgeld for governor. He campaigned hard in Chicago for the labor vote. In the prairie towns of southern Illinois, he spoke to farmers as he used to speak to the Grangers in Missouri. When an audience was mostly German, Altgeld delighted them by speaking in their native language. Illinois elected its first foreign-born governor. Altgeld was also the first Chicago resident to hold the office, and the first Democrat elected since the Civil War.

As governor, Altgeld wanted to be a "good government" reformer. He was a humanitarian whose heart ached over corruption and injustice. He planned to make reforms regarding labor disputes, child labor, prison conditions, taxes, public education, public ownership of utilities, factory safety, and other problems of the day. Always, too, there was in his mind the U.S. Senate. He believed that his greatest influence would be in a national forum—in Washington.

(Engraving from Frank Leslie's Illustrated News, November 19, 1887, p. 217. Courtesy of Chicago Historical Society [ICHi 03668])

The Law Vindicated—Four of the Chicago Anarchists Pay the Penalty of Their Crime

Sick with fever during the early months of his term, the governor accomplished little. He got well by summer only to find that he was being haunted by the matter of the imprisoned anarchists. Clarence Darrow and a few other friends came to the capital to urge the new governor to pardon the trio still in prison. To Darrow, Altgeld said, "If I conclude to pardon those men, it will not meet with the approval you expect . . . from that day I will be a dead man politically."

Tormented by the case of the anarchists, the governor finally had his secretary bring him the Haymarket trial transcripts. Late into the nights he studied more than eight thousand pages of testimony. His study of the record convinced him that the accused anarchists had not received a fair trial. He had three reasons for his conclusions: (1) the jury was prejudiced in favor of a conviction, (2) the judge was biased against the defendants, and (3) the accused were not proven guilty of the crime for which they were charged.

In June 1893, Governor Altgeld signed an order pardoning the three men and setting them free. While watching the governor sign the pardon message his secretary said, "The storm will break now." "Oh yes," replied Altgeld, "I was prepared for that. It was merely doing right. . . . No man has the right to allow his ambition to stand in the way of the performance of a simple act of justice."

The pardon triggered an explosion second only to the Haymarket bomb itself. Very few approved of the governor's action. Rarely had anyone been so fiercely attacked in the press. Local papers and those from across the country denounced Altgeld. In editorials he was called "Anarchist," "slimy demagogue," "apologist for murder," "foreigner," "a disgrace to our American Republic," and a great deal more. Typical was an editorial that appeared in the Chicago *Tribune:* "He has apparently not a drop of true American blood in his veins. He does not reason like an American, does not feel like one, and consequently does not behave like one."

Altgeld had committed political suicide. In 1896 he was defeated for a second term as governor, and he never held public office again.

The major sources for this story were:

Bernard, Harry. *Eagle Forgotten: The Life of John Peter Altgeld.* New York: Bobbs-Merrill, 1938.

Ginger, Ray. *Altgeld's America.* New York: Funk & Wagnalls, 1958.

Fast, Howard. *The American: A Middle Western Legend.* New York: Duell, Sloan and Pearce, 1946.

ACTIVITIES FOR "A SIMPLE ACT OF JUSTICE"

Write all answers on a separate sheet of paper.

Historical Understanding

Answer briefly:

1. Who were the *Know-Nothings*?

2. After the Civil War what were two factors that attracted easterners to the West?

3. Briefly describe the Granger movement.

4. What kind of a city was Chicago during the late nineteenth century?

5. Briefly describe the relationship between employers and Chicago's early labor unions.

6. What kind of society did the anarchists seek?

Reviewing the Facts of the Case

Answer briefly:

1. How did Altgeld pay back the neighboring farmer who bought him a new suit and overcoat?

2. Why did Altgeld leave Ohio?

3. What were three reforms Governor Altgeld planned for Illinois?

4. What happened at Haymarket Square?

5. What sentence was handed down by the judge in the Haymarket trial?

6. What were Altgeld's reasons for pardoning the anarchists?

Analyzing Ethical Issues

Considering punishment.   People may agree that someone ought to be punished, but their purposes for punishing may differ. Following are four commonly stated purposes for punishment:

Retribution: to pay someone back in return for a wrong that was done by that person; to get even

Disablement: to prevent someone from repeating a harmful action; to protect society from danger by rendering someone incapable of committing another offense

Deterrence: to prevent others from doing similar harm; to set an example for others

Rehabilitation: to prepare offenders for a constructive place in society; to teach good judgment to offenders so that they will regret their actions and choose to do them no more

Some arguments made about punishing those convicted of murder at Haymarket Square are presented below. Indicate the purpose for punishment that is implied in each of these arguments. For example:

Some of these anarchists must be killed in order to prevent a revolution.   *Deterrence.*

1. The right to life of the policemen killed was not respected by the murderers. Now they must forfeit their own lives.

2. Whether these anarchists are guilty or not, hanging them will restore calm in our city between employers and workers.

3. Executing these men is unnecessary. By putting them in prison for life we will be safe from their violent deeds.

4. Those who try to destroy the American way of life should not be allowed to enjoy it. Hang the revolutionaries.

5. Send the anarchists back where they came from. It is the only way to protect our society from their alien ideas.

6. What they need is education about democracy. If they were taught how our Constitution and laws work, they would learn respect for government authority. While in jail they must discover the errors of their ways.

Expressing Your Reasoning

1. Should Governor Altgeld have granted a pardon to the three imprisoned anarchists? Why or why not?

2. The governor's critics offered reasons against the granting of a pardon by Altgeld. Some are presented below. Which do you think is the best reason? Which is the worst? Explain your basis for evaluating these reasons.

   a. Altgeld could have become a great reformer in Illinois and then in the Senate. The nation needed him. By pardoning the anarchists, he denied the country his political leadership.

   b. It would have been better to "let sleeping dogs lie." Very few people wanted a pardon. Why stir things up and make trouble? Altgeld should have avoided conflict by keeping his silence.

   c. The Democratic party was seriously harmed by the pardon. Its nominees were widely defeated at the next election. The party had supported Altgeld, and he owed them allegiance in return. Party loyalty demanded that he not pardon the anarchists. He could have protected the Democrats from being labeled "the party of anarchy."

   d. By pardoning the anarchists Altgeld showed disrespect for our legal system. He publicly ridiculed the lower court decision that was upheld by the state supreme court. The governor, by his pardon, undermined confidence in American justice.

   e. It would have been better to allow the executions to take place even if the men were innocent. The executions would be a warning to those inclined toward lawless violence. Better for three anarchists to die than for many more citizens to be killed in street violence.

3. Some claim the Haymarket anarchists were punished for their beliefs and not their actions. Could it ever be right to punish someone for his or her beliefs? Express your position in writing.

4. *Seeking Additional Information.* In making decisions about questions such as those above, we often feel we need more information before we are satisfied with our judgments. Choose one of the above questions about which you would want more information than is presented in the story. What additional information would you like? Why would that information help you make a more satisfactory decision?

Throne Overthrown

HAWAIIAN REVOLUTION

(*Courtesy of the Library of Congress*)

Queen Liliuokalani Wearing the Order of Kalakaua
Photograph Signed for Josephus Daniels, Secretary of the Navy

In 1778, the British explorer Captain Cook discovered a beautiful group of islands in the Pacific Ocean. He named them the Sandwich Islands in honor of the Earl of Sandwich, an English nobleman. They are known today as the Hawaiian Islands.

In the 1820s, U.S. *missionaries* (those sent to do religious work in a foreign place) came to Hawaii. They established schools and churches and converted many natives to Christianity. They also created a written form of the spoken Hawaiian language. In addition, they taught native Hawaiians mechanical skills and U.S. agricultural practices.

The missionary influence extended to politics. At the time, Hawaii was a monarchy ruled by a king and a group of chiefs. Partly because of the missionary influence, formal laws were written against murder, theft, and other crimes. In the 1840s, a constitution was written, and courts and other governmental agencies were created. An American, William Lee, was named as the first chief justice of Hawaii.

Americans were not the only foreigners who had an impact on Hawaii. The location of the islands made them a convenient place for ships of many nations to stop for fresh water and other supplies. Honolulu, the capital of the islands, became a busy seaport.

Businessmen from England, Germany, the United States, and elsewhere came to the islands. Large scale agriculture, especially sugar cane, became an important feature of the economy. Workers from as far away as China and Portugal came to find jobs on the sugar plantations.

Foreign influence was good for the economy but had some harmful effects on the native Hawaiians. Contact with foreigners brought new diseases that the islanders had difficulty fighting off. By one estimate, there were about 300,000 islanders at the time of Captain Cook's arrival. By 1866 there were about 57,000 native Hawaiians. By 1890 there were only about 34,000 native Hawaiians among the over 90,000 people living in Hawaii.

The economic good times of the mid-century fell off in the 1870s. The United States had enacted *tariffs* (taxes on imports) to protect the sugar industry in the United States from foreign competition. Because of these tariffs, Hawaiian sugar growers had difficulty selling in the U.S. market, and their profits dwindled.

There were growing political difficulties as well. When the king died without naming a successor, the legislature met to select a new monarch. The legislature was following the rules set out in the constitution. They elected David Kalakaua king. Opponents of Kalakaua rioted. A mob attacked the legislature. The native police were politically divided and could not be counted on to control the rioters. The new king asked that U.S. troops on a warship in the harbor be brought ashore to restore peace. Over one hundred marines were brought ashore and the riot ended. Later about seventy British troops were landed to help maintain order.

At the request of business leaders, King Kalakaua arranged a reciprocity treaty with the United States in 1875. *Reciprocity* means exchange. According to the treaty, certain Hawaiian products such as sugar could be sold in the United States without a tariff. In exchange, U.S. products could be sold in Hawaii without a tariff. In addition, Hawaii had to agree not to make similar treaties with any other country. The treaty was to be in effect for seven years.

One reason the United States was willing to make the treaty was to counteract the influence of other nations in Hawaii. England and Germany, for example, had been acquiring colonies in the Pacific. The United States did not want foreign powers too close to its western shore. Also, there were many Americans living in Hawaii, and many of the sugar plantations were owned by Hawaiian-born Americans. The United States believed it had a special interest in Hawaii.

Business leaders in Hawaii were delighted with the treaty, and a new era of prosperity began. The leaders were not delighted with Kalakaua, however. They accused him of being high-handed, spendthrift, and corrupt. For example, if his cabinet officers disagreed with his ideas, he would dismiss them without the consent of the legislature. He frequently allowed the government to go into debt. He also allowed his closest personal advisor, Walter Gibson, to hold several governmental posts and to receive a salary for each one.

Business leaders were especially hostile toward Gibson. He coined the phrase "Hawaii for Hawaiians," and did as much as he could to stir antiforeign feelings among the native Hawaiians. In part through bribery and in part through appeals to Hawaiian nationalism, Kalakaua and Gibson were able to secure control of the government. In the election of 1880 and 1882, almost no whites were elected to the legislature. When those legislatures enacted laws that put the government into debt, the business leaders were infuriated. They paid virtually all of Hawaii's taxes but had little influence on how the money was spent.

In December 1886, a semisecret organization called the Hawaiian League was formed. About four hundred men, mostly planters and other businessmen, joined. The members pledged themselves to work to improve the government. The league publicized charges against the king, sent petitions asking for reform, and did whatever it could to express dissatisfaction with the king and Gibson.

The league also began obtaining weapons, and soon a revolutionary faction in the group began to argue for overthrowing the monarchy. Some members, including the respected lawyer Sanford Dole, resigned because they opposed violence.

By June 1887, the league believed it had enough strength to overthrow the king. When it was discovered that the king had taken bribes from men seeking a license to sell opium in Hawaii, the league took action.

On June 30, a mass public meeting was called. Resolutions were read and acclaimed by the crowd. Among the resolutions were demands that the king dismiss Gibson, return the bribery money, and promise not to interfere with the elections for the legislature.

Kalakaua recognized the explosive situation and hastily agreed to meet the demands. With the assistance of Sanford Dole, members of the league drew up a new constitution that dramatically reduced the king's powers.

Supporters of the king called the new constitution the Bayonet Constitution because it was brought into being by the threat of force. Many native Hawaiians resented what had happened and were distressed that their king had been so humiliated. In 1889, a group of them attempted to take over the government by force. Gunfire was exchanged, but the group was not powerful enough to succeed. American marines were again brought ashore to restore order.

When King Kalakaua died in January 1891, his sister Liliuokalani became queen. The 53-year-old monarch was an intelligent and talented woman. Many Americans were concerned, however, because the queen was a great admirer of the British monarchy. It was known that she had resented her brother's signing of the 1887 constitution. There were fears that she might refuse to take the necessary oath to support the constitution. The fears were unfounded, for the queen swore to uphold the constitution.

For some years, pro-American groups in Hawaii had hoped the United States would take over the Hawaiian Islands through a procedure known as *annexation* (incorporating territory into an existing country). In part their reasons were economic. The McKinley Tariff of 1890 eliminated the advantages Hawaiian sugar had in the U.S. market and caused a *depression* (a severe economic slump) in Hawaii. If Hawaii were annexed to the United States, the tariff would not apply to Hawaiian products. It was clear, however, that the queen opposed annexation.

In 1892, a small group of businessmen formed a secret organization called the Annexation Club. Members of the club wanted annexation to the United States. They were also opposed to the rule of the queen. It was rumored that the queen was planning to overturn the constitution of 1887 and to install a new one that would increase her royal powers. If she made such an attempt, the members of the club planned to take forceful action against her.

The leaders of the club were eager to know what policy the United States would follow if the queen were overthrown. They knew that John Stevens, the U.S. minister to Hawaii, was in favor of annexation, but they needed to know how officials in Washington would react.

One of the club's leaders went to Washington to determine the attitude of the U.S. government. President Harrison's message was: "If conditions in Hawaii compel you people to act as you have indicated and you come to Washington with an annexation proposition, you will find an exceedingly sympathetic administration here."

The queen took a number of actions that hardened the determination of her opponents. She wanted a lottery company to set up a form of gambling in the islands. The company would pay the government $500,000 a year for the privilege. The company had been expelled from the United States. If it became influential in Hawaii, it would probably be anti-American. In addition, the queen signed an opium license bill similar to the one that Kalakaua had supported. It was reported that legislators had been bribed for their support. When the queen signed the lottery bill, John Stevens was furious. He said it was an attack on the United States.

The club soon discovered that the queen was planning a new constitution. She had received petitions, mainly from native Hawaiians, asking for a constitution that would reduce foreign influence. In the constitution she prepared, foreigners would not be allowed to vote unless they became official citizens of Hawaii. There were other changes in the new constitution, and Sanford Dole estimated that if they were enacted, the owners of 90 percent of Hawaii's property would not be allowed to vote.

On January 14, 1893, the club met to decide what action to take. The members were convinced that John Stevens would call in U.S. marines to support a plan to take over the government.

Hearing of the opposition, the queen dropped her plans for a new constitution. Nonetheless, heavily armed U.S. marines landed in Honolulu and set up camp. Officially the troops were landed to protect American lives and property in case of violence. Unofficially, their landing symbolized support for the Annexation Club.

The queen's government objected, saying it could maintain order and did not require assistance. The objections were ignored.

The club told Sanford Dole of its plans and asked him to serve as leader of a new government when the queen was overthrown. Dole did not favor the queen's policies, but he wanted to install a new monarch whom he believed would be more reasonable. Nonetheless, he agreed to think about the offer. The following morning he agreed to serve.

On January 17, a nervous delegation from the club marched to the main government building. There were only a few clerks working in the building, and they turned it over to the delegation. From the steps of the building, a member of the delegation read a proclamation saying that the monarchy was overthrown and that a provisional government was now in charge. Soon some armed supporters of the new government took positions around the building. United States troops were not involved, although they were stationed nearby. Their presence may have persuaded the queen not to call on her military forces.

When the queen heard of the efforts to establish a new government, she asked John Stevens what he intended to do. He said that, as representative of the United States, he officially recognized the new government. Liliuokalani stepped down from the throne saying: "Now, to avoid any collision of armed forces and perhaps the loss of life, I do under this protest . . . yield my authority until such time as the Government of the United States shall . . . undo the action . . . and reinstate me in authority." She would not, however, officially recognize the authority of the provisional government.

As soon as the provisional government was established, a group was sent to Washington to negotiate a treaty annexing Hawaii to the United States. In the meantime, the queen was ordered to leave her palace and to lower the royal flag. With tears in her eyes she did both. Sanford Dole was not happy with the impolite treatment given the queen, but the deed was done.

In the United States, Grover Cleveland had defeated Benjamin Harrison for president in the 1892 election. Cleveland would not take office until March 1893, however, and Harrison was still president.

He agreed to an annexation treaty and sent it to the Senate for its approval.

The pros and cons of annexation created intense debate in the Senate. When Cleveland took office, he withdrew the treaty from the Senate. He had questioned the legality of Stevens' actions and believed more facts were needed. He sent a special commissioner, James Blount, to Hawaii to investigate.

In the meantime, the provisional government feared that the British or Japanese might attempt forcibly to restore the queen to power. The government asked Stevens to declare Hawaii under the protection of the United States. Stevens agreed and the U.S. flag was raised on February 1, 1893.

When Blount arrived in late March, he ordered that the flag be lowered and that the marines be returned to their ship. He then began his investigation. In July, Blount wrote his report. In it he said that the revolution could not have succeeded without the presence of U.S. marines. He said that Stevens was not justified in calling in troops or declaring a protectorate. In addition, he said the revolution was not supported by a majority of the Hawaiian people.

President Cleveland had a difficult decision to make. Military strategists generally approved of U.S. control over Hawaii. England and other powers had been colonizing in the Pacific. Hawaii was a key to the North Pacific, and the military leaders believed the United States would be in a hazardous position if a foreign nation got control of Hawaii.

In spite of arguments favoring annexation, Cleveland was persuaded by Blount's report that wrong had been done. He sent Albert Willis to Hawaii with instructions to tell the queen of his "sincere regret that the reprehensible conduct of the American minister and the unauthorized presence on land of a military force of the United States . . . had led to her downfall." He said she could "rely on the justice of this government to undo the flagrant wrong."

Willis was told that the queen must agree to pardon all of those who had been involved in the revolution. If she agreed, Willis was to return authority to the queen.

At first the queen refused to agree. She indicated that under Hawaiian law, the punishment for treason was death. She was told that Cleveland would not work on her behalf unless she agreed to the pardons. Finally she agreed.

After the queen's agreement, Willis requested that the provisional government turn over its authority to the queen. He asked the government: "Are you willing to abide by the decision of the President?"

Sanford Dole sent a lengthy reply to Willis. In it, he argued that the United States had previously recognized the authority of the provisional government. Dole said that he hoped for annexation to the United States sometime in the future, but, until then, the provisional government would remain in power.

After this reply, the provisional government placed sandbags around the government buildings, and prepared to defend itself in case of attack. No U.S. troops were called in. The president had ordered Willis to take no action if the provisional government refused to step down.

Cleveland decided he did not have legal authority to take further action. He turned the matter over to Congress, asking for advice. Congress debated but could not agree on further action. It was clear, however, that the United States would not use force to restore the queen to her throne.

The provisional government decided to place itself on a more permanent basis. A constitution, similar to that of the United States, was put into effect. On July 4, 1894, the Republic of Hawaii was declared. The July 4th date symbolized the government's hope for eventual annexation to the United States.

The hopes were finally fulfilled. William McKinley took office as president in 1897. The Spanish-American War persuaded many Americans of the strategic importance of Hawaii and, on July 6, 1898, the Senate approved a treaty of annexation. A monarch would never again rule Hawaii.

The major sources for this story were:

Dole, Sanford B. *Memoirs of the Hawaiian Revolution* (edited by Andrew Farrell). Honolulu: Advertiser, 1936.
Kuykendall, Ralph S., and Day, A. Grove. *Hawaii: A History.* New York: Prentice-Hall, 1948.
Liliuokalani. *Hawaii's Story by Hawaii's Queen.* Rutland, Vt.: Charles E. Tuttle, 1964.
Loomis, Albertine. *For Whom Are the Stars?* Honolulu: University of Hawaii Press, 1976.
Tate, Merze. *The United States and the Hawaiian Kingdom.* New Haven, Conn.: Yale University Press, 1965.

ACTIVITIES FOR "THRONE OVERTHROWN"

Write all answers on a separate sheet of paper.

Historical Understanding

Answer briefly:

1. Describe one social, one economic, and one political effect of foreign influence in Hawaii.

2. In addition to its natural beauty, why was Hawaii attractive to foreign nations?

3. How did the United States' tariffs affect the Hawaiian economy?

4. Why did Americans believe the United States had a special interest in Hawaii?

Reviewing the Facts of the Case

Answer briefly:

1. What was the Hawaiian League? Why did its members oppose King Kalakaua?

2. What was the Bayonet Constitution?

3. What were the provisions of the 1875 reciprocity treaty?

4. What was the Annexation Club? Why did its members oppose Queen Liliuokalani?

5. Who was John Stevens?

6. What did James Blount conclude as a result of his investigation?

7. What reason did Sanford Dole give for refusing to yield the authority of the provisional government to the queen?

Analyzing Ethical Issues

There is agreement about the answer to some questions. For other questions there is disagreement or uncertainty about the answer. We call these questions issues. Issues can be categorized as factual or ethical. A factual issue asks whether something is true or false, accurate or inaccurate. An ethical issue asks whether something is right or wrong, fair or unfair. Factual issues ask what *is*; ethical issues ask what *ought to be*. For example:

> How much influence did missionaries have in Hawaii? *Factual.*
>
> Was James Blount wrong in ordering the U.S. flag to be lowered? *Ethical.*

For each of the following questions, decide whether the issue is factual or ethical.

1. Did native Hawaiians benefit from the existence of sugar plantations?

2. Should Walter Gibson have been allowed to hold more than one government office?

3. Was Sanford Dole right in accepting the leadership of the provisional government?

4. Would the Hawaiian revolution have succeeded without the landing of U.S. troops?

5. Should Queen Liliuokalani have taken an oath to support the 1887 constitution?

6. Would passage of a lottery bill have made the Hawaiian government anti-American?

7. Was President Harrison right in supporting a treaty of annexation?

8. Would U.S. national security have been endangered if Hawaii had not been annexed?

Expressing Your Reasoning

1. When asked to do so, should Sanford Dole have returned authority to the queen? Why or why not?

2. Should the United States have annexed Hawaii? Why or why not? Explain your position.

3. One issue in Hawaii was who should be allowed to vote. Various criteria were discussed in deciding who should qualify for voting. Which of the following people should have been allowed to vote?

Give a reason for each of your judgments.
a. People under the age of 18.
b. People living in Hawaii for less than five years.
c. Those born in Hawaii.
d. People who owned no property.
e. People unable to read or write.

4. *Seeking Additional Information.* In making decisions about such questions as those above, we often feel we need more information before we are satisfied with our judgments. Choose one of the above questions about which you would want more information than is presented in the story. What additional information would you like? Why would that information help you make a more satisfactory decision?

Sinking Into War

WILLIAM JENNINGS BRYAN

(*State Historical Society of Wisconsin*)

William Jennings Bryan

Thousands cheered as the new president, Woodrow Wilson, finished his inaugural address on March 4, 1913. Then the crowds began to chant: "Bryan! Bryan! Bryan!" They wanted a speech from the new secretary of state, William Jennings Bryan, one of the most popular and dramatic orators of the time. The secretary was a bit embarrassed because the day belonged to the president. He was also flattered and said to his wife, Mary: "It is worth sixteen years of hard work to have devotion like this, isn't it?" Mary agreed.

William Jennings Bryan had been a leading figure in U.S. politics for more than 16 years. He was born in Illinois on March 19, 1860 and reared in a devoutly religious family. He soon became interested in politics and believed that he could apply his religious principles in the making of policy. He moved to Nebraska and was elected to Congress in 1890. He became a part of the *Populist* movement. Among other things, Populists believed that the influence of wealthy easterners should be reduced. Bryan's popularity was such that he was nominated for president three times by the Democrats, but was defeated in each election.

Bryan worked hard to elect Woodrow Wilson, who appointed him secretary of state. Before accepting the appointment, he asked the president to agree to two conditions. One was that Bryan not be expected to serve any alcoholic beverages at diplomatic dinners, where it was traditional to serve wine and other spirits. Bryan opposed drinking on principle and later in his life became an ardent *prohibitionist* (one who believed that alcohol should be outlawed). Wilson agreed that Bryan did not have to serve such drinks.

Bryan was also a *pacifist* (one who opposes war). In a 1909 speech he firmly argued: "When you believe war was the sum of all evils and that no good whatever can come from it, you should be true to that belief not only in times of peace but when war came." Bryan's second condition for accepting appointment as secretary of state was that Wilson be a strong advocate of world peace. Wilson said that he would, and Bryan accepted the appointment.

Bryan's high ideals quickly became a source of controversy. At his first diplomatic luncheon, grape juice was served instead of wine. There were many who supported Bryan's break with tradition, but many others pictured him as a ridiculous character. He was soon known as the "grape juice diplomat." Bryan stood by his beliefs and would not change.

Further controversy followed Bryan. For many years he had earned money giving speeches and he planned to continue now that he was secretary of state. He said his $12,000 salary was not enough to cover his personal expenses, which included generous donations to charities and churches. President Wilson did not object, but many others did. Critics said that Bryan was using his important position for personal gain. They said that he knew what his salary would be and should not have accepted the position if he felt the salary was not high enough. Bryan argued that he was speaking for good causes, and that he would be away from his office for only short periods of time. He continued his public speaking. The controversy died down as more significant events faced the nation.

Neither President Wilson nor Secretary Bryan had much experience in foreign affairs. After his election, Wilson said to Bryan that it would be unfortunate if they had to face many serious international problems. Wilson's fears became reality.

In Europe, tensions between the Triple Alliance (Germany, Austria-Hungary, and Italy) and the Triple Entente (England, France, and Russia) led to war in 1914. When war came, the alliances shifted somewhat. The Triple Entente plus Italy and a few other nations became known as the Allies. The Triple Alliance with Germany, Austria-Hungary, Bulgaria, and Turkey became known as the Central Powers. The war between the Allies and the Central Powers soon affected the United States.

In the United States, a day of prayers for peace was organized. In a speech on that day, Bryan said: "Most of the errors which man commits in international affairs arise from a failure to understand the fundamental truth—that moral principles are as binding upon nations as upon individuals. . . . 'Thou shalt not kill' applies to nations as well as to individuals." The pacifist Bryan was pleased that President Wilson said the United States would not take sides in the war. Wilson urged Americans to be neutral in both their words and actions.

As the war progressed, it became difficult for Americans to remain neutral. Two of the warring nations, England and Germany, took actions that violated traditional rules of war and the neutral rights of the United States.

One of the generally accepted rules of war was that the fighting should only be among the troops of each side. Civilians of the warring nations were not to be harmed unless it was unavoidable. Early in the war, England, with superior naval power, declared a blockade of Germany. England wanted to prevent Germany from obtaining military supplies. In addition, England tried to prevent food from going to Germany; food that would be used to feed the civilian population as well as soldiers. England even stopped neutral ships from sailing to neutral European ports, because supplies might be taken overland to Germany.

In carrying out its policy, England frequently stopped U.S. ships and took them into British ports where the cargoes were inspected and often detained. U.S. business leaders were outraged, as were many other Americans. The United States protested, but England continued stopping ships.

In retaliation against the British blockade, Germany declared a war zone around England. The Germans intended to use a modern weapon of war—the submarine. The German government warned all neutral nations to keep ships out of the war zone because they might be torpedoed by submarines. British ships often flew the flags of neutral countries such as the United States. England hoped to protect its ships by flying such flags. As a result, Germany said it would not be safe for neutral ships to travel in the war zone.

The United States sent a message to Germany. The message said that Germany should not violate the traditional rules of naval warfare. One of those rules required that ships be stopped and searched to determine if they were carrying supplies for an enemy. Another rule required that a ship's passengers and crew be given time to get into lifeboats before the ship was attacked.

The United States insisted in the message that Germany respect its neutrality. The U.S. government would hold Germany to a "strict accountability" on these matters and would "take any steps it might be necessary to take to safeguard American lives and property and to secure to American citizens the full enjoyment of their acknowledged rights on the high seas."

Finally, the message said that the United States was sending a protest to England over the use of the American flag on British ships. The message was signed by Secretary of State Bryan.

The German government responded by saying it had no intention of harming neutrals. Because the British blockade was intended, in part, to starve innocent German civilians, Germany believed it was justified in striking back with submarines. Submarines could not be expected to follow traditional rules of naval warfare because they could easily be sunk if they showed themselves on the surface. Germany reminded the United States that it had given a general warning to neutrals to stay out of the war zone and that England continued to use neutral flags to disguise its ships.

The United States remained angry at England's violation of neutral rights. The most severe tensions, however, developed between Germany and the United States. On March 28, 1915, the British liner *Falaba* was torpedoed by a German submarine. One of the passengers who was killed was a U.S. citizen, an engineer on his way to a job in West Africa.

Details of the sinking were unclear, but an American life had been lost and the United States had to respond. Robert Lansing, Wilson's chief legal advisor, argued that Germany's actions were legally and morally indefensible. He said the United States should insist that Germany apologize for the sinking, punish the submarine commander, and pay money for the death of the American.

Bryan disagreed with Lansing. Germany had warned neutrals to stay off British ships, said Bryan, so the American knew he was taking a risk. He said the American was putting his private business interests above the interests of his country. He asked:

[Should a citizen,] by putting his business above his regard for his country, assume for his own advantage unnecessary risks and thus involve his country in international complications? Are the rights and obligations of citizenship so one-sided that the government which represents all the people must bring the whole population into difficulty because a citizen, instead of regarding his country's interests, thinks of himself and his interests?

President Wilson was impressed with the arguments of both Bryan and Lansing, but tended to side with Lansing. Wilson was disgusted with Germany's use of the submarine. He believed Americans had the right to travel where they wished, and the government should protect them when they legally acted on that right. He also noted that England violated U.S. property rights by detaining ships and cargoes; Germany, according to Wilson, was violating rights of life, a more fundamental human right.

Before a final decision was made on how to respond to the *Falaba* incident, a more disastrous event occurred. On May 1, 1915, the following notice was printed in New York newspapers:

Travellers intending to embark on the Atlantic voyage are reminded that a state of war exists between Germany and her allies and Great

Britain and her allies; that the zone of war includes the waters adjacent to the British Isles; that, in accordance with formal notice given by the Imperial German Government, vessels flying the flag of Great Britain, or any of her allies, are liable to destruction in those waters and that travellers sailing in the war zone on ships of Great Britain or her allies do so at their own risk.

The notice had been published by the German embassy. Next to the notice in many of the newspapers was another notice announcing the sailing of the huge British liner, the *Lusitania*. On May 7, 1915, the *Lusitania* was torpedoed without warning in the war zone around Great Britain. About 1,200 people died, including 128 Americans.

William Jennings Bryan, like most Americans, was shocked by the news of the sinking. He feared it would bring war. As he thought about the matter, one idea began nagging him. He said to his wife: "I wonder if that ship carried munitions of war! I will have to investigate that! If she did carry them, it puts a different face on the whole matter! England has been using our citizens to protect her ammunition!" In fact, the *Lusitania* had been carrying four to five thousand cases of ammunition.

Bryan was determined to maintain U.S. neutrality in the face of the *Lusitania* crisis. In discussion with Wilson and others, Bryan argued that Americans should have been prevented from traveling on British ships. He said Germany had a right to prevent ammunition from reaching England. He was angered because he said England was trying to use American citizens to protect shipments of war goods.

President Wilson listened to Bryan's arguments but was more influenced by other advisors. He continued to object to submarine warfare. He said the United States must protect its citizens when they were within their rights to travel on British passenger ships.

On May 13, the United States sent a note to Germany. The note included five major points: (1) submarines cannot be used in war "without an inevitable violation of many sacred principles of justice and humanity"; (2) American citizens had a right to expect their government to protect them in their rights to free travel; (3) the warning in the newspapers could not excuse the "unlawful and inhumane act" that had occurred; (4) Germany should recognize a wrong had been done, prevent it from happening again, and pay for the loss of life; and (5) the United States would not "omit any act necessary to the performance of its sacred duty of maintaining the rights of the United States and its citizens."

Bryan was not pleased with the harsh tone of the note but, as secretary of state, he signed it. Nonetheless, he feared that Germany might think the United States was siding with the Allies.

It is difficult to tell how many Americans supported Bryan's ideas. There was strong sentiment against entering the war. Many believed England had violated the rules of neutrality and hurt the U.S. economy by interfering with trade. There were also those who were outraged by German war methods, such as the use of poison gas and the killing of civilians in Belgium.

It was becoming more difficult for Americans to remain neutral. Former President Theodore Roosevelt believed Germany was acting immorally. He said the nation should take action against wrong-doing. "More and more I come to the view that in a really tremendous world struggle, with a great moral issue involved, neutrality does not serve righteousness; for to be neutral between right and wrong is to serve wrong."

Germany responded to the U.S. protest note by saying the *Lusitania* should not be considered an innocent passenger ship. Germany regretted the loss of American lives but said it was acting "in just self-defense when it seeks to protect the lives of its soldiers by destroying ammunition destined for the enemy." Finally, Germany said the ship's company was to blame for the deaths because it knew it was placing passengers in a dangerous situation.

The German response had failed to address the main points in the U.S. protest note. Nonetheless, Bryan renewed his struggle to preserve neutrality. To protect U.S. citizens he said the United States was "compelled by duty to do what we can to prevent our citizens incurring unnecessary risks." He wanted Wilson to agree that Americans should be prohibited from traveling on British ships, especially those that carried ammunition. He also said a law should be passed preventing passenger ships from carrying ammunition.

Wilson rejected Bryan's advice. For some time, the president had been more influenced by his friend Colonel House and by Robert Lansing. Wilson was convinced that Germany's actions were more severe violations of human rights than the British actions.

Wilson prepared a second protest note to Germany. In it he said the sinking of the *Lusitania* without warning was unacceptable. The German warning to stay away from the war zone could not justify a restriction of the rights of Americans legally to travel on the high seas. Wilson said that the "United States is contending for something much greater than mere rights of property or privileges of commerce. It is contending for nothing less high and sacred than the rights of humanity."

Bryan had reluctantly signed the first protest note to Germany. He believed he should not sign the second one. His advice had been rejected. To resign from office during a time of international crisis would be a dramatic act. If he resigned, he would probably be called a quitter, a coward, or worse.

As Bryan grappled with these thoughts and feelings, he sought advice from his friend William McAdoo, secretary of the treasury. McAdoo said: "I think you could not make a graver mistake than to resign. I am sure that the note that the President proposes to dispatch to Germany will not lead to war. But if you resign, you will create the impression that there is a difference of opinion in the Cabinet over this serious situation, and you will, I think, contribute to the very result which you are anxious to avoid." President Wilson, upon hearing of Bryan's possible resignation, shared McAdoo's concern and hoped that Bryan would remain in office.

McAdoo also told Bryan that resignation would end his political career. Nonetheless, after careful thought, Bryan responded: "I believe you are right: I think this will destroy me; but whether it does or not, I must do my duty according to my conscience, and if I am destroyed, it is, after all, merely the sacrifice that one must not hesitate to make to serve his God and country."

On June 9, 1915, it was announced that Bryan had resigned. People at home and abroad were startled. There were those who respected his decision and others who were angered. He was called disloyal and a "second Benedict Arnold." One newspaper editorial accused him of being selfish; another claimed it would be a long time before "Americans forgive the man who sulked and ran away when honor and patriotism should have kept him in his post."

Although Bryan was saddened by much of the public response to his resignation, he was determined to work for neutrality and peace. He began a campaign of public speaking, hoping to arouse public opinion against war. He said it would be wrong for the United States to send millions of young men to possible death because a hundred people died on a sinking ship.

Bryan publicly opposed President Wilson's policy of *preparedness*. Wilson wanted to strengthen the military in case of war. Bryan argued that building up the military violated the principle that

America should "influence others by example rather than by exciting fear."

Bryan's efforts for peace could not stop the flow of events that led to America's entrance into the war. Germany continued its policy of submarine warfare. Early in 1917 it was discovered that, in case the United States entered the war, Germany was planning an alliance with Mexico. If Mexico accepted the alliance, Germany would provide support for an invasion of the southwestern United States. The secret German offer, in what was called the Zimmerman note, had been intercepted by British intelligence agents, and sent to the United States.

President Wilson finally decided that the United States must enter the war. On April 2, 1917, he asked Congress to declare war. He said America must help make the world "safe for democracy." Wilson loved peace but, he said: "The right is more precious than peace." By a huge majority, Congress declared war.

Like many pacifists of the time, Bryan faced a dilemma. Now that his country had declared war, should he support the decision or continue to argue against it? Bryan chose to support the president and urged all Americans to unite in working to end the war quickly.

With America's help, the Allies were able to defeat the Central Powers. Over 100,000 Americans died in the war. A truce agreement with Germany was signed on November 11, 1918.

The major sources for this story were:

Coletta, Paolo E. *William Jennings Bryan, II: Progressive Politician and Moral Statesman, 1909–1915.* Lincoln: University of Nebraska Press, 1969.

Devlin, Patrick. *Too Proud to Fight: Woodrow Wilson's Neutrality.* New York: Oxford University Press, 1975.

Koenig, Louis W. *Bryan: A Political Biography of William Jennings Bryan.* New York: G. P. Putnam's Sons, 1971.

Scott, James B. *Diplomatic Correspondence Between the United States and Germany: August 1, 1914–April 6, 1917.* New York: Oxford University Press, 1918.

ACTIVITIES FOR "SINKING INTO WAR"

Write all answers on a separate sheet of paper.

Historical Understanding

Answer briefly:

1. What was one desire of the Populists?

2. In what ways did Germany and England violate America's neutral rights?

3. What was *preparedness*?

4. Identify two events that led the United States to enter World War I.

Reviewing the Facts of the Case

Answer briefly:

1. What two conditions did President Wilson have to agree to before William Jennings Bryan was willing to become secretary of state?

2. How did Bryan and Robert Lansing disagree over what the United States' response should be to the sinking of the *Falaba*?

3. In what ways did Wilson and Bryan disagree about what should be done after the sinking of the *Lusitania*?

4. What did the United States demand from Germany after the sinking of the *Lusitania*? How did Germany respond?

5. What advice did William McAdoo give Bryan about resignation?

6. What was one reason Bryan resigned?

Analyzing Ethical Issues

There are a number of times in this story where ethical decisions were made. An ethical decision is one in which the rights or well-being of others are involved. List three instances where ethical decisions were made in this story. For example one instance is:

Bryan's decision to resign as secretary of state was an ethical decision.

Expressing Your Reasoning

1. Was Bryan right or wrong to resign as secretary of state?

2. Bryan once said that moral principles should regulate the conduct of nations. A *principle* is a general rule for deciding right or wrong. Indicate whether each of the following activities was right or wrong, and state a principle in support of your judgment.
   a. The British effort to prevent food from reaching Germany.
   b. Germany's sinking of the *Lusitania*.
   c. England's efforts to protect its ships by flying the American flag.
   d. Wilson's refusal to prohibit U.S. citizens from traveling on British ships.
   e. America's policy of preparedness.

3. Former President Theodore Roosevelt said, "To be neutral between right and wrong is to serve wrong." Do you agree with Roosevelt? Why or why not? Write a paragraph stating your position.

4. *Seeking Additional Information.* In making decisions about such questions as those above, we often feel we need more information before we are satisfied with our judgments. Choose one of the above questions about which you would want more information than is presented in the story. What additional information would you like? Why would that information help you make a more satisfactory decision?

Speaking His Peace

EUGENE V. DEBS

(Brown Brothers)

Eugene V. Debs Clutching a Bouquet of Carnations at the
Atlanta Penitentiary After Being Notified of His Nomination
as Socialist Party Candidate for President, 1920

One day in May 1920, a small group of people waited in the warden's office of the Atlanta Federal Prison. A man wearing an inmate's uniform, convict number 9653, entered the room. He cordially greeted the group waiting for him. The group's spokesperson told the prisoner that he had been nominated for president. If he accepted the nomination, he would be the first person in U.S. history to run for president while in prison.

The prisoner's name was Eugene Victor Debs. Four times before, the Socialist party of the United States had nominated him for president. The last time had been in 1912. In the presidential election of that year, almost a million voters had cast their ballots for Debs. Now, eight years later, Debs again accepted the nomination of his party. How had it come to pass that a serious candidate for the presidency was conducting his campaign from a jail cell?

The answer to that question begins in Terre Haute, Indiana. It was in that town on the Wabash River that Eugene Debs was born in 1855. He was one of ten children. His mother and father had come to Terre Haute from France six years before Gene's birth. Gene's middle name, Victor, was taken from his father's literary hero, Victor Hugo. Young Gene loved reading that great French novelist's works. He was especially fond of the novel *Les Miserables*. His father read it to him as a child, and Gene read it time after time throughout his life. The book captured Gene's emotions. In it he learned of poverty and other forms of human misery.

When he was 14, Gene quit high school. He felt the lure of the railroad, which ran through his home town. He found his first job with the Vandalia line, cleaning grease from freight engines. Railroading soon lost some of its glamour, but Gene was proud to bring home a paycheck on Saturday night.

One winter night Gene was pressed into service as a night fireman on the train between Terre Haute and Indianapolis. In an open cab, biting cold on one side of him and furious heat on the other, Gene threw wood on the roaring flames. He wrote later that as a fireman he learned "of the ceaseless danger that lurks along the iron highway, the uncertainty of employment, scant wages and altogether trying lot of the workingman, so that from my very boyhood I was made to feel the wrongs of labor."

Along with thousands of others, Gene was laid off as a result of the economic depression known as the Panic of 1873. In search of work, he rode a freight to St. Louis. There, for the first time in his life, he encountered large-scale suffering. He saw homeless drunks in the city streets, wandering families, and people living in shacks near the Mississippi. It was misery he had known before only in the pages of Victor Hugo's *Les Miserables*. What he as an individual could do about such conditions, he did not know. He burned with a determination to do something.

In St. Louis, Gene was lucky enough to find a job as a railroad fireman. Railroading was a very hazardous trade. One of Gene's friends slipped under a locomotive and was killed in 1874. After that Gene's mother begged him to come home. He returned to Terre Haute and became a billing clerk for a wholesale grocery firm. Railroad life, however, continued to fascinate Gene. The wholesale grocery business did not.

One day an official of the Brotherhood of Locomotive Firemen came to Terre Haute to organize a local chapter of his union. Gene knew nothing of unions but decided to attend the evening meeting called by the visitor. What he learned about unions appealed to Gene. The idea of workers united to improve their wages, hours, and working conditions inspired him. After the meeting, he joined the new local chapter of the union, which was called Vigo Lodge.

A short time later, Gene took over as secretary of Vigo Lodge. He worked tirelessly for the local union. Soon he was asked to head the national union. He accepted, and the Brotherhood of Locomotive Firemen moved its national headquarters to Terre Haute. Under Debs' leadership the union flourished. New members flooded in.

A railroad strike in 1877 had almost wiped out the young railroad unions. During that strike, union workers had been replaced by *scabs* (workers who take strikers' jobs). Railroad management also used the *blacklist* (a list of workers not to hire, passed among employers) to fight the infant unions. *Yellow-dog contracts* (agreements that required a worker not to join a union while employed) became common as well.

Debs worked day and night to rebuild the railroad unions, but he moved cautiously. He believed that a spirit of compromise and fair play could settle labor difficulties. He was opposed to strikes. He traveled from state to state drumming up membership for his union.

Gene was unusually generous, and money had a way of slipping through his fingers. Railroad workers who came to him for food and money were never turned away. Once, during his travels, Debs heard that a railroad employee could not be promoted to conductor for lack of a watch, and he gave the man his own. At least once he gave away his overcoat. After he visited strikers' families, his pockets were empty of cash. People liked Gene Debs. His reputation for kindness became widespread.

Gradually, Debs altered his approach to trade unionism. He began to sympathize with bold tactics by unions. He changed his mind about strikes. Hurrying to the scene of a strike by engineers of the Chicago, Burlington, and Quincy Railroad, he said to the assembled strikers: "When . . . we come in contact with a narrow minded, bigoted and infamous railroad official, who will not accord us our common rights, then I am in favor of strikes."

Railroad workers could win their rights, Debs believed, only if they united. He urged the separate unions of switchmen, brakemen, firemen, engineers, and conductors to merge. An alliance of all railroad workers into one big industrial union became Debs' goal. He worked tirelessly to bring about a giant federation.

In 1889, Debs announced the formation of the American Railway Union (ARU). It took in all white railroad workers from engineer to engine wiper. Debs' proposal to include nonwhite workers was voted down. Within a year, despite the bitter opposition of the railroad owners, the union had a membership of 150,000. Debs was elected president of the ARU.

The new union's first test of strength came when it launched a strike in 1894 against James Hill's Great Northern Railroad. Wages on that line had been cut twice that year. When Hill announced a third cut from his office in St. Paul, Debs called a strike. Within days the Great Northern was brought to a standstill. Nine thousand railroad workers refused to work. Hill agreed to *arbitration* (turning the dispute over to an impartial third party for settlement).

The arbitrator granted the strikers most of their demands. It was the greatest union victory the nation had witnessed. The idea of one industrial union had succeeded. In only 18 days the ARU had triumphed.

Not two months after the victory of the ARU over the Great Northern Railroad, another strike was at hand. It was to go down in history as the Pullman Strike. At the time it was called "Debs' strike."

George M. Pullman was president of the Pullman Palace Car Company, which produced dining cars, chair cars, and the famous sleeping cars (often called Pullmans) for trains. Just outside Chicago, Pullman had built what he considered a model town where his workers were expected to live. Compared with the grimy factory neighborhoods of Chicago, the Pullman town was a pleasant place. It had neat brick homes, shaded streets, grassy yards, and a small lake beside which the Pullman band gave summer concerts.

It was a "company town." Pullman owned almost everything in it. One Pullman worker scornfully declared: "We are born in a Pullman house, fed from the Pullman shop, taught in the Pullman school, catechized in the Pullman church, and when we die we shall be buried in the Pullman cemetery and go to the Pullman hell." No union activity was tolerated in Pullman.

In 1893, a deep-seated economic depression settled upon the nation. During 1893–1894, Pullman discharged over a third of his workers and cut the wages of the others by up to one-half. Prices in the company stores and rents for company houses were not lowered. During the same year, *dividends* (a share of profits) paid to Pullman stockholders were increased.

It was a harsh Illinois winter that year, and suffering became unbearable in the town of Pullman. Children lacked the shoes and coats they needed to go to school. In some houses they were kept in bed to keep warm because there was no coal in the house. Families often had no food for dinner.

Pullman workers decided to become members of the ARU. In the spring of 1894 they rushed to join. Their first act was to call a strike. Debs visited the town and was appalled by what he saw. He said, "I believe a rich plunderer like Pullman is a greater felon than a poor thief."

Debs wanted to avoid a strike. He preferred arbitration, but Pullman refused to discuss the matter. "Nothing to arbitrate" was his reply.

Finally, Debs proposed a strike plan that was approved by the ARU. Beginning in June, switchmen refused to switch Pullman cars on to trains. The country was soon facing the most extensive strike it had yet known. More than one hundred thousand workers walked out. Twenty railroads in 27 states were shut down.

The ARU had intended to have a peaceful strike. Debs urged strikers to "commit no violence." Violence did flare up, however. Some railroad cars were overturned and burned. Debs claimed it was the work of thugs and riffraff and not ARU members. The strike soon captured newspaper headlines coast to coast.

President Cleveland, believing the situation critical, sent federal troops to Chicago. Some mob violence erupted after the troops arrived. The attorney general of the United States responded by obtaining an *injunction* (court order) in federal court. Union leaders were forbidden by the injunction to take part in or even discuss the strike.

If Debs obeyed the injunction, the strike would be broken and the power of his union destroyed. If he disregarded the injunction, he would be putting himself outside the law and would probably be jailed. He decided to ignore the court order. To the strikers he said, "Let every man stand pat. Troops cannot move trains." Debs was arrested, tried, and convicted for contempt of court. Troops took over the city. The strike was broken, the ARU crushed, and Debs was on his way to jail to serve a six-month sentence.

The actions of the president and the attorney general during the Pullman Strike led Debs, a Democrat, to lose faith in the political system. He believed that the two major parties were controlled by big businessmen like George Pullman. Labor unions, he became convinced while in jail, would have to look elsewhere for political support. The Debs who emerged from jail was a changed man. Socialist ideas were beginning to take hold of him.

In 1897, Debs, now the most famous labor leader in the United States, announced that he was a socialist. Several socialist ideas appealed to him. One of them was the notion of *class struggle*. According to this notion the upper and lower classes in society could not live in harmony. Rich *capitalists* (owners of businesses) would always enslave poor workers. Debs came to share these beliefs.

Another socialist idea that Debs adopted was "collective ownership of the means of production and distribution." To Debs this meant that factories, railroads, banks, and mines should be taken away from private owners and placed under government ownership. Debs believed further that interest and profit from all private investments should be eliminated.

Debs captured the hearts of the rank-and-file members of the Socialist party. As a speaker he was superb, one of the best orators of the day. Tall, gaunt, and modest, he reminded many of Lincoln. Party members made him their nominee for president. Among other measures, his party's platform supported free medical care, old-age insurance, woman suffrage, and an end to race discrimination and child labor.

During the presidential election campaigns, Debs drew enormous crowds across the country. Several times the crowds that came to hear him were larger than those drawn by the Republican or Democratic candidates when they had been in the same city. At each succeeding election, beginning in 1900, his vote total increased.

The bright hopes of U.S. socialists were soon clouded over by the First World War. The war split the Socialist party. Some socialists, moved by feelings of patriotism, supported U.S. loans and supplies for the Allies. Some even urged that the United States join the war against Germany. Other socialists, including Debs, were fiercely opposed to U.S. involvement in the war. Debs saw the war as an example of the class struggle. He believed that the capitalist class started the war out of greed for empire, but that it would be the working class that fought and died in the war. The workers of the world, Debs concluded, had no interest in the bloody conflict: "Let the capitalists go out and slaughter one another on the battlefields."

Meanwhile, the United States was moving toward war. The economy of the country became tied to the war effort of the Allies. Workers drew large salaries from munitions plants. Bankers granted huge war loans to the English and French governments. Farmers exported food to feed the soldiers of the Allied armies.

In February 1917, Germany resumed unrestricted submarine warfare against all shipping. In response, President Wilson broke off diplomatic relations with Germany. The United States was now poised on the brink of war. The inevitable soon occurred. A German submarine sank a U.S. ship, killing Americans, and the United States declared war in April.

President Wilson rallied all Americans to support the war effort. He said, "No government can afford to tolerate open dissent in wartime." A majority in Congress agreed with the president. On June 15, 1917, the Espionage Act was passed. This law made it a crime to speak or otherwise act against the war. All over the United States many who openly opposed the war were imprisoned.

Debs wondered publicly how a country fighting a war "to make the world safe for democracy" could deny the democratic right of freedom of speech to its citizens at home. He knew that it had become dangerous to criticize the war. Nonetheless, he was determined to defy the Espionage Act.

In Canton, Ohio, on June 16, 1918, Debs addressed the state convention of the Socialist party. A crowd of twelve hundred heard him deliver a vigorous antiwar speech. A government agent in the crowd frantically wrote down every word Debs spoke. During the speech, Debs made several statements condemning the war, including the following: "The master class has always declared the wars; the subject class has always fought the battles. The master class has had all to gain and nothing to lose, while the subject class has had nothing to gain and all to lose—especially their lives."

Two weeks later, Debs was arrested for violating the Espionage Act. The jury at his trial decided that Debs was guilty of trying to obstruct the draft. The judge imposed a sentence of ten years in prison. Debs' conviction was upheld by the U.S. Supreme Court.

From his cell in the Atlanta Penitentiary, Debs, then 64 years old and in failing health, conducted his fifth and final campaign for president. In the election, he rolled up his largest vote, but it amounted to only 3.5 percent of the total. One socialist leader accurately sensed that the campaign was "the last flicker of a dying candle."

World War I ended in November 1918. Peace brought a softening of American attitudes toward the war critics. Sentiment grew for release of those in prison for having protested the war. A group sympathetic to Debs recommended to President Wilson that Debs' sentence be shortened. After carefully reading the recommendation, President Wilson replied:

> I will never consent to the pardon of this man. While the flower of American youth was pouring out its blood . . . this man, Debs, stood behind the lines, sniping, attacking, and denouncing them. Before the war he had a perfect right to exercise his freedom of speech and to express his own opinion, but once the Congress of the United States declared war, silence on his part would have been the proper course to pursue. . . . This man was a traitor to his country and he will never be pardoned during my administration.

A new administration replaced Wilson's in 1921. The new president, Warren Harding, agreed to Debs' release on Christmas day of that year.

The major sources for this story were:

Ginger, Ray. *Bending Cross.* New Brunswick, N.J.: Rutgers University Press, 1949.
Morais, Herbert, and Cahn, William. *Gene Debs: The Story of a Fighting American.* New York: International Publishers, 1948.
Russell, Francis. "As Warm a Heart As Ever Beat." *American Heritage* 26(5): 77-81.

ACTIVITIES FOR "SPEAKING HIS PEACE"

Write all answers on a separate sheet of paper.

Historical Understanding

Answer briefly:

1. What was the American Railway Union?

2. What do the following terms mean: *scab, yellow-dog contract, injunction,* and *arbitration.*

3. How did the Pullman Strike come to an end?

4. What did socialists mean by *class struggle*?

5. How did American socialists differ regarding U.S. involvement in World War I?

Reviewing the Facts of the Case

Answer briefly:

1. How did George Pullman respond to the depression of 1893–1894?

2. Why was Debs jailed during the Pullman strike?

3. What was the purpose of the Espionage Act?

4. Why was Debs arrested after his speech in Canton, Ohio?

5. What reasons did President Wilson give for denying a pardon to Debs?

Analyzing Ethical Issues

Examining the value of property.   Property is a value concerning what people should be allowed to own and how they should be allowed to use it. We cannot be sure how Debs regarded all the various forms of private property in the United States. We know that he believed in public ownership of "the means of production" and that he opposed interest and profits from private investments. Given these beliefs, try to determine whether the following examples of private property would have been acceptable or unacceptable to Debs. Explain your thinking in a sentence or two. For example:

An investor's stock dividend.

Probably unacceptable to Debs, because dividends were profits he opposed.

1. A saver's interest on a bank account.
2. A union official's salary.
3. A person's wristwatch.
4. A farmer's land.
5. A couple's house.
6. A child's inheritance upon the death of a parent.
7. A fisherman's catch.
8. An inventor's patent.
9. A landlord's rental income.

Expressing Your Reasoning

1. Should Debs have made his Canton, Ohio, speech opposing United States involvement in World War I? Why or why not?

2. The First Amendment of the U.S. Constitution guarantees citizens the right to freedom of speech. Throughout the nation's history there has been debate over the limits of free speech. Answer with a "yes" or a "no" whether you think a citizen should have the right to:
   a. Criticize a public official.
   b. Make false statements that harm someone's reputation.
   c. Make true statements that damage someone's reputation.
   d. Falsely yell "fire" in a crowded theater.
   e. Use obscene language.
   f. Urge someone to act violently.
   g. Reveal the name of an American secret agent.
   h. Encourage someone to break a law.

3. Should President Wilson have pardoned Debs when World War I ended? Why or why not?

4. During the ARU strikes of both the Great Northern Railroad and the Pullman Company, scabs took the jobs of some strikers. Was it right of them to do this? Why or why not?

5. Some Pullman workers were laid off during the depression. Should the workers who kept their jobs have been willing to accept pay cuts in order to prevent the layoffs? State your position in a paragraph.

6. Debs said, "I believe a rich plunderer like Pullman is a greater felon than a poor thief." Perhaps Debs was thinking about his favorite novel, *Les Miserables*, when he spoke those words. The main character of the novel is a poor thief named Jean Valjean. The following is a summary of what happened to Valjean:

> Jean Valjean was an orphan in France who had been brought up by his older sister. When he was 25, his sister's husband died. Valjean took the father's place in supporting his sister's seven children.
>
> It was a wretched group. They were very poor and their lives were miserable. During the severe winter of 1795 the family had no bread whatsoever to eat. Valjean could find no work and the family was starving. One Sunday night Valjean broke the window of a local bakery and seized a loaf of bread. He was caught and arrested, his arm still bleeding. Valjean was found guilty of burglary and sentenced to five years in jail. His sentence was increased after several unsuccessful escape attempts. After 20 years he was finally released. Bitter from his years in prison Valjean committed two robberies. He stole candlesticks from a priest and money from a young boy.
>
> Soon after Valjean's release from prison, a stranger settled in a small village. In the village there was a workshop that produced bracelets. The stranger figured out an improved way to manufacture the bracelets. His idea had an enormous effect. It reduced the price of the bracelets, increased the wages of the workers, and improved the quality of the product. In less than three years, the inventor of the new process became rich. He built a large factory that offered a job to anyone who needed one. The stranger made a fortune for himself, and the whole region prospered.
>
> One night there was a fire in one of the village town houses. Risking his life, the stranger, now called Mr. Madeline, rushed into the fire and saved two children. Another time he risked getting crushed by using his own body to save the life of a man pinned

beneath a wagon. Mr. Madeline became very popular and was appointed mayor of the village.

The village police chief was jealous of Mr. Madeline. He also had a feeling that he knew Mr. Madeline from somewhere else, but he could not place him. Suddenly, one day it dawned on the police chief that Mr. Madeline was Jean Valjean, the convict wanted for two robberies committed years earlier. The police chief arrested Valjean and turned him over to the authorities.

  a. Should Valjean have stolen the bread from the bakery? Why or why not?
  b. The law required a five-year sentence for burglary. Was it right of the judge to sentence Valjean for stealing? Why or why not?
  c. Should the police chief have turned Valjean over to the authorities? Why or why not?

7. *Seeking Additional Information.* In making decisions about such questions as those above, we often feel we need more information before we are satisfied with our judgments. Choose one of the above questions about which you would want more information than is presented in the story. What additional information would you like? Why would that information help you make a more satisfactory decision?

PART 2

Normalcy and Depression (1919-1940)

Bay State Blues

BOSTON POLICE STRIKE

Massachusetts Governor Calvin Coolidge (left) and
Boston Police Commissioner Edwin Curtis Reviewing Police Parade,
October 15, 1920

In the early 1900s, the Boston police were ranked among the best law enforcement groups in the world. They had a long tradition of pride in their work and were courteous, honest, and courageous. The men in blue were respected and admired. According to one police official, the men understood that they did not have jobs as such, but rather special positions for which they had been selected.

Beneath the cool blue surface of police dignity, however, all was not well. Most of the police stations were old and deteriorating. Many were infested with mice and rats. The rodents chewed leather from policemen's helmets. For years the city government had done nothing to improve these old stations.

A policeman also worked long hours, seven days a week. Depending on his duty, an officer would work from 70 to 90 hours a week. Every two weeks he would have a day off but could not leave the city without permission. In addition, there were times he would be assigned to keep order during parades, a duty for which he received no pay.

Compared with other workers in the city, policemen's pay was low. For example, some shipyard workers earned from $75 to $100 a week while many policemen earned only $23. The starting salary for a policeman was $900 a year. After six years, he could reach the maximum of $1,400 a year. Carpenters and street car conductors earned approximately twice that amount. Policemen also had to pay about $200 a year for uniforms and equipment.

The policemen had not received raises in salary for many years. Frequently they asked for raises and improvements in working conditions but received neither. In 1918, Mayor Andrew Peters promised the policemen a substantial raise. When the raise was announced, the men were disgusted. Depending on their years of service, some men received $200, some $100, and many nothing at all.

Although most of the policemen liked their jobs, many found it hard to survive. The federal government said that $1,575 a year was the minimum necessary to support a family of five. Very few of the officers earned that much. Some had to borrow money to make ends meet.

One reason that policemen were having trouble surviving on their salaries was high *inflation* (a continuing rise in prices). During and after World War I, prices for food, housing, and other products and services went up and up. While living expenses increased dramatically, the policemen's salaries remained the same.

Throughout the nation workers were joining labor unions. As

members of unions, workers could bargain for higher wages and better working conditions. If necessary, they would go on strike until their demands were met. In Boston, the telephone operators and employees of the elevated railway had gone on strike and received better wages as a result. Policemen began talking of joining a union.

The idea of policemen joining a union and possibly going on strike caused many people to see red. Some opponents of labor unions feared that workers who joined them would be influenced by communists, who might try to overthrow the government by calling strikes and disrupting society. Little more than a year earlier, revolutions in Russia had brought communists to power. Communists often said that workers should organize and overthrow their governments.

There were other reasons some opposed a policemen's union. Police were supposed to maintain law and order. If they were members of a union, would they be willing to maintain order when other unions went on strike? Also, what would happen if the police went on strike? In Montreal, Canada, the police had gone on strike. In the absence of police enforcement, there was looting and violence before the strike was settled.

In Boston, one of those opposed to police unions was the commissioner of police, Edwin Curtis. Under Massachusetts law, the commissioner, appointed by the governor, was in charge of the Boston police. Although Boston taxpayers paid the expenses of the police department, their city's mayor had no legal authority over the operations of the department.

Commissioner Curtis knew that the police were talking of joining a union. In July 1919, he told his men he was not opposed to labor unions for most workers, but that he was opposed to police unions. He said police were sworn to protect law and order and might not perform their duties to the public if they were torn by loyalty to their union. He warned his men not to join a union.

In spite of Curtis' warning, a large majority of the police voted to form a union and become part of the American Federation of Labor (AFL). The AFL was a national organization of many labor unions. When he learned of the policemen's preferences, the commissioner issued a ruling. The rule was more than a warning; it said clearly that no policeman was to join the union.

Many of the policemen thought Curtis' action was extreme. They believed they could perform their duties while being members of a union. Labor leaders urged the governor, Calvin Coolidge, to remove

Curtis from office. Governor Coolidge replied: "Mr. Curtis is the Police Commissioner of Boston invested by law with the duty of conducting the office. I have no intention of removing him as long as he is Commissioner and am going to support him."

Curtis would not back down from his opposition to the union. In mid-August, after the policemen had elected union officers, Curtis called in eight union leaders. He asked them about their activities in the union, and reminded them of the rule against joining the union. On August 21, Curtis announced that charges of violating the rule would be brought against the eight men. He would make a decision as to their guilt and possible punishment in about one week.

Leaders of Boston's labor unions were angered at Curtis' action and believed he was trying to destroy the new police union. The leaders supported a policemen's union and said that all labor unions in Boston would go on strike if the eight policemen were punished.

More and more it seemed likely there would be a police strike. A former superintendent of police, possibly with Curtis' consent, began recruiting volunteers to protect the city in case of a police strike.

The eight policemen were brought to trial before Commissioner Curtis. Their lawyers said membership in the AFL would not prevent them from performing their duties. Besides, the lawyers said, the commissioner would have a legal right to take action against any policeman who failed to perform his duty. One of the lawyers said that Curtis' rule was "the greatest invasion of a man's personal freedom of action I have ever known."

Curtis listened to the arguments and said he would announce his judgment in a few days. In the meantime, more policemen were charged with violating the rule.

The commissioner and the union had taken strong, opposing stands. Mayor Peters hoped a compromise could be worked out. He appointed a citizens' committee, headed by a businessman named James Storrow, to investigate the situation and to make recommendations.

There was not much time to find a compromise. Curtis' decision would soon be made. Some union leaders said the police would go on strike if the officers charged with violating the rule were dismissed or even officially scolded by the commissioner.

The Storrow Committee hurriedly came up with a compromise plan. Three of the recommendations in the plan were: (1) the Boston police should withdraw from the AFL and create their own local organization; (2) wages and working conditions should be investigated by a citizens' committee that would recommend changes; and (3) no member of the police force should be punished for past involvement with the AFL.

Mayor Peters approved the compromise plan, and sent it to Curtis urging him to accept the plan. Curtis would not approve the plan. He told the mayor that he would carry out his legal duty to decide how the suspended officers would be treated.

On Monday, September 8, Curtis announced that the 19 men would be suspended from duty. Later the policemen began taking a strike vote. A vast majority of the men voted to strike. Over one thousand policemen eventually went on strike; a few hundred remained on the job.

Storrow and Peters met with Governor Coolidge before the strike began. If the governor would support the compromise plan, it seemed likely that Commissioner Curtis would have to go along with it or lose his job. Coolidge refused. Curtis had told him the strike would not amount to much, and the Governor stood by the commissioner's prediction.

Sadly for Boston, the strike amounted to a great deal—a great deal of violence. It did not take long for law and order to break down. On Tuesday, as the striking policemen left their stations, illegal dice games began in the streets and parks. Some of those who won money were attacked and robbed. Mobs moved through the streets. As the dark, rainy night fell, an ugly mood came over some of the crowd. Some striking policemen were hit with clumps of mud, eggs, and bottles. A few policemen were assaulted by men they had arrested in the past.

The toughest mobs gathered in Scollay Square and in South Boston. Store windows were broken, and gangs stole liquor, food, clothing, jewelry, and whatever else they could grab. Like the orange flames of a forest fire, the violence spread. From time to time gunfire could be heard. It was not until early Wednesday morning that the rampage stopped.

The violence had shocked the city. Some citizens had volunteered to work as police during the strike. Now more and more signed up. The president of Harvard University urged students to offer their services. The head football coach called off practice and told his players to help protect Boston. Volunteers reported to police stations and were given instructions and guns.

Mayor Peters was furious over Governor Coolidge's refusal to call out the state guard. Peters discovered an old law that permitted the mayor to take charge of state guardsmen stationed in Boston if there was an emergency. On Wednesday morning, the mayor announced that he was taking charge of the guard in Boston. He also asked the governor to call up additional troops from around the state. Coolidge agreed to do so.

As the mobs gathered for the second evening's action, members of the state guard prepared to maintain order. The volunteers were unable to control the streets. In some cases crowds surrounded police stations and prevented the volunteers from coming out. Volunteers in the streets were sometimes attacked by gangs of toughs.

When the state troops reached the streets late on Wednesday, some of the mobs broke up. Smaller groups continued the rioting. As the troops took control of the city, there were violent confrontations in which bayonets and guns were used. By Thursday the state guard had restored order. Eight people had died. More than seventy had been wounded or injured. Many thousands of dollars worth of property had been stolen or destroyed.

Throughout the nation, newspapers reported the news with headlines such as "Riots in Boston" and "Terror Reigns in City." President Wilson spoke out. He said, "A strike of the policemen of a great city, leaving that city at the mercy of an army of thugs, is a crime against civilization."

Although order had been restored, problems remained. Boston labor leaders were considering a general strike of all unions to show support for the policemen's union. Governor Coolidge was worried that Mayor Peters would attempt to have the striking policemen rehired as a way to avoid a general strike. Coolidge said he felt sympathy for the policemen's low wages, but he agreed with Curtis that the men had violated their duty by striking. For Coolidge it was a matter of principle that the men not be rehired. He decided to act.

Governor Coolidge announced that, as commander-in-chief of the state guard, he was now taking charge of the troops in Boston. Mayor Peters had been pushed aside. Coolidge was now in control.

The national president of the AFL, Samuel Gompers, hoped the labor problems in Boston would be settled quickly. He knew the police strike was unpopular with the public and did not want all labor unions to become unpopular. In a telegram to Governor Coolidge, Gompers wrote that Curtis' tough stand was responsible for the strike. He urged the governor to take a broad, generous view of the situation. Gompers was angry because Curtis had announced that the striking policemen would never be rehired. He hoped Coolidge would find a satisfactory solution.

In response to Gompers, Coolidge said that he supported the commissioner's views. He said enforcement of the law should not be placed back in the hands of the men who had gone on strike. In a sentence that was to become famous, the governor said, "There is no right to strike against the public safety by anybody, anywhere, any time."

The striking policemen were not rehired. Other AFL unions decided not to call a general strike. By the end of the year, over one thousand new policemen had been hired and trained. They were given the raises that the strikers had originally requested and no longer had to pay for their uniforms. The former policemen had to find new jobs to support their families.

The once unknown governor of the Bay State became a national hero. To many he seemed a cool and courageous man of principle. At the Republican convention of 1920, Coolidge was nominated for vice-president. After President Harding's death, Calvin Coolidge became president of the United States. In 1924 he was elected president. His handling of the Boston police strike helped bring him to the highest office in the nation.

The major sources for this story were:

Russell, Francis. *A City of Terror: 1919, The Boston Police Strike.* New York: The Viking Press, 1975.

White, William A. *A Puritan in Babylon: The Story of Calvin Coolidge.* New York: Macmillan, 1938.

Ziskind, David. *One Thousand Strikes of Government Employees.* New York: Columbia University Press, 1940.

ACTIVITIES FOR "BAY STATE BLUES"

Write all answers on a separate sheet of paper.

Historical Understanding

Answer briefly:

1. What is *inflation*?

2. What did workers hope to accomplish by joining unions?

3. What is a *general strike*?

4. How did the Boston police strike help Calvin Coolidge become president?

Reviewing the Facts of the Case

Answer briefly:

1. What were three job improvements sought by the Boston police?

2. Why did inflation cause special hardships for Boston police?

3. What were two reasons some people opposed police unions?

4. What rule did Edwin Curtis make about police unions?

5. What recommendations were made by the Storrow Committee? How did Curtis, Peters, and Coolidge react to the recommendations?

6. What specific event triggered the police strike?

7. What was Governor Coolidge's response to Samuel Gompers?

Analyzing Ethical Issues

Examining the value of authority. This story presents problems involving the value of authority. Authority is a value concerning what rules or people should be obeyed and the consequences for disobedience. When people or groups make decisions or rulings, they claim to have the proper authority to make those decisions. Often there is disagreement over whether the people or groups do have the proper authority. At such times these decision makers may identify the basis or source of their authority to make decisions that others should obey. For example, the president might decide to send U.S. troops on manuevers. If asked by what authority he made that decision, the president might claim that the Constitution makes him commander-in-chief of all the armed forces.

Constitutional law is a basis for authority, but there are others that could be claimed. For each of the following statements, identify a source or basis of authority that could be claimed for the decision, as illustrated by this example:

A doctor might insist that a patient take certain medicines.

The doctor might claim that he is an expert in human health.

1. Edwin Curtis ruled that the Boston police were not to join the AFL.

2. Mayor Peters took charge of the state guardsmen in Boston.

3. The Storrow Committee made certain recommendations.

4. Most of the Boston policemen went on strike.

5. Governor Coolidge took charge of the state guardsmen in Boston.

6. Samuel Gompers sent a telegram to Governor Coolidge on behalf of the AFL.

Expressing Your Reasoning

1. Should Coolidge have permitted rehiring of the striking policemen? Why or why not?

2. One policeman who went on strike said afterward:

   "I want to say that I joined the union because we could not get our grievances redressed, or even listened to, any other way.

   "I didn't want to strike, and I don't know any other man who did want to. I went out because 19 men were discharged by the commissioner because I and others had elected them officers of the union. They were no more guilty than I was and I wouldn't be yellow enough to leave them to be the goats for all of us. I'm proud of it.

   "I wouldn't have gone on strike if I thought the city was undefended and there was going to be a riot, and neither would the rest of the fellows."

   Should the Boston police have gone on strike? Why or why not? State your position in writing.

3. Governor Coolidge said there was no right to strike against the public safety at any time. Each of the following groups provide a service that can be seen as affecting the public safety. Would it be wrong in general for members of any of these groups to strike? Present reasons for your positions.

a. Nurses
b. Trash collectors.
c. Air traffic controllers.
d. Soldiers.
e. Doctors.

4. *Seeking Additional Information.* In making decisions about such questions as those above, we often feel we need more information before we are satisfied with our judgments. Choose one of the above questions about which you would want more information than is presented in the story. What additional information would you like? Why would that information help you make a more satisfactory decision?

Stealing North

RICHARD WRIGHT

(*Courtesy of the Library of Congress*)

Segregated Movie Theater

Before the Civil War, race relations in the United States were shaped by the experience of slavery. In the South, black slaves were considered property and treated as inferiors by whites. Most Northern whites opposed slavery, but believed blacks should be put in a lower class and kept separate from whites. Although his ideas would later change, Abraham Lincoln, foremost spokesperson of the Republican party, expressed such a view in an 1858 speech:

> I am not, nor ever have been in favor of bringing about in any way the social and political equality of the white and black races . . . that I am not nor ever have been in favor of making voters or jurors of negroes, nor of qualifying them to hold office, nor to intermarry with white people; and I will say in addition to that there is a physical difference between the black and white races which I believe will for ever forbid the two races living together on terms of social and political equality. . . . While they do remain together there must be the position of superior and inferior, and I as much as any other man am in favor of having the superior position assigned to the white race.

After the Civil War, during Reconstruction (1865-1876), the Constitution was amended to prohibit slavery and guarantee blacks the right to vote. During this period there was increased mixing of the races in Southern states. The presence of federal soldiers in the South and changes in the law brought expanded contact between blacks and whites. Black faces began to appear where they had been absent: in the jury box, on the judge's bench, in legislatures, at the polls, in the marketplace, and even in the best staterooms of steamships. These contacts were not to endure.

Toward the end of the nineteenth century, racism gripped the South. Gradually a pattern of complete *racial segregation* (separation of the races) emerged in the old Confederacy. This period marks the beginning of what has come to be called the "Jim Crow era." (The name "Jim Crow" came from a character who ridiculed blacks in a song and dance act.)

At the dawn of the new century, a wave of Jim Crow laws swelled in the South where 90 percent of the nation's blacks lived. These state laws were intended to segregate the races and keep blacks in an inferior social position. Those Southerners who favored racial equality were swept aside by the tide of racism.

One type of Jim Crow law provided for *disenfranchisement* (denial of the vote) of blacks. Disenfranchisement took several forms. In some Southern states only those who owned a considerable amount of property were allowed to vote. Most blacks were excluded by this qualification. The literacy test was also used to keep blacks out of voting booths. It pretended to limit the vote to people who could read. Blacks usually failed the tests because those given to them were much more difficult than those given to whites. Another obstacle to black voting was the poll tax. By this device, one had to pay a tax in order to vote. Most blacks were so poor that they could not afford the few dollars for the tax. Even if a black paid the tax, the election judge would usually find some mistake in the receipt to keep the black person from voting.

These devices were enormously effective. For example, in Louisiana in 1896, there were 130,334 registered black voters. By 1904 there were 1,342. Between the two dates, the literacy, property, and poll tax qualifications were adopted. Blacks soon disappeared from legislatures. Juries also became all white because jurors were selected from lists of eligible voters.

Jim Crow laws drew the color line almost everywhere. Along the avenues and byways of Southern life, signs appeared that read: "Whites Only" or "Colored." These signs could be seen over entrances and exits at theaters and boarding houses, toilets and water fountains, waiting rooms and ticket windows. In South Carolina, a 1915 law prohibited workers of different races from working together in the same room. A Mississippi law segregated patients in hospitals. Alabama prohibited white female nurses from attending black male patients. Prisoners were separated by race in ten states. Blacks were barred from white public parks by a 1905 Georgia law. Local ordinances in Virginia excluded blacks from living in white neighborhoods. In North Carolina and Florida, the law required that textbooks used by public school children of one race be kept separate from those used by the other. In all Southern states, the law required separate schools for black and white children. In Atlanta, baseball teams of different races were prohibited from playing each other. It was unlawful for a black person and a white person to play checkers in Birmingham, Alabama. And so it was across the South at soda fountains, bars, waiting rooms, street cars, circuses—even in cemeteries.

Jim Crow cars rattled across the tracks of sourthern railways. By law, railroads kept separate cars for black and white passengers. On June 7, 1892, Homer Plessy walked into a New Orleans station and bought a first-class ticket. He boarded the train and took a seat. Suddenly the conductor informed him that he had to move to the next coach. The car Plessy occupied was for white passengers only. Plessy, who was one-eighth black, was not allowed to ride in it. When told to leave, however, he refused. The conductor called a police officer, who forcibly removed Plessy from the car and took him to jail. Plessy was charged with violating the Louisiana law that required "separate accommodations for the white and colored races."

Plessy's case became a stormy landmark. His lawyers argued in a Louisiana court that railway segregation ran contrary to the U.S. Constitution's guarantee of equal protection of the laws. The judge denied their arguments and found Plessy guilty. Plessy's lawyers appealed to the Louisiana Supreme Court, which upheld the lower court decision of Judge Ferguson. A final appeal was then made to the U.S. Supreme Court. In *Plessy* v. *Ferguson* (1896), the highest court in the land ruled against Homer Plessy by a vote of 7 to 1. The justices said that "separate but equal" facilities for white and black people were constitutional. This decision placed racial segregation under the protection of the federal government. Jim Crow laws were to thrive for more than one-half century following the Plessy decision.

Jim Crow era racism appeared in forms other than segregation laws. During the first year following World War I, for example, 70 blacks were lynched, several of them veterans still in uniform. During these years the Ku Klux Klan flourished. The Klan, a white organization, inflamed race prejudice and encouraged race violence.

What was it like to be black in the Jim Crow South? In his autobiography, Richard Wright describes his experiences as a youth in Jackson, Mississippi, during the 1920s.

He lived with his mother, grandmother, and brother. They were very poor. Richard had shabby clothes and little to eat. In school he wrote a story that was published by the local black paper. Encouraged by this recognition of his talent, Richard began dreaming of a career as a writer. He believed that it would be impossible to succeed in the South. The North symbolized opportunity for him. To get there, he had to raise money for train fare.

At school, Richard inquired about jobs and heard of a white family who wanted a boy to do chores. He went to the address after school and was hired. He was to work mornings, evenings, and all day Saturday for two dollars a week plus breakfast and dinner.

The first morning on the job Richard chopped wood, lugged coal, washed the front porch, swept the kitchen and back porch, helped wait on the table, washed the breakfast dishes, and went to the store to shop. Richard recalls his discussion with the woman of the house upon his return from the store:

"Your breakfast is in the kitchen."

"Thank you, ma'am."

I saw a plate of thick, black molasses and a hunk of white bread on the table. Would I get no more than this? They had had eggs, bacon, coffee . . . I picked up the bread and tried to break it; it was stale and hard. Well, I would drink the molasses. I lifted the plate and brought it to my lips and saw floating on the surface of the black liquid green and white bits of mold . . . I can't eat this, I told myself. The food was not even clean. The woman came into the kitchen as I was putting on my coat.

"You didn't eat," she said.

"No, ma'am," I said. "I'm not hungry."

"You'll eat at home?" she asked hopefully.

"Well, I just wasn't hungry this morning, ma'am," I lied.

"You don't like molasses and bread," she said dramatically.

"Oh yes, ma'am, I do," I defended myself quickly, not wanting her to think that I dared criticize what she had given me.

"I don't know what's happening to you niggers nowadays," she sighed, wagging her head. She looked closely at the molasses. "It's a sin to throw out molasses like that. I'll put it up for you this evening."

"Yes, ma'am," I said heartily.

Neatly she covered the plate of molasses with another plate, then felt the bread and dumped it into the garbage. She turned to me, her face lit with an idea.

"What grade are you in school?"

"Seventh, ma'am."

"Then why are you going to school?" she asked in surprise.

"Well, I want to be a writer," I mumbled, unsure of myself; I had not planned to tell her that, but she had made me feel so utterly wrong and of no account that I needed to bolster myself.

"A what?" she demanded.

"A writer," I mumbled.

"For what?"

"To write stories," I mumbled defensively.

"You'll never be a writer," she said. "Who on earth put such ideas into your nigger head?"

"Nobody," I said.

"I didn't think anybody ever would," she declared indignantly.

As I walked around her house to the street, I knew that I would not go back. The woman had assaulted my ego; she had assumed that she knew my place in life, what I felt, what I ought to be, and I resented it with all my heart. Perhaps she was right; perhaps I never would be a writer; but I did not want her to say so.

In 1924, when Richard was 15, he took a summer job as a water boy in a brickyard. For a dollar a day he carried a pail of water from one laboring gang of black men to another. The owner's dog went about the brickyard snapping and growling at the workers. Richard was afraid that the dog would bite him. One afternoon, while getting water from the pond, he felt something sharp sink into his thigh. He had been bitten; the teeth marks showed deep and red. Afraid of infection, Richard reported the bite to the office and returned to work. Later in the afternoon, the boss, a tall white man, came toward Richard:

"Is this the nigger?" he asked a black boy as he pointed at me.

"Yes sir," the black boy answered.

"Come here, nigger," he called me.

I went to him.

"They tell me my dog bit you," he said.

"Yes, sir."

I pulled down my trousers and he looked.

"Humnnn," he grunted, then laughed, "A dog bite can't hurt a nigger."

"It's swelling and it hurts," I said.

"If it bothers you, let me know," he said. "But I never saw a dog yet that could really hurt a nigger."

He turned and walked away and the black boys gathered to watch his tall form disappear down the aisles of wet bricks.

Soon afterward, the brickyard went out of business, and Richard was again out of work. He graduated from junior high school first in his class. Now he would look for a full-time job. Richard found employment as a porter and delivery boy in a clothing store operated by a white man. The store sold cheap goods on credit. Richard watched several times, frightened but tight-lipped, as his employer beat black customers who had not paid their bills. The boss' son cornered Richard one morning:

> "Say, nigger, look here," he began.
> "Yes, sir."
> "What's on your mind?"
> "Nothing, sir," I said, trying to look amazed, trying to fool him.
> "Why don't you laugh and talk like the other niggers?" he asked.
> "Well, sir, there's nothing much to say or smile about," I said, smiling.
> His face was hard, baffled; I knew that I had not convinced him. He whirled from me and went to the front of the store; he came back a moment later, his face red. He tossed a few green bills at me.
> "I don't like your looks, nigger. Now, get!" he snapped.
> I picked up the money and did not count it. I grabbed my hat and left.

Richard held a series of petty jobs for short periods after leaving the clothing store. He was usually driven off because whites did not like his attitude. Most of the money he earned went to support his family. Nearing his seventeenth birthday, he was no closer than ever to his goal of saving enough money to head northward. One night a friend told Richard about a job at the local black movie theater. "The girl who sells tickets is using a system," he explained. "If you get the job, you can make some good gravy."

In his autobiography, Richard describes what happened at his last job in Mississippi:

> My chances for getting the job were good; I had no past record of stealing or violating the laws. When I presented myself to the Jewish proprietor of the movie house I was immediately accepted. The next day I reported for duty and began taking tickets. The boss man warned me:
> "Now look, I'll be honest with you if you'll be honest with me. I don't know who's honest around this joint and who isn't. But if you are honest, then the rest are bound to be. All tickets will pass through your hands. There can be no stealing unless you steal."
> I gave him a pledge of my honesty, feeling absolutely no qualms about what I intended to do. He was white, and I could never do

to him what he and his kind had done to me. Therefore, I reasoned, stealing was not a violation of my ethics, but of his; I felt that things were rigged in his favor and any action I took to circumvent his scheme of life was justified. Yet I had not convinced myself.

During the first afternoon the Negro girl in the ticket office watched me closely and I knew that she was sizing me up, trying to determine when it would be safe to break me into her graft. I waited, leaving it to her to make the first move.

I was supposed to drop each ticket that I took from a customer into a metal receptacle. Occasionally the boss would go to the ticket window and look at the serial number on the roll of unsold tickets and then compare that number with the number on the last ticket I had dropped into the receptacle. The boss continued his watchfulness for a few days, then began to observe me from across the street; finally he absented himself for long intervals. . . .

While I was eating supper in a near-by cafe one night, a strange Negro man walked in and sat beside me.

"Hello, Richard," he said.

"Hello," I said. "I don't think I know you."

"But I know *you*," he said, smiling.

Was he one of the boss' spies?

"How do you know me?" I asked.

"I'm Tel's friend," he said, naming the girl who sold the tickets at the movie.

I looked at him searchingly. Was he telling me the truth? Or was he trying to trap me for the boss? I was already thinking and feeling like a criminal, distrusting everybody.

"We start tonight," he said.

"What?" I asked, still not admitting that I knew what he was talking about.

"Don't be scared. The boss trusts you. He's gone to see some friends. Somebody's watching him and if he starts back to the movie, they'll phone us," he said.

I could not eat my food. It lay cold upon the plate and sweat ran down from my armpits.

"It'll work this way," he explained in a low, smooth tone. "A guy'll come to you and ask for a match. You give him five tickets that you'll hold out of the box, see? We'll give you the signal when to start holding out. The guy'll give the tickets to Tel; she'll re-sell them all at once, when the crowd is buying at the rush hour. You get it?"

I did not answer. I knew that if I were caught I would go to the chain gang. But was not my life already a kind of chain gang? What, really, did I have to lose?

"Are you with us?" he asked.

I still did not answer. He rose and clapped me on the shoulder and left. I trembled as I went back to the theater. . . . I took the tickets with my sweaty fingers. I waited. I was gambling; freedom or the chain gang. There were times when I felt that I could not breathe. I looked up and down the street; the boss was not in sight. Was this a trap? If it were, I would disgrace my family.

The man I had met in the cafe came through the door and put a ticket in my hand.

"There's a crowd at the box office," he whispered. "Save ten, not five. Start with this one."

Well, here goes, I thought. He gave me the ticket and sat looking at the moving shadows upon the screen. I held onto the ticket and my body grew tense, hot as fire; but I was used to that too. Time crawled through the cells of my brain. My muscles ached. I discovered that crime means suffering. The crowd came in and gave me more tickets. I kept ten of them tucked into my moist palm. No sooner had the crowd thinned than a black boy with a cigarette jutting from his mouth came up to me.

"Gotta match?"

With a slow movement I gave him the tickets. He went out and I kept the door cracked and watched. He went to the ticket office and laid down a coin and I saw him slip the tickets to the girl. Yes, the boy was honest. The girl shot me a quick smile and I went back inside. A few moments later the same tickets were handed to me by other customers.

We worked it for a week and after the money was split four ways, I had fifty dollars. Freedom was almost within my grasp. Ought I risk any more? I dropped the hint to Tel's friend that maybe I would quit; it was a casual hint to test him out. He grew violently angry and I quickly consented to stay, fearing that someone might turn me in for revenge, or to get me out of the way so that another and more pliable boy could have my place. I was dealing with cagey people and I would be cagey.

I went through another week. Late one night I resolved to make that week the last. . . . Saturday night came and I sent word to the boss that I was sick. My mother sat in her rocking chair, humming to herself. I packed my suitcase and went to her.

"Mama, I'm going away," I whispered.

"Oh, no," she protested.

"I've got to, mama. I can't live this way."

"You're not running away from something you've done?"

"I'll send for you, mama. I'll be all right."

"Take care of yourself. And send for me quickly. I'm not happy here," she said.

"I'm sorry for all these long years, mama. But I could not have helped it."

I kissed her and she cried.

"Be quiet, mama. I'm all right."

I went out the back way and walked a quarter of a mile to the railroad tracks. It began to rain as I tramped down the crossties toward town. I reached the station soaked to the skin. I bought my ticket, then went hurriedly to the corner of the block in which the movie house stood. Yes, the boss was there, taking the tickets himself. I returned to the station and waited for my train, my eyes watching the crowd.

An hour later I was sitting in a Jim Crow coach speeding northward, making the first lap of my journey to a land where I could live with a little less fear. Slowly the burden I had carried for many months lifted somewhat. My cheeks itched and when I scratched them I found tears. In that moment I understood the pain that accompanied crime and I hoped that I would never have to feel it again. I never did feel it again, for I never stole again; and what kept me from it was the knowledge that, for me, crime carried its own punishment.

The major sources for this story were:

Woodward, C. Vann. *The Strange Career of Jim Crow*. 3rd rev. ed. New York: Oxford University Press, 1974.

Wright, Richard. *Black Boy*. New York: Harper & Row, 1966.

ACTIVITIES FOR "STEALING NORTH"

Write all answers on a separate sheet of paper.

Historical Understanding

Answer briefly:

1. What was Abraham Lincoln's position on racial equality before the Civil War?

2. What were the two major purposes of Jim Crow laws?

3. Give three specific examples of Jim Crow laws.

4. What precedent was set by the case of *Plessy* v. *Ferguson*?

Reviewing the Facts of the Case

Answer briefly:

1. Why did Richard quit his job doing chores for a white family?

2. For what purpose was Richard trying to save money?

3. How was Richard treated by the owner of the brickyard?

4. Why was Richard fired from the clothing store?

5. What agreement did Richard reach with the theater owner?

6. Describe how the ticket scheme worked.

Analyzing Ethical Issues

Considering equal protection.   Plessy's lawyers argued unsuccessfully that their client had been denied "equal protection of the laws" as provided in the Fourteenth Amendment to the U.S. Constitution. The equal protection clause prohibits state governments from discriminating unfairly against citizens. It does not, however, prevent private citizens from discriminating against one another. A private act of discrimination is not illegal unless it is prohibited by a specific local, state, or federal law.

For each example below, indicate whether the racial discrimination involved results from government or private action and explain your reasoning. For example:

A homeowner signs an agreement not to sell his home to a black buyer.

Private action (because the homeowner is acting as a private individual and not as an agent of a government).

1. A restaurant hires white waitresses only.

2. An athletic club excludes whites from membership.

3. A school board requires black and white children to attend separate schools.

4. Prisoners in a state prison are segregated by race.

5. A city police department favors black job applicants.

6. A religious group excludes blacks from its clergy.

7. The Navy hires only black cooks.

8. A landlord rents to whites only.

9. A county board accepts bids to build a new office building only from black-owned construction firms.

Cite two examples of racial discrimination from the story, one that involves government action and one that involves private action.

Expressing Your Reasoning

1. Should Richard have participated in the ticket scheme? Why or why not?

2. Suppose that before Richard joined in the ticket scheme the owner had approached him and asked if he knew whether anything dishonest was happening among the employees. Would it have been right for Richard to tell the theater owner about the ticket scheme and who was involved in it? Why or why not?

3. Read the following case and respond to the question following it:

MRS. WEBSTER'S ROOMING HOUSE

Ever since her husband died, Mrs. Webster had struggled to eke out a living from the small rooming house she operated. She didn't really like members of minority groups, especially blacks. But, more important, Mrs. Webster felt that if she rented rooms to such people her regular boarders might get angry and move out. "It's my property," she told her neighbors, "and no one has the right to tell me whom I must allow to sleep in my house."

One night Mrs. Webster was interrupted at dinner by the ring of her doorbell. "A traveler to occupy my vacant room," she thought happily. When she opened the door she saw the face of a black man.

"My name is Mr. Jones. I've looked all over town. Do you have a vacant room for me tonight?" he asked.

Mrs. Webster hesitated. "No, sorry, we're all full."

Was it wrong of Mrs. Webster to reject Mr. Jones? Why or why not?

4. *Seeking Additional Information.* In making decisions about such questions as those above, we often feel we need more information before we are satisfied with our judgments. Choose one of the above questions about which you would want more information than is presented in the story. What additional information would you like? Why would that information help you make a more satisfactory decision?

Rebel Without a Pause

ZELDA FITZGERALD

(Reprinted by permission of Harold Ober Associates Incorporated)

Zelda Fitzgerald

On a lazy summer day in Montgomery, Alabama, a young girl was looking for excitement. She called the fire department. She reported that a little girl was stranded on the roof of a tall house. She then climbed a ladder to the top of her house and kicked the ladder away. With an impish smile she watched the flurry of activity as the fire fighters rushed to her rescue.

The little girl, Zelda Sayre, had created a scene, and it was exciting. It would not be the last time she created a commotion by violating commonly expected standards of behavior. In the 1920s she would become the symbol of a new way of life for young people—a way of life that was admired by some and despised by others.

During the 1920s, waves of change crashed through U.S. society. The Nineteenth Amendment guaranteed women the right to vote. After decades of struggle, women had finally won a basic democratic right. Another amendment placed a restriction on Americans: the Eighteenth Amendment to the Constitution made it illegal to sell, transport, or manufacture alcoholic beverages.

When Warren Harding was elected president in 1920, he hoped the troubled waters of the war years would be calmed. He said the United States wanted to return to "normalcy." In fact, many behaviors and beliefs that had once seemed normal were engulfed by the tides of change.

The U.S. economy was strong during the early 1920s and, after the sacrifices of the world war, many Americans simply wanted to have a good time. In spite of the Eighteenth Amendment, alcohol was widely available. Gangsters made huge amounts of money *bootlegging* (illegally smuggling and selling liquor). Illegal nightclubs, called *speakeasies*, were popular in most cities. Law enforcement officials could not stop the flow of alcohol.

Americans sought entertainment. Interest in sports spurted to a new high. Golfer Bobby Jones, boxing champion Jack Dempsey, baseball player Babe Ruth, and football player Red Grange were among the popular heroes of the time. In the cities, people poured into nightclubs to learn new dances such as the Charleston and the Black Bottom. Throughout the country, people began listening to radio shows and watching movies. There had never been times like these.

One of the most visible changes occurred in the behavior and thinking of young women. To many it seemed that proper standards for women had eroded almost overnight. Short dresses became the fashion—dresses that went as high as the knee. According to one joke, a little boy got lost in the city because he could not reach high enough to hold onto his mother's skirt. Not everyone saw fashion as a joking matter. In one state, a bill was introduced to make it illegal for a woman's dress to be more than three inches above her ankles.

Perhaps more shocking than the rise in hemlines was the rise in smoking and drinking among women. It had always been considered indecent for women to smoke or drink alcohol, especially in public. Now such behavior was becoming common. Many parents worried about their daughters hopping into automobiles and driving off to wild parties where drinking and smoking were likely to occur.

Zelda sailed with the tides of change, making plenty of waves herself. Born in 1900, she grew into an extraordinarily beautiful young woman. As an Alabama teenager she was extremely popular with boys. Constantly she went to parties and dances. She loved to swim and was fearless when it came to taking high dives. Whatever she felt like doing she did. One night, she saw a picture of one of her boyfriends in a local photography shop. Without hesitation, she broke the store window and walked away with his picture.

Zelda had many boyfriends, but one became dominant. At a country club dance during the war, she met a handsome young lieutenant, F. Scott Fitzgerald. Scott was unlike other men she had known. He was from the North and had been a student at Princeton University. He dreamed of becoming a great writer of novels. Zelda was also artistic and intelligent. She and Scott became intensely attracted to one another.

Scott's first novel, *This Side of Paradise*, was published in 1920. In April of that year, he and Zelda were married in New York City. For Zelda and Scott Fitzgerald the Roaring Twenties, or what he later called the Jazz Age, had begun.

The couple jumped into the swim of New York social life. Scott's novel was a great success, and he and Zelda became two of the best-known people in the city. They partied endlessly and wildly. People loved to be around them, for no one could tell what might happen. For example, one night Zelda jumped into a water fountain for a cooling dip.

Their behavior and ideas were symbols of a new pleasure-seeking era. Zelda was called by one observer "without doubt the most

brilliant and most beautiful young woman I've ever known." Young
women of the 1920s were often called flappers. Zelda wrote about her
ideas of what a flapper should be like.

Zelda said flappers should experiment with life. Young women
should get as much enjoyment from life as possible. She said the
flapper "refused to be bored chiefly because she wasn't boring. She
was conscious that the things she did were the things she had always
wanted to do." According to Zelda, to be a flapper was to rebel
against all the stuffy old traditions that had made women unhappy.

Scott knew there were those who resented Zelda. He wrote: "No
personality as strong as Zelda's could go without criticism . . . I've
always known that, any girl who gets stewed in public, who frankly
enjoys and tells shocking stories, who smokes constantly and makes
the remark that she has 'kissed thousands of men and intends to kiss
thousands more,' cannot be considered beyond reproach." Nonetheless, he loved "her courage, her sincerity and her flaming self-respect."

Zelda spoke for and tried to act for a new generation of women.
Scott's novels also spoke to a new generation. They described the
lives, ideas, and troubles of the young.

In his novels, Scott often described, through fictional characters,
the lives that he and Zelda were leading. He often put Zelda's words
into the mouths of his female characters. A writer friend asked if he
could buy Zelda's diary, but Scott would not permit it. Her diary was
too useful to him in his own writing.

They were leading figures of their time, envied and admired. Once
newspapers around the nation ran a full-page photograph of them.
The photo would fade, however, as would their glamour.

Both Zelda and Scott were heavy drinkers, and some friends worried
about their wild behavior. One evening in a speakeasy, Scott was
drunk and a bouncer refused to let him return to the bar. Zelda urged
Scott to stand up to the bouncer. The fearless Zelda could not stand
the idea that Scott would ever act in a way that she thought cowardly.
Scott returned to the bar, where the powerful bouncer gave him a
thorough beating.

When Zelda discovered she was going to have a baby, she returned
to Montgomery, planning for the child to be born there. She had
gained a large amount of weight. At that time it was unusual for
pregnant women to walk about in public. Zelda did more than walk.
One day she decided to go for a swim. She squeezed herself into a tight

bathing suit and went to the local pool. Such behavior was considered improper, and she was asked to leave the pool. Eventually she did. She also left Alabama. The baby was born in Scott's hometown of St. Paul, Minnesota.

Their baby daughter did not slow down the Fitzgeralds' pace. Soon they were off to Europe. The parties continued. They met many of the most famous writers and artists of the time. Scott's writings continued to be successful, but the couple spent money as fast as it flowed in. Scott often wrote short stories for U.S. magazines to bring in extra money. The stories were well received, but he was more interested in writing novels.

Zelda was also a writer and occasionally was able to sell her work to U.S. magazines. She was not as famous a writer as Scott, however, and did not receive as much money for her writing as he did. Typically, Zelda would receive a few hundred dollars for each of her stories. At one point, a magazine publisher said he would pay $4,000 for one of her stories if Scott's name appeared as the author. The Fitzgeralds agreed, and the story, although completely written by Zelda, appeared in Scott's name.

In addition to being a writer, Zelda was also a painter. The form of art that came to dominate her life, however, was dancing. She began taking lessons from the finest dance instructors available. Her dream was that one day she might be a ballerina. There was not much of a chance that she could succeed, because most great dancers began serious study and practice when very young. This did not stop Zelda. She studied and practiced for hours on end. Nothing seemed more important in her life.

Sadly, Zelda's dreams turned nightmarish. She began acting strangely. Friends noticed that she often did not make sense when she talked. Once, while she was watching a movie about underwater life, the sight of an octopus caused her to scream and panic. People could not believe the fearless swimmer would react that way. Something was wrong.

Zelda began to have a series of mental disorders that would put her in and out of hospitals for the rest of her life. In 1930, she entered a hospital in Paris and later was moved to a special clinic in Switzerland. Scott was distressed. He willingly paid heavy expenses. He spent time discussing her treatment with the doctors.

Frustration compounded Scott's distress. In 1925, his novel, *The*

Great Gatsby, had been published, but he had been unable to finish another novel since then. He was to be delayed even longer by having to deal with Zelda's illness.

Zelda wanted to know what her chances of future success as a dancer might be, so she asked Scott to write to her teacher for an honest opinion of her ability.

Her doctor did not want Zelda to be encouraged to continue dancing. He was convinced that her relentless drive to become a dancer was causing her to sink deeper into a pool of despair.

In her response to Scott's letter, Zelda's teacher said that Zelda could become a good dancer and dance in some important roles. She would not, however, ever become a great dancer. The doctor decided, and Scott agreed, that the teacher's opinion would not be made known to Zelda.

The doctor was also convinced that the couple's drinking was a cause of their problems. For years, the intensity of their love was matched by the intensity of their arguments, especially after bouts of heavy drinking. The doctor said that Zelda must never drink again, and urged Scott to quit as well. Scott was addicted to alcohol but was unwilling to admit it. In part he blamed Zelda, saying drinking "was almost a necessity for me to be able to stand her long monologues about ballet steps." He also said that for years he had worked hard at his writing and at providing for Zelda and that drinking was something of a reward. He was willing to cut down and perhaps quit for short periods of time, but he would not give up drinking.

From time to time Zelda was allowed to leave the hospital for short trips and occasional visits with Scott. In 1931, they returned to the United States and Zelda was taken to Montgomery. Her Alabama friends were shocked at her appearance. The once beautiful and lively Zelda was aged and hardened by her suffering.

It was not long before Zelda was again in a hospital. Scott was still unable to devote time to his novel. He wrote short stories to help pay for the costs of her treatment and their daughter's education. In the hospital Zelda painted and resumed her writing. In a remarkably short time she finished a novel, *Save Me the Waltz*. She did not show Scott the novel but sent it directly to the publishing company that had published Scott's earlier works.

Before the book was published, Scott saw a copy. He was furious. In their writing both Scott and Zelda often described scenes from their own lives, but this time Scott believed she had gone too far.

During the many years he had been working at *Tender Is the Night*, his as yet uncompleted new novel, Zelda had been aware of its contents. In her novel, Scott said, she had used many of the major ideas and sections of his work—work he had been unable to complete because of her illness.

Scott's rage would not subside. He insisted that Zelda change certain portions of the novel. Unhappily, she agreed to make the changes.

Scott arranged for publication of Zelda's book. He asked the publisher not to praise her work excessively, for fear the excitement might endanger her mental health. He had the publication contract written so that one-half of the book's earnings would go to pay off $5,000 he had borrowed from the publisher.

Save Me the Waltz was published in 1932. The book was neither an artistic nor a financial success. Zelda earned only about $120 from it, and Scott's debt remained unpaid.

Zelda planned to continue writing. The theme of her next novel was again similar to Scott's work in progress. Hostility bubbled forth when they were together. Scott had delayed completion of his novel to provide for Zelda's care. The stuff of their lives, he claimed, belonged to him to use in his fiction: "That is all my material. None of it is your material." Scott insisted that Zelda think of his interests as a novelist and stop her writing. The matter was not settled between them, and resentment persisted.

The sweetness of Scott and Zelda's earlier success had soured. Zelda chose not to pursue novel writing, although she did work on shorter pieces. Scott finally published *Tender Is the Night* in 1934. Although it was a best-seller for a while, it did not, perhaps because of the Depression, sell as many copies as hoped.

Scott did not complete another novel. He had lived hard and his health had suffered. In December 1940, at the age of 44, he collapsed and died. The troubled waters of Zelda's life were stilled in March 1948. She died in a fire at her mental hospital.

The major sources for this story were:

Allen, Frederick L. *Only Yesterday*. New York: Bantam Books, 1959.
Milford, Nancy. *Zelda*. New York: Avon, 1970.

ACTIVITIES FOR "REBEL WITHOUT A PAUSE"

Write all answers on a separate sheet of paper.

Historical Understanding

Answer briefly:

1. What were the provisions of the Eighteenth and Nineteenth Amendments?

2. Name three forms of entertainment popular in the 1920s.

3. What were two ways in which women of the 1920s rebelled against tradition?

4. What was *bootlegging*? What were *speakeasies*?

Reviewing the Facts of the Case

Answer briefly:

1. What were Zelda's ideas about how flappers should live?

2. What were three characteristics of Zelda that Scott adored?

3. Identify two things that Zelda did that showed she rebelled against tradition.

4. Why did Scott not want Zelda to sell her diary?

5. What did Zelda's doctor urge Scott to do when Zelda wanted to know her chances of becoming a great dancer?

6. Why was Scott angry with Zelda about the writing of her novel?

Analyzing Ethical Issues

Examining the value of truth. There are a number of incidents in this story in which decisions involving the value of truth were made. Truth is a value concerning the expression, distortion, or withholding of accurate information. For example:

> *Zelda allowed Scott to appear as the sole author of one of her stories.*

The value of truth was involved because accurate information about who really wrote the story was withheld.

Identify one other decision in this story involving the value of truth, and explain how it was involved.

Expressing Your Reasoning

1. Should Zelda have stopped writing because Scott demanded it? Why or why not?

2. Was it wrong of Scott to mislead Zelda about her teacher's opinion of her dancing ability? Why or why not? Some argue that patients have a right to know the truth about their medical condition. Are there any circumstances in which patients should not be told the truth? Explain your thinking.

3. Scott and Zelda, like some other people, went to illegal nightclubs. Was it wrong for them to have done that? Why or why not? Write a paragraph stating your position.

4. *Seeking Additional Information.* In making decisions about such questions as those above, we often feel we need more information before we are satisfied with our judgments. Choose one of the above questions about which you would want more information than is presented in the story. What additional information would you like? Why would that information help you make a more satisfactory decision?

Bad News

NEAR v. MINNESOTA

United States Supreme Court, 1930

In 1880, iron ore was discovered in the Mesabi Range near Duluth, Minnesota. Iron ore was vital to the making of steel. The growing U.S. steel industry had an endless hunger for the ore, and the Mesabi Range seemed to have an endless supply of ore to feed that hunger. Thousands of workers, many of them European immigrants, came to work the rich mines. Railroads were built to bring the ore to Duluth. From Duluth, the ore was shipped across the Great Lakes to the steel mills of Pennsylvania and Ohio.

Duluth became a boom town. Wealthy shippers and mine owners built mansions on the hills overlooking Lake Superior. The city had a newfound elegance, but it also had a newfound roughness. Many miners and other workers spent rowdy evenings in saloons and coarse hotels. Professional gamblers came to get a share of the workers' wages. When the sale of alcoholic beverages was made illegal in the early 1900s, gangsters came to supply liquor to those who ignored the law.

John Morrison, an intensely religious man, was disgusted by the law-breaking. He was convinced that many of the local police and politicians were cooperating with the criminal element by taking bribes to overlook illegal activities. He decided to publish a newspaper, the *Rip-saw*, which would expose corruption.

The pages of the *Rip-saw* were filled with charges of scandal. Morrison was not always careful about what he printed. He was willing to publish rumors as though they were true. He accused a judge of being unfit to hold office, a former mayor of being a drunkard, and a senator of threatening to kill him. Later, Morrison was charged with *libel* (printing untrue statements that damage someone's reputation). In court he admitted that some of his charges were false. He was fined $100 and set free.

Many public officials believed newspapers like the *Rip-saw* should not be published. Owners of major newspapers in Minnesota agreed. They thought that newspapers like Morrison's were simply "scandal sheets" that gave the newspaper business a bad name. The publishers of the major newspapers helped draft a law to prevent publication of papers like the *Rip-saw*. In 1925, the Minnesota legislature passed the Public Nuisance Law.

According to the law, anyone who regularly published an obscene, scandalous, or *defamatory* (insulting to a person's reputation) newspaper could be found guilty of being a public nuisance. If the publisher could show intent to print the truth without malice, there would be no

penalty. If publishers knowingly printed false and damaging information, however, they could be ordered by a judge to stop printing
their newspapers.

Morrison protested the new law but died soon after it went into
effect. He would not be heard from again, but the law was soon to
become national news.

The scene now shifted to Minneapolis, the state capital. Minneapolis,
like Duluth, was afflicted with corruption. When the Eighteenth
Amendment to the Constitution, which prohibited the sale, manufacture, or transportation of alcoholic beverages went into effect in
1920, crime increased in Minneapolis. The city's location made it an
ideal place for the distribution of illegal liquor. Whiskey smuggled
from Canada could be shipped conveniently to Chicago and St. Louis.

One observer wrote that gangsters and crooked politicians worked
together to run gambling houses, the whiskey business, and other
illegal activities. It was rumored that Mose Barnett, a leading gangster,
had made a deal with the police chief allowing gambling houses to
operate. In addition, Barnett was said to have paid the chief a portion
of the gambling profits.

Like Morrison in Duluth, Jay Near and Howard Guilford began
publishing charges of corruption and scandal in Minneapolis. Their
stories and headlines were designed to shock the public. Some people
claimed that the publishers blackmailed politicians and gangsters.
Some scandal sheets did accept money in exchange for a promise not
to print charges, though it was never proved that Near or Guilford
did so.

In September 1927, the first edition of their paper, the *Saturday
Press*, charged that gangsters had threatened the publishers. The
following day, while out for a drive, Guilford was shot by men in a
speeding car. Guilford was not killed and said he could identify the
gunmen. Strangely, he refused to bring charges against the mobsters
when they apologized and paid his hospital expenses.

The *Saturday Press* was often filled with hatred, lies, and prejudice.
Among others, Jay Near hated Jews, blacks, Catholics, labor unions,
and the Salvation Army. His writing publicly insulted these groups.
He also claimed that Jewish gangsters, like Barnett, were ruining
Minneapolis.

Barnett was no source of civic pride to Minneapolis. In addition to
his gambling operations, he served as an "enforcer" for a group of dry
cleaners. As an enforcer, Barnett prevented other cleaning businesses

from getting started. Sam Shapiro, a Jewish immigrant, started his own cleaning business and refused to deal with the mobsters. Barnett told him to close the shop, but Shapiro refused. In August 1927, four of Barnett's men entered Shapiro's store. They poured acid over the customers' clothing and pistol-whipped Shapiro.

Shapiro told his story to law enforcement officials, but no action was taken. Shapiro knew that Jay Near hated Jews, but he decided to tell him what had happened. Near took advantage of Shapiro's story to lash out against the police chief and other officials. As usual, Near's writing was filled with anti-Jewish phrases:

> It is Jew thugs who have "pulled" practically every robbery in this city.
>
> Practically every vendor of vile hooch, every owner of a moonshine still, every snake-faced gangster . . . is a Jew.
>
> It was a Jew who employed JEWS to shoot down Mr. Guilford. It was a Jew who employed JEWS to assault that gentleman when he refused to yield to their threats.

Near said that the Jewish community should get rid of the criminal element in their midst. The *Saturday Press* accused County Attorney Floyd Olson of failing to take action against the criminals who attacked Shapiro. It was suggested that Olson was tied in with Jewish criminals.

Olson, later to become a popular governor of Minnesota, was fed up with insults to himself and the Jewish community. He decided to take action under the Public Nuisance Law. As a result of his complaint, a judge ordered Near and Guilford to stop publishing the *Saturday Press*.

The judge's decision was generally popular in Minneapolis, but Near protested. He said the state constitution guaranteed freedom of the press and claimed his constitutional rights had been violated. Eventually, his case went to the state supreme court. There, in 1928, the court ruled against Near. In its decision, the court said freedom of the press has limits: "Liberty of the press does not mean that an evil-minded person may publish just anything any more than the constitutional right of assembly authorizes and legalizes unlawful assemblies and riots." The court ruled that the Public Nuisance Law was not in violation of the state constitution.

Near had lost his case but refused to quit fighting. The newspaper seemed to be the only way he could make a living, and he wanted to continue publishing. If his case could be appealed to the United States Supreme Court, he thought he might be able to win. He did not have enough money to pay for the expenses of a Supreme Court appeal. The major newspaper publishers in Minneapolis would not help him, so he asked Colonel Robert McCormick, publisher of the *Chicago Tribune*, for assistance.

McCormick was a flashy, swaggering, controversial man. He was also a millionaire with a deep commitment to freedom of the press. He believed the Minnesota law was a "gag" law intended to prevent the press from criticizing government officials. He feared that other states might follow Minnesota's example and try to shut down newspapers that tried to expose political corruption. If the U.S. Supreme Court would strike down the Minnesota law, McCormick believed freedom of the press would be strengthened.

Near complained bitterly to McCormick, saying he resented the long legal proceedings. He told McCormick that he was in need of money. McCormick was willing to provide money and lawyers for the Supreme Court appeal, but he had no interest in Near's personal financial situation.

Many publishers of major U.S. newspapers opposed McCormick's plans. Some argued that a sleazy publication like the *Saturday Press* should not be given publicity by going to the Supreme Court. Others feared that if the Supreme Court upheld the Minnesota law, legislatures in their states might enact similar laws restricting press freedom. McCormick was not persuaded by his opponents.

In 1930, the case of *Near* v. *Minnesota* reached the Supreme Court of the United States. There were strong arguments on both sides. Chief Justice Hughes believed the law was a violation of freedom of the press. He said the law allowed judges to prevent, in advance, the publication of newspapers. This was called *prior restraint*, which Hughes said was a type of censorship not permitted by the First Amendment to the Constitution. After all, argued Hughes, if a newspaper published something that unfairly injured someone's reputation, that person could sue for libel. Furthermore, freedom of the press was necessary in a democracy to expose corruption by public officials. In Hughes' opinion the Minnesota law should be declared unconstitutional.

Justice Butler held a different view. In his opinion the law did not violate freedom of the press. He said there was no prior restraint because Near had published enough issues of his paper so that one could tell that future publications would continue to be outrageous and a threat to community peace. He said that few people would go through the trouble of filing libel complaints, and that those who were unfairly treated by the paper might seek violent revenge like the shooting of Guilford. Freedom of the press was supposed to protect those with good intentions who wanted to print the truth. According to Justice Butler, Near and his newspaper were not protected by the constitutional guarantee of a free press.

In June 1931, the Supreme Court declared the Minnesota Public Nuisance Law unconstitutional. The vote was 5 to 4 in favor of striking down the law.

It was good news for Near, but bad news for those he hated. He resumed publishing the *Saturday Press*. In the paper he bragged that the Supreme Court had proved him right. He continued his anti-Jewish writing. His old partner Guilford was killed by gangsters after announcing plans to expose the influence of organized crime on government. Near himself died quietly in 1936.

The major source for this story was:

Friendly, Fred W. *Minnesota Rag.* New York: Random House, 1981.

ACTIVITIES FOR "BAD NEWS"

Write all answers on a separate sheet of paper.

Historical Understanding

Answer briefly:

1. Identify two effects the discovery of iron ore had on the city of Duluth.

2. What were the provisions of the Eighteenth Amendment? How did it contribute to an increase in crime?

3. What is meant by *prior restraint*?

Reviewing the Facts of the Case

Answer briefly:

1. How did the publication of the *Rip-saw* lead to the 1925 Public Nuisance Law?

2. What were the provisions of the 1925 Public Nuisance Law?

3. Why did gangsters attack Sam Shapiro?

4. Why did Floyd Olson try to shut down the *Saturday Press*?

5. Why did the Minnesota Supreme Court say the 1925 law was constitutional?

6. Why did Colonel McCormick want to take Near's case to the Supreme Court of the United States?

Analyzing Ethical Issues

There is agreement about the answer to some questions. For other questions there is disagreement or uncertainty about the answer. We call these questions issues. Issues can be categorized as factual or ethical. A factual issue asks whether something is true or false, accurate or inaccurate. An ethical issue asks whether something is right or wrong, fair or unfair. Factual issues ask what *is*; ethical questions ask what *ought to be*. For example:

> If the Supreme Court had upheld the Minnesota Public Nuisance Law, would other states have enacted similar laws? *Factual.*

> Was it wrong for McCormick not to help Near with his personal money troubles? *Ethical.*

For each of the following questions, decide whether the issue is factual or ethical.

1. Would Near have won his case without McCormick's support?

2. Should the *Saturday Press* nave been forced to stop publishing?

3. Should Shapiro have resisted Barnett's demands?

4. Would most people sue newspapers that insulted their reputations?

5. Was it fair of Near to charge that Olson cooperated with gangsters?

Write an example of one more factual and one more ethical issue raised by the story.

Expressing Your Reasoning

1. Should prejudiced people like Jay Near be allowed to publish papers like the *Saturday Press*? Why or why not?

2. Some people believe that freedom of the press means that a publisher always has the right to print the truth. Others disagree and say that there are times when it would be wrong to print the truth. Would it be wrong to print the truth in any of the following examples? Explain your reasoning.
   a. A community leader in a small town is a generous and respected middle-aged woman. A reporter discovers that she had been convicted of shoplifting 20 years ago. The local newspaper prints the story.
   b. A newspaper editor, during wartime, learns that U.S. troops are going to be sent on a secret mission into enemy territory. The editor prints the story.
   c. An informant tells a reporter who committed a murder in town. The informant tells the reporter not to print the story and the reporter agrees. Later the reporter has a change of mind and prints the story, naming the person who supposedly committed the murder.
   d. Before a criminal suspect is brought to trial, a local newspaper reports evidence against the accused.

3. Should the U.S. Supreme Court have upheld the Minnesota Public Nuisance Law? Write a paragraph stating your position.

4. *Seeking Additional Information.* In making decisions about such questions as those above, we often feel we need more information before we are satisfied with our judgments. Choose one of the above questions about which you would want more information than is presented in the story. What additional information would you like? Why would that information help you make a more satisfactory decision?

Soldiers of Misfortune

BONUS ARMY

(Herbert Hoover Presidential Library)

Members of Bonus Army Battling Police

It has been called the Great Depression, but there was nothing great about it. It probably should have been called the Terrible Depression. From the late 1920s through the 1930s, the U.S. economy suffered its worst setback. Banks closed, businesses failed, farm prices fell, and millions of Americans lost their homes and jobs.

Throughout the nation people struggled to survive. For shelter, some people built rickety shacks from scraps of wood and cardboard. Some took to the road, moving from town to town seeking food and jobs. In cities it was common to see long lines of people waiting for free meals of soup and bread donated by charities. Once prosperous workers now suffered the pains of poverty.

Included among the unemployed were tens of thousands of World War I veterans—men who little more than a decade before had fought to defend democracy. Now many of these men decided to fight a new battle. They would go to Washington and demand that Congress provide some financial relief from their woes of poverty.

Most nations have a tradition of rewarding those who fought their wars. In keeping with that tradition, Congress passed a law in 1924 providing medical and other benefits for veterans. Included in the law was a provision that veterans would receive a payment of money in 1945. This payment became known as the bonus and would amount to a few hundred dollars for each veteran. Faced with the unemployment and hunger brought on by the Depression, many veterans believed they should receive their bonuses at once and not have to wait until 1945.

In May 1932, a few hundred veterans in Portland, Oregon decided to march to Washington. They intended to demonstrate in favor of a bill before Congress that would provide immediate payment of the bonus. The veterans did not march the entire way. When possible they got into freight trains headed east. Because the marchers could not pay, railroad officials tried to prevent them from getting on board. In such instances, the veterans would block the tracks or engage in other disruptive actions until they were permitted back on the trains.

The marchers soon received publicity. As other unemployed veterans heard of the march, many decided they, too, would go to Washington. Soon there were reports of thousands of veterans, a "Bonus Army," moving toward the capital.

In Washington, city officials were worried. What would they do with thousands of unemployed, former soldiers? It appeared the veterans were not coming for a short visit. Walter W. Waters, the man selected by the veterans as their leader, had announced: "I don't know when we'll get to Washington, but we're going to stay there until the bonus bill is passed if it takes until 1945."

Waters seemed the ideal leader for the veterans. In his mid-thirties, he was tall, energetic, and a stirring public speaker. The former army sergeant had also suffered from the Depression. Unable to find steady work, he and his wife had only fried potatoes for their Christmas dinner. He was determined to get the bonus he believed the veterans deserved.

Washington officials became even more worried when they heard that Communists were involved in the veterans' movement. There was a small Communist party in the United States at that time, and some veterans were members. The Communists supposedly hoped for violent confrontations that would lead to an overthrow of the government. Officials feared what might happen if thousands of angry ex-soldiers in the streets of Washington became influenced by the Communists.

Police Chief Pelham D. Glassford was not as concerned as some other Washington leaders. At that time, the city was governed by three district commissioners appointed by President Hoover. One of the commissioners, Glassford's superior, wanted to use force to move the veterans out of the city. Glassford disagreed. He believed more harm than good would come from using force. He argued that order could be maintained by trying to control the Bonus Army rather than fighting it. The commissioner reluctantly gave in to Glassford—at least for a while.

By early June thousands of veterans had entered the city. A West Point graduate, Glassford had been a general during the war. Now he met with ex-sergeant Waters who had become, in effect, the general of the Bonus Army. For a time the two men were able to work together.

Waters organized the army into military units to help maintain order. Each marcher had to show papers proving he was a veteran. Waters also organized a military police force to help assure that no Communists were allowed into the ranks of the Bonus Army.

Chief Glassford tried to prepare the city for what was to come. He told the citizens that the veterans, like other Americans, had a right to come to Washington. As for the Communists, they were a legal political party. Although they advocated the overthrow of the government, the chief believed he had to protect their rights to demonstrate as long as they did not break the law.

The chief arranged places for the Bonus Army to stay. The largest group was to camp on the Anacostia Flats, a few miles from the center of the city. Glassford thought this a good site because, in the event of trouble, a drawbridge across the Anacostia River could be raised to prevent easy access to the downtown area.

Some groups of marchers were allowed to stay in abandoned old buildings that were soon to be demolished for new construction. Glassford made sure that those who said they were Communists were separated from the rest of the veterans. About two hundred Communists were housed in a building away from the main body of veterans. There it was easier for the police to keep a watch on them.

Glassford also helped provide food, beds, and medical services for the growing Bonus Army. Waters tried to prevent food from going to the Communist veterans. Although he opposed the politics of the Communists, Glassford said they had to be fed like the other veterans.

Glassford's success in obtaining donations of supplies from Washington citizens and the government were appreciated by most of the veterans. He was often cheered as he rode his motorcycle through the camps checking on conditions. For a while he even served as the treasurer of the Bonus Army.

Glassford and his police had a difficult job. The president believed control and care of the Bonus Army was the responsibility of local Washington officials and not a matter for the federal government. Glassford's job was made somewhat easier because the vast majority of the veterans were patriotic and law-abiding. Their number was menacing, however. By mid-June about twenty thousand veterans were camped in the city.

The sight of hungry, often ragged veterans living in makeshift shelters brought much public sympathy. It was discouraging to see the former war heroes struggling to survive. Sympathy for the marchers did not translate into support for the bonus bill then being debated in Congress. Opponents of the bill said the cost of the bonus would virtually deplete the federal treasury. They said the veterans were only a small proportion of unemployed Americans and should not be singled out for special treatment at the expense of others. Those who favored the bonus bill said the veterans had risked their lives for their country and deserved the bonus in advance. Some also argued that the bonus would stimulate the economy by giving the veterans more spending power.

There was little chance that the bonus bill would pass in Congress. Even if it could have passed, President Hoover would probably have vetoed it as an expense the nation could not afford during a depression.

The veterans demonstrated for their bonus, talked with members of Congress, and packed the galleries to listen to the debates on the bill. The final Senate vote occurred June 17, 1932, and about eight thousand veterans waited outside the Capitol to hear the outcome.

After the Senate vote, Walter Waters stepped out to announce the news to the veterans. They were stunned; the Senate had voted down the bonus bill. During the tense silence that followed, some observers feared the Bonus Army might riot or attack the capitol. It did not. Waters led the disappointed veterans in singing a patriotic song after which they returned to their camps.

After the defeat of the bonus bill, many thought the veterans would leave the city, but the old soldiers would not fade away. Some left, but more came. Waters repeated his pledge that they would stay until 1945 if necessary.

Glassford was torn. He continued to provide aid to the Bonus Army, but he also wished they would leave. In speeches he tried to persuade the marchers to go home. In meetings with the district commissioners, however, he urged the establishment of semipermanent housing. Glassford was convinced that a hard core of the veterans planned an indefinite stay.

The commissioners were unimpressed with Glassford's suggestion. They said the chief's kindness was one reason the veterans were staying. Also, the government needed to get to work demolishing the old buildings so that new construction could begin. Occupation of the old buildings meant construction and demolition workers would be without work. The commissioner said that Glassford must move the veterans out.

Glassford continued to try to persuade the veterans to leave. Congress helped by providing money to help pay the veterans' expenses for traveling back to their homes. Some veterans did leave, but many others probably felt the same as one man who wrote: "Why should we go home? My savings were exhausted in the Summer of 1931; since that time I don't know how I and my family lived, that's not the word—existed—no home—no money—I might as well be here, and here I shall stay even if in jail."

Waters did what he could to keep the men in Washington. His military police reportedly threatened any veteran who wanted to leave. Nerves became strained as the hot summer wore on. More and more there were fears of a violent clash between the veterans and the authorities. A Communist group attempted to march around the White House but was pushed back by the police. Adding to the tension were rumors that members of the non-Communist Bonus Army were gathering weapons.

Federal officials decided it was time to act. Authorities prepared orders to evict the veterans from the downtown buildings. Glassford hoped the eviction would be peaceful. On July 27, he brought Waters to meet with the district commissioners so that the eviction could be planned. The commissioners refused to meet Waters face-to-face. As a result, Glassford carried messages from one room to another. Eventually Waters agreed to order the men out of the buildings. He later said that he had been given a few days to complete the removal. That was not the official plan, however. Federal officials were to order the veterans out the following day. Glassford was ordered to protect the officials.

The buildings occupied by the veterans, as well as Camp Anacostia, were federal property. Glassford had arranged for these places to be temporarily used by the Bonus Army. Advisors to President Hoover were concerned that local police would not be able to maintain order if the veterans resisted removal. Hoover was persuaded to call on federal troops if it became necessary. He insisted, however, that troops not be used unless requested by Glassford and the commissioners.

On the morning of July 28, Waters urged the veterans to leave one of the downtown buildings. He was booed and called a traitor to the Bonus Army. The men refused to leave. Federal officials and Glassford's police then came to the scene. The veterans were led, one at a time, out of the building. A few struggled but were quickly subdued. A large crowd had gathered to watch, but no violence occurred. By noon the first building was cleared.

When veterans at Anacostia heard of the eviction, many of them hurried to the area to protest. An angry crowd began milling around. Then, suddenly, a group of veterans, one carrying an American flag, attempted to reoccupy the building. Glassford and his men headed them off and a fight began. Some people in the crowd threw bricks at the police. After about five minutes peace was restored.

The crowd remained in an ugly mood. Many police officers feared they could no longer control the situation. Chief Glassford, however, did not call for federal troops. The commissioners, on the other hand, did request troops. In their request to the president, the commissioners said that the chief agreed troops were needed. Glassford later denied that he said it.

Early in the afternoon there was another fight between the police and a group of veterans. One officer being attacked began firing his gun. Glassford arrived and ordered the shooting stopped. Two veterans were hit. One was killed immediately; the other died later. It was the first time firearms had been used during the many weeks of the Bonus Army's presence.

The federal troops had been well prepared. General Douglas MacArthur, chief of staff of the army, was in command. President Hoover wanted use of the troops to be limited. His orders to MacArthur were as follows:

> You will have United States troops proceed immediately to the scene of disorder. Cooperate fully with the District of Columbia police force which is now in charge. Surround the affected area and clear it without delay.
>
> Turn over all prisoners to the civil authorities. In your orders insist that any women and children who may be in the affected area be accorded every consideration and kindness. Use all humanity consistent with the due execution of this order.

MacArthur had his orders, but he also had his own ideas. Like the commissioners, he believed Glassford's methods had helped create the problem. He was also convinced that the Bonus Army had become dominated by radicals and was a threat to law and order. To MacArthur it was time to drive them completely out of the city.

Late in the afternoon the troops, including cavalry and tanks, began clearing the downtown area. When veterans resisted, tear gas was used. Soldiers also used bayonets to keep the veterans moving.

By evening the troops reached Camp Anacostia. Hoover sent orders that the army should not cross into the camp. MacArthur claimed it was too late to stop the operation. After a brief delay, the troops moved into the camp. Soon the night blazed with fire. The shacks of the Bonus Army were aflame. Some were set afire by retreating veterans; others were fired by the troops. By early the following morning, the Bonus Army had been driven from the capital.

In a news conference General MacArthur said the Bonus Army had become a mob that might have attempted a revolution. He praised his troops and reminded listeners that no one had been killed during the eviction.

President Hoover was angry at MacArthur's disobedience, but he did nothing to punish the general. Hoover did not publicly admit that MacArthur had gone beyond his orders. Instead he said, "There is no group, no matter what its origin, that can be allowed to violate the laws of this city to intimidate the government." People believed that Hoover had ordered the total eviction of the veterans from Washington.

Many Americans were disgusted with the treatment of the Bonus Army. One editor wrote: "What a pitiful spectacle is that of the American Government, mightiest in the world, chasing unarmed men, women and children with Army tanks." Chief Glassford, eventually fired by the district commissioners, wrote articles blaming the president for mishandling the Bonus Army.

President Hoover, in part because of the Bonus Army episode, became an unpopular president. He was easily defeated by Franklin D. Roosevelt in the November elections.

The major sources for this story were:

Daniels, Roger. *The Bonus March: An Episode of the Great Depression.* Westport, Conn.: Greenwood, 1971.

Lisio, Donald J. *The President and Protest: Hoover, Conspiracy and the Bonus Riot.* Columbia, Mo.: University of Missouri Press, 1974.

ACTIVITIES FOR "SOLDIERS OF MISFORTUNE"

Write all answers on a separate sheet of paper.

Historical Understanding

Answer briefly:

1. Identify three effects of the Great Depression.

2. What did Congress provide World War I veterans in 1924?

3. Why were many Washington authorities worried about Communists?

Reviewing the Facts of the Case

Answer briefly:

1. Why did the Bonus Army come to Washington?

2. In what way did Chief Glassford and the district commissioners disagree on how the Bonus Army should be treated?

3. What did Glassford do to help maintain order during the stay of the Bonus Army?

4. What were two arguments in favor of the bonus bill and two arguments against it?

5. What was Walter Waters' attitude toward Communists?

6. Why did Washington officials want the Bonus Army to leave after the Senate voted against the bonus?

7. Why were federal troops called out?

8. How did General MacArthur and President Hoover differ on how troops should be used?

Analyzing Ethical Issues

Difficult decisions are often a mix of factual and ethical issues. A factual issue is a question that asks what *is* or what might be. Factual issues are concerned with whether a statement is true or false, accurate or inaccurate. An ethical issue is a question that asks what *ought to be*—whether something is right or wrong, fair or unfair. One difficult decision that Chief Glassford faced was whether or not to provide the Communist veterans with food and supplies just as he did for the non-Communist veterans. He had to consider both factual and ethical issues. For example:

DECISION: *Whether or not to feed the Communist veterans.*

FACTUAL ISSUE: *Would feeding the Communists encourage more of them to come to Washington?*

ETHICAL ISSUE: *Is it right to treat the Communist veterans the same as the non-Communist veterans?*

Find another instance in this story in which a difficult decision had to be made. Identify the decision and one factual and one ethical issue involved.

Expressing Your Reasoning

1. Should the Bonus Army have been driven out of the capital? Why or why not?

2. After the defeat of the bonus bill, Waters did all that he could to keep the men in Washington to continue demonstrating for the bonus. Was Waters wrong to do that? Why or why not?

3. President Hoover was angered that General MacArthur did not obey his orders but did not publicly tell anyone that it had happened. Instead he publicly said that he supported MacArthur's actions and reasons. We do not know why Hoover acted that way. Should the president have punished MacArthur for disobedience? Why or why not? Write a paragraph expressing your opinion.

4. One of the controversies surrounding the Bonus Army concerned what special benefits should be awarded military veterans by the government. There was general agreement that veterans should get some benefits but disagreement as to what those benefits should be. Which, if any, of the following types of benefits do you think should be given to veterans? Explain your reasoning for each benefit.
    a. Medical expenses for injury or illness suffered while in the military.
    b. Medical expenses for any injury or illness whether or not suffered while in the military.
    c. Money to help pay for the higher education of veterans.
    d. Preferential treatment when competing with nonveterans for government jobs.

5. *Seeking Additional Information.* In making decisions about such
   questions as those above, we often feel we need more information
   before we are satisfied with our judgments. Choose one of the
   above questions about which you would want more information
   than is presented in the story. What additional information would
   you like? Why would that information help you make a more
   satisfactory decision?

United We Sit

FLINT SIT-DOWN STRIKE

(Courtesy of the Library of Congress)

Sit-down Strikers, Fisher Body Number One, 1937

The time was early evening of a bitterly cold winter day, December 30, 1936. The place was General Motors' key plant in Flint, Michigan. The event was an attempt by the autoworkers employed in the factory to shut it down. When the starting whistle blew to begin the evening shift, there was no roar of machinery. There was only silence. Then a third-floor window swung open. A worker leaned out and shouted, "She's ours!"

Thus began the great General Motors sit-down strike. For six weeks the attention of Americans was riveted on Flint. The sit-down strike was a lead story in newspapers, newsreels, and radio newscasts. One historian has called this strike the most significant conflict between U.S. labor and management in the twentieth century. What prompted the small and weak United Automobile Workers union (UAW) to challenge the giant and powerful General Motors Corporation (GM)?

Automobile manufacturing was the number one industry in the United States, and GM was the number one automaker. GM's 1936 sales of 1,500,000 Chevrolets, Pontiacs, Oldsmobiles, Buicks, La-Salles, and Cadillacs made it the largest manufacturer in the world. It was also the most profitable—$284 million in pretax profits in 1936.

These profits were widely distributed to GM's *stockholders* (those who own shares of the company's stock). There were hundreds of thousands of them across the country. They were pleased with the performance of the company they owned. They opposed any changes that might threaten the production of so many golden eggs.

Unions were considered a disruptive new influence at GM. Plant managers were allowed to meet with employee representatives to discuss wages, hours, and working conditions at local plants. The company refused, however, to recognize a labor union formally or to enter into a written contract with one. To prevent the union from gaining worker support, GM hired private detectives to spy on union workers in its factories.

Although autoworkers received high hourly wages and other benefits, their work schedule was irregular. Automobile production was seasonal. During periods of low production fewer workers were needed. The fear of being laid off during these periods hung over the head of every worker. The plant foreman usually decided who would be kept and who would lose their jobs. He often showed favoritism. Length of service did not protect a worker against lay-off. The company could fire anyone it wished.

In 1936, 15 percent of GM's hourly workers had been laid off for part of the year. For those who were laid off, high hourly wages did not translate to high annual income. A study by the federal government in 1936 estimated that a family of four needed an annual income of $1,435. Average earnings for those laid off that year were below $1,150.

Workers not only felt insecure about keeping their jobs. They were also dissatisfied about the nature of their work. The major complaint was that the work schedule was exhausting: nine hours a day, five days a week. The wife of a Chevrolet plant worker put it this way: "My husband, he's a torch solderer. . . . You should see him come home at night, him and the rest of the men in the buses. So tired like they was dead, and irritable. . . . And then at night in bed, he shakes, his whole body, he shakes."

One cause of fatigue was the *speed-up* (increasing the pace set on the assembly line). As the workers stood in their places, tools in hand, the line monotonously moved one car after another past them. A foreman holding a stopwatch would sometimes yell at the workers to hurry. A Buick worker complained, "We didn't have time to go to the toilet. . . . You have to run to the toilet and run back." The faster the line moved, the higher the output. GM workers believed that the company was always trying to increase profits by getting more production with fewer workers. A Fisher Body plant worker protested bitterly: "You might call yourself a man if you was on the street, but as soon as you went through the door and punched your card, you was nothing more or less than a robot. . . . It takes your guts out, that line."

During the Great Depression, some workers began to turn to unionism as the best hope for improving their lot. Through unions they hoped to increase wages and benefits, improve job security, and slow down the pace of their work.

The autoworkers' union was not well established during the early thirties. By 1935 only 5.4 percent of the wage earners employed in the auto industry had joined the UAW.

Union leaders recognized that if the automobile workers were to be organized, the UAW would have to penetrate GM's Flint stronghold. If the union could prove its strength in Flint, autoworkers everywhere would be more willing to join the UAW. By the summer of 1936 the UAW had only 150 members in Flint. That drab industrial city was the home of GM's Fisher Body Number One, the largest automobile body plant in the world. Chevrolet, Buick, and AC Spark Plug factories were also located there. More than one-half of the city's labor force was made up of GM autoworkers. Eighty percent of Flint's families were dependent upon the GM payroll.

In November 1936, the UAW leadership announced its goals for the autoworkers. These goals included elimination of speed-up, *seniority* based on length of service alone (last hired, first fired, when layoffs were necessary), an eight-hour day and forty-hour week, time-and-a-half pay for overtime, and improved safety measures. One goal, however, stood high above the others: recognition by GM of the UAW as the only labor union with which they would bargain. As 1936 drew to a close, GM leaders remained as opposed as ever to unions.

The hopes of UAW leaders were raised by the landslide re-election of Franklin Roosevelt in 1936. The president was considered a friend of organized labor. "You voted New Deal at the polls and defeated the Auto Barons—Now get a New Deal in the shop," a UAW official told the autoworkers.

Recent changes in federal law further increased the optimism of labor leaders. In 1935, Congress passed, and the president signed into law, the National Labor Relations Act (NLRA), sometimes referred to as the Wagner Act after its chief sponsor Senator Robert Wagner of New York. The Wagner Act required employers to bargain with their workers. It also prohibited employers from using "unfair labor practices," including firing union members and interfering with union organizing efforts. The new law also set up the National Labor Relations Board. Among other things, it held elections among the workers of a company to find out if they wished to be represented by a particular union.

Renewed efforts in the last months of 1936 to organize the autoworkers of Flint were unsuccessful. By late December only 10 percent of the city's GM workers had joined the UAW. Union leaders were convinced that if an election under the NLRA were held, the UAW would lose it. It seemed that a dramatic display of union strength would be required to get the majority of workers to embrace the UAW. The majority of the workers were not necessarily opposed to the UAW. They were waiting to see how the union would fare in a struggle with the giants of the industry.

Even if the UAW could have won an election under the NLRA, GM would not have accepted the results. The company expected the

Supreme Court to declare the Wagner Act unconstitutional and had decided not to obey it in the meantime.

The stage was set for a strike. But what kind of strike? Normally, when workers went on strike, they walked off their jobs. Carrying signs, they usually marched in picket lines around the outside of the building where they worked. In the past, this kind of strike had often been smashed by police breaking through the line of pickets.

UAW leaders decided upon a special kind of strike in Flint—a sit-down. Instead of walking off their jobs, strikers would remain at their machines overnight and refuse to operate them. An attempt by police to break the strike might lead the strikers to damage expensive company machinery. Also, in a sit-down strike, it would be very difficult for strikebreakers to replace the strikers at their jobs.

A union leader at Flint's Fisher One was asked if his workers were ready for a sit-down strike. "Ready? They're like a pregnant woman in her tenth month!" On December 30, 1936, it happened. Workers at Fisher Body One and nearby Fisher Two sat down inside the plants. David was trying out a new weapon against Goliath. The fate of the UAW rested upon the outcome of the contest.

A strike in one key automobile plant could paralyze other factories that depended on its product. During the first few weeks of the sit-down strike in Flint, parts shortages caused closings of 50 other plants. Production of Chevrolets and Buicks was grinding to a halt just as the new year began. Across the country the total number of idled GM workers soon reached 136,000. Nonstrikers complained about being deprived of work by the striking minority.

Although the strike had spread to other places, the spotlight remained on Flint, the principal seat of GM's power. A proud GM worker wrote to his wife: "We have the key plant of the General Motors and the eyes of the world are looking at us. We shure done a thing that GM said never could be done."

Sit-down strikers conducted themselves with military discipline inside the struck plants. Strike committees drafted and enforced strict rules of conduct. Dining halls were established in the plant cafeterias. Sleeping quarters were improvised from car seats. For recreation there were lectures and games of ping-pong and volleyball. Some strikers went roller skating between the long lines of idle machinery. A feeling of solidarity grew among the strikers inside the plants. Morale was high.

GM insisted that the sit-downers were illegally trespassing on company property. The company refused to bargain with the strikers until the plants were evacuated. General Motors' president, Alfred Sloan, said the UAW was seeking a labor dictatorship. His company would not accept any union as the sole bargaining agent for its employees.

Tension mounted in Flint. On January 11, 1937, it exploded into violence. General Motors cut off heat to the Fisher Two plant. The temperature outside was 16 degrees. At dinner time, company guards refused to let the dinner meal be delivered to the strikers. In response, UAW leaders decided to bring in union members from other cities to take over the main gate of the plant. At 8:30 P.M. a squad of men, armed with billy clubs, approached the company guards blocking the gate. The guards fled. Their commander telephoned Flint police headquarters for help. Riot-equipped police officers were dispatched to the scene.

The police stormed the plant entrance. Tear gas crashed through the closed windows. The strikers fought back with bottles, bolts, steel car-door hinges, and torrents of water from the plant's fire hoses. The police were turned away. By the end of the battle, 13 strikers suffered gunshot wounds. Eleven policemen were also injured. Most of them had gashed heads. Heat and food were restored after the violent incident.

The outbreak of violence brought Michigan's new governor, Frank Murphy, to Flint. Throughout his career, Murphy had demonstrated a genuine sympathy for the afflicted and the unfortunate. Born and raised in Michigan, Murphy had graduated from the University of Michigan with a law degree. In a paper for a course he took at the university Murphy had written: "If I can only feel, when my day is done, that I have accomplished something toward uplifting the poor, uneducated, unfortunate, ten hour a day, laborer from the political chaos he now exists in, I will be satisfied that I have been worthwhile."

Frank Murphy's secret ambition was to become president of the United States. During the early 1930s, he had been mayor of Detroit and then governor-general of the Philippine Islands. When he won the 1936 race for governor of Michigan, one newspaper noted that Murphy would be a presidential possibility in 1940. The thought had already occurred to the newly elected governor.

Unlike many public officials of his time, Murphy sympathized with workers. He believed that workers had the right to join unions and to strike. He favored *arbitration* (settlement of conflicts by an impartial third party) rather than force as a way to settle labor disputes. He was determined to avoid violence during strikes. The government, he believed, must not take sides during a strike. According to Murphy, police ought to keep peace without favoring either strikers or their employers.

Murphy received strong support for his election from labor unions. While campaigning he declared, "I am heart and soul in the labor movement." Upon his election, he received a congratulatory message from the president of the American Federation of Labor. Murphy responded, "My administration in Lansing will mark a new day for labor in Michigan."

The new governor arrived in Flint the day after violence had broken out. Murphy ordered National Guard troops and state police into the city. "Peace and order will prevail," the governor vowed.

By the end of the day, 1,289 guardsmen, most of them in their late teens and early twenties, had arrived. Their number would double by the end of the month. The troops blockaded the area near the struck plants. They made no attempt to eject the strikers or deny them access to food.

In the past, strikers throughout the United States had reason to fear the arrival of troops. They had been used to break strikes, often violently. In Flint, however, strikers cheered the arrival of soldiers because they trusted the man who sent them. "Under no circumstances," Murphy declared, "would the troops take sides."

Critics of the governor charged that it was his obligation to take sides. The governor, they claimed, ought to employ the power of the state to restore GM property to its rightful owners. Some said Murphy's neutrality was really a prostrike policy.

Murphy wanted to break the stalemate by negotiation between the UAW and GM. His first efforts to bring about a negotiated settlement broke down. A major obstacle was the stance of GM's President Sloan. He refused to bargain with "a group that holds our plants for ransom without regard to law or justice."

The strikers were unlawfully occupying GM property. Governor Murphy was urged to enforce the law and eject the strikers by force. An attempt by troops to drive out the sit-downers would produce certain bloodshed. On February 2, the pressure mounted on Murphy to evict the strikers forcibly. A Flint judge issued an *injunction* (court order) requiring evacuation of the Fisher Body plants within 24 hours.

After the judge's order was read to the strikers at Fisher Two, they sent the following telegram to the governor:

> We have decided to stay in the plant. We have no illusions about the sacrifices which this decision will entail. We fully expect that if a violent effort is made to oust us many of us will be killed and we take this means of making it known to our wives, our children, and to the people of the state of Michigan and of the country that if this result follows from the attempt to eject us you are the one who must be held responsible for our deaths.

The responsibility to act was thrust upon the governor by the injunction. Would he order an assault on the occupied plants? "I'm not going down in history as Bloody Murphy," the governor declared. "It would be inconsistent with everything I have ever stood for in my entire life." Murphy refused to use bullets and bayonets to drive the strikers from the plants.

Instead, the governor brought GM and UAW leaders to Detroit for negotiations. Murphy personally served as mediator. Like a jackrabbit, he jumped back and forth between the two parties carrying proposals and counterproposals. After a final grueling 16-hour session, the deadlock was broken. The 40-day sit-down strike came to an end. GM had lost production of 280,000 cars, valued at $175 million.

As part of the settlement, the UAW agreed to evacuate the plants. In exchange, GM recognized the UAW and agreed to bargain exclusively with it. The union had won a major victory. The settlement opened the floodgates of union membership. UAW membership swelled rapidly. In the wake of the sit-down strike, the UAW was recognized by Chrysler, Ford, and the smaller automobile manufacturers.

Governor Murphy, more than anyone else, affected the outcome of the strike. He had insisted that welfare payments be made to the strikers' families. He had dispatched troops to Flint, not to break the strike, but to prevent violence. He had delayed enforcement of a court order that could have broken the strike. He had personally kept the strike talks going day and night until a settlement was reached.

When the dispute finally ended, reactions were mixed. Labor leaders applauded Murphy for his handling of the strike. "A great achievement of a great American," was the praise offered by President Roosevelt. Many others were sharply critical of the governor for failure to enforce the law and protect GM property. Critics emphasized that the sit-downers had broken the law by committing criminal trespass. A member of Congress accused Murphy of having "sowed the seeds of armed rebellion and anarchy."

Soon after the settlement of the GM sit-down strike, a rash of sit-down strikes spread across the country, especially in Michigan. Workers of every stripe—garbage collectors, waitresses, hospital workers, dime store clerks—sat down on their jobs. There were 477 sit-down strikes during 1937. A group of civic leaders in Boston wired the Senate in March 1937:

> It is rapidly growing beyond control . . . if minority groups can seize premises illegally, hold them indefinitely, refuse admittance to owners and managers, resist by violence and threaten bloodshed all attempts to dislodge them, and intimidate properly constituted authority to the point of impotence, then freedom and liberty are at an end, government becomes a mockery, suspended by anarchy, mob rule, and ruthless dictatorship.

In 1939, the U.S. Supreme Court outlawed the sit-down strike as a violation of property rights. The citizens of Michigan rendered a verdict of their own a year earlier. Frank Murphy was defeated for re-election as governor. The sit-downs had been a major cause for his defeat. According to one newspaper, the voters carried "pictures of 1937 in the back of their heads when they went to the polls." Frank Murphy's hopes of becoming president had been dealt a shattering blow. He was never to hold elective office again. President Roosevelt, however, appointed Murphy attorney general of the United States and later justice of the U.S. Supreme Court.

The major sources for this story were:

Fine, Sidney. *Frank Murphy: The New Deal Years*. Chicago: University of Chicago Press, 1979.

Fine, Sidney. *Sit-Down: The General Motors Strike of 1936–37*. Ann Arbor: University of Michigan Press, 1969.

Sear, Stephen W. "Shut the Goddam Plant!" *American Heritage* 33(3) (April–May 1982):49–64.

ACTIVITIES FOR "UNITED WE SIT"

Write all answers on a separate sheet of paper.

Historical Understanding

Answer briefly:

1. During the 1930s what was the leading industry in the United States and which corporation was the largest manufacturer in that industry?

2. In a labor dispute, what is *arbitration*?

3. What were two goals of the UAW in the 1930s?

4. What were the major provisions of the National Labor Relations Act of 1935?

Reviewing the Facts of the Case

Answer briefly:

1. What was GM's policy toward labor unions during the 1930s?

2. Identify two complaints autoworkers had about their jobs.

3. Why did the UAW choose Flint as the location for the sit-down strike?

4. Why was the sit-down type of strike chosen as a tactic by the UAW?

5. In what ways did Governor Murphy influence the outcome of the GM sit-down strike?

6. What effects did the GM sit-down strike have upon (a) the organized labor movement and (b) Frank Murphy's political career?

Analyzing Ethical Issues

Examining the value of property.   Property is a value concerning what people should be allowed to own and how they should be allowed to use it. Identify two incidents in the story that involve the value of property. For example:

The UAW demanded a greater share of GM profits.

Expressing Your Reasoning

1. Should Governor Murphy have forcibly ejected the sit-down strikers from the plants they occupied in Flint? Why or why not?

2. In deciding whether to use force to evict the sit-down strikers, which of the facts below do you think should have been most important to the governor? Which should have been the least important to him? Explain your choices.

a. Removal of the strikers would have caused bloodshed.
b. Most General Motors executives had opposed Murphy's election, and the UAW had supported his candidacy.
c. A governor's oath of office includes a duty to enforce the laws of the state.
d. Murphy wanted to become president of the United States.
e. GM had refused to bargain collectively with the UAW.
f. The premises occupied by the strikers belonged to GM.
g. Murphy owned GM stock valued at $105,000.
h. A poll showed that 65 percent of Michigan citizens thought the government should use force to remove sit-down strikers.

3. Uncertainty of employment was one of the concerns of GM workers. Because auto production was seasonal and unpredictable, workers were in danger of being laid off their jobs. To protect themselves, the workers wanted GM to accept a seniority system. Under such a system workers would be laid off based on their length of service alone; last hired, first fired. Would it be fair for GM to follow a seniority system in determining the order of layoff? Write a paragraph expressing your position. Before writing consider whether marital status, number of dependents, or quality of work should be taken into account in deciding which employees should be kept on the job at a time of cutbacks.

4. During the sit-down strike in Flint, Governor Murphy ordered that public relief be paid by the state government to nonstrikers and strikers alike. Do you think he was right to grant welfare payments to the families of striking workers? State a reason for your position.

5. *Seeking Additional Information.* In making decisions about such questions as those above, we often feel we need more information before we are satisfied with our judgments. Choose one of the above questions about which you would want more information than is presented in the story. What additional information would you like? Why would that information help you make a more satisfactory decision?

Yearning to Breathe Free

JEWISH REFUGEES

(Courtesy of Stern Archives)

Passengers on the **St. Louis** Leaving Germany

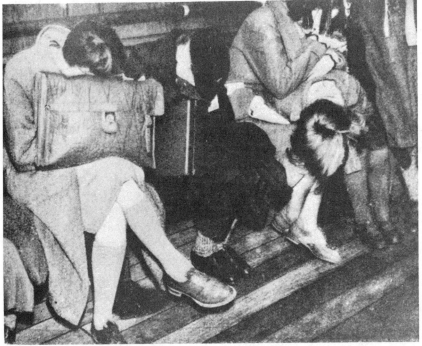

(*Courtesy of Stern Archives*)

Passengers on the St. Louis Returning to Europe

On May 27, 1939, the big German ocean liner *St. Louis* steamed into Cuba's Havana Harbor. The decks were crammed with happy German passengers eager and anxious to leave the ship after the voyage from Hamburg, Germany. The passengers all carried Cuban *visas* (legal documents allowing them to enter another country). After staying for a time in Cuba, the passengers expected to immigrate to the United States. Most of the passengers were elated. Why were they so happy? Why were they leaving their homeland? The story of the *St. Louis* and its cargo of over nine hundred people illustrates the social, economic, and political turmoil of the times.

Most of the passengers were German Jews fleeing the horrors of Nazi Germany. When Adolf Hitler and the Nazi party took control of

Germany in 1933, they were determined to rid Germany of all Jews. The Nazis blamed the Jews for Germany's problems and wanted to create a "pure" German race. Jews were not to be included.

Over the years, Nazi policies toward the Jews became increasingly severe. Jews were not permitted to hold certain types of jobs, jobs that they had worked at for years. Jewish businesses and property were taken by the government. Jews were prohibited from using public facilities such as parks and swimming pools. The Nuremberg Laws of 1935 declared that Jews were no longer German citizens. Many Jews were imprisoned in concentration camps or simply dumped over the border into neighboring nations.

Early in November 1938, a night of terror known as *Kristallnacht* (Night of Broken Glass) occurred. Nazi mobs destroyed Jewish businesses and burned synagogues. Jews were beaten in the streets. The police did nothing to stop the violence. To add to the outrage, the government blamed the Jewish victims for the destruction. A heavy tax was placed on Jews to pay for the damage done to them! Even the most patriotic German Jews began to realize they would not be safe unless they left Germany.

President Franklin Roosevelt was shocked by the events of *Kristallnacht*. He said he "could scarcely believe that such things occur in a twentieth century civilization." In reaction, the president extended the time limit on visitors' visas for about fifteen thousand German Jews then visiting the United States. By his action, the German Jews could remain in the United States for an additional six months. He doubted that "we have a right to put them on a ship and send them back to Germany under the present conditions."

The president's action showed his disgust with Hitler's Nazis. Some Americans wished he would do more. Thousands of Jews were fleeing Germany seeking safety. Many wanted to come to the United States. Under U.S. law, however, the number of people who could immigrate to the United States was strictly limited. Some wanted the president to try to change the law. The vast majority of Americans favored the law, so it was unlikely that the Congress could be persuaded to change it.

Traditionally, the United States had been a haven for immigrants. Since the 1800s, however, the government had placed restrictions on immigration. The law in effect in the 1930s was the National Origins Immigration Act of 1924. The law set limits on the number of people who were allowed to immigrate from various countries. Each nation received a quota stating the number of immigrants who could come to the United States each year. The highest quotas were given to nations in northern and western Europe. No immigrants from Asia were permitted. The quota for Germany was about twenty-six thousand a year.

People who wanted strict limitations on immigration were known as *restrictionists*. Some restrictionists even favored the complete elimination of immigration. During the 1920s and 1930s, restrictionist sentiment ran high. Three general factors help explain the rise in restrictionist feeling: isolationism, unemployment, and nativism.

Isolationists wanted the United States to avoid involvement with foreign nations. Placing limits on immigration was one way isolationists sought to avoid getting entangled in the affairs of other countries. As one Senator put it: "Let Europe take care of its own people. We cannot take care of our own, to say nothing of importing more to care for."

As a result of the Depression, millions of Americans were unemployed. Many workers feared immigrants would compete with them for jobs. Some said that every job taken by an immigrant was one less job for an American citizen.

Nativists were people who endorsed slogans like "America for Americans," or spoke of the need for citizens to be "100 percent" American. Nativists looked down on immigrants. One man commented in disgust at "the babble of foreign tongues, . . . the filth of the streets, the greasy lives of the people, the utter disregard for American standards of morality" that he associated with immigrants. Nativists believed the United States would be threatened by an influx of immigrants. According to one book on immigration, "No living nation need permit its own conquest by unselected immigrants."

Some Americans believed that immigration contributed to the quality of American life. They pointed out that virtually all Americans were descended from immigrants. They argued that purchases by immigrants would stimulate the economy and reduce unemployment. They also stressed that the number of immigrants entering the United States was small compared to the nation's total population of about 130 million. From their point of view, immigrants were no threat to the United States. Besides, the poem on the Statue of Liberty was an invitation to all people "yearning to breathe free."

Although there were people who defended immigrants, public opinion polls showed that close to 70 percent of Americans consistently favored the restricting of immigration. Politicians were well aware of anti-immigrant feelings. One Senator said opposing foreigners "is perhaps the best vote-getting argument in present-day politics. The politician can beat his breast and proclaim his loyalty to America. He can tell the unemployed man that he is out of work because some alien has a job."

Disagreement about immigration was not confined to the United States. England, France, and many other nations struggled with the problem of how to handle the thousands of refugees fleeing Germany. Many nations believed they had already taken in more refugees than they could handle.

As Germany took control of other countries, including Czechoslovakia and Austria, the stream of refugees rapidly became a river and threatened to become a flood. Not all the refugees were Jews, although Jews were the special target of the Nazis. To many people, however, all refugees were Jews. This made the refugee problem even more complicated.

For centuries Jews throughout the world had often been subject to a form of prejudice known as *anti-Semitism*. Anti-Semites distrusted Jews and blamed them for causing problems. In the United States, for example, anti-Semites leveled many false charges against Jews. They claimed that Jews controlled the economy and the government. They accused Jews of being more loyal to their religion than to the United States. Some anti-Semites feared that American Jews, in their efforts to help German Jews, might try to drag the United States into European problems.

Anti-immigrant feelings placed President Roosevelt and many other world leaders in a difficult position. The president condemned the terror tactics of the Nazis publicly. Political pressures, however, made it difficult for him to solve the problem of the refugees. Many people believed that any efforts to increase the quota would lead Congress to make immigration policy even more restrictive.

The president would not take action to change the quota law. He did, however, call an international conference to consider what could be done about the refugee problem. Representatives of over thirty nations met at Evian, France, early in 1938. Many statements of sympathy for the refugees were made, but no significant way of dealing with them came from the meetings.

Germany was quick to point out that the nations would not take all the Jewish refugees. One German newspaper taunted America by saying: "The United States, which initiated the Evian Conference, should be reminded of its moral duty to set other immigration countries a good example with a generous gesture." Hitler said with a sneer that Germany was willing to let all Jews leave, "even on luxury ships."

The *St. Louis* was a luxury ship, but the passengers had faced great hardships to get on board. Some of them had once been prosperous professionals, but the Nazi government had taken virtually all their money and property. Others had been abused in other ways by the Nazis. About one-half of the passengers were women and children. All had managed to pull together enough money to buy Cuban visas and a ticket to Cuba. About seven hundred of them had been accepted as future immigrants into the United States. Because of the quota system, most would have to wait in Cuba for a few months to a few years before they could enter the United States.

Each passenger could tell his or her own story of suspense and fear before boarding the *St. Louis* on May 13, 1939. Would 13 be a lucky number? They knew the German government might, at any time, refuse to allow them to leave. No wonder there were sighs of relief when the ship pulled away from the dock.

The passengers were pleasantly surprised at how well they were treated by the German crew. They did not know that the captain, Gustav Schroeder, had ordered the crew, some of whom were Nazis, to treat the passengers with care and respect.

Soon many passengers began relaxing and enjoying the good life aboard the liner. Captain Schroeder had made certain that they would receive the same fine food and entertainment for which his ship was known. There were many things, however, that the captain could not control.

Captain Schroeder had been assured by his superiors that Cuba would admit his passengers. He was not told that the Cuban visas had been cancelled! The visas had been illegally written and sold by a Cuban immigration official. Cuba's president, Federico Bru, had discovered the visa scheme and issued a decree making the visas worthless.

President Bru's action was popular in Cuba. Cuba had already accepted a few thousand Jewish refugees, and many Cubans believed they should take no more. There were also rumblings of anti-Semitism.

Referring to the *St. Louis'* passengers, one newspaper editorial said: "Against this invasion we must react with the same energy as have other people of the globe."

When the *St. Louis* entered Havana Harbor, passengers crowded on the decks thrilled to be so close to safety at last. On shore were crowds of onlookers, including relatives of some of the passengers. On board, ten-year-old Marianne Bardeleben strained her eyes for a glimpse of her father. Her mother stood with her.

The passengers had packed their luggage and were prepared to leave the ship. Hours passed. No announcement to disembark had been made. Why the delay? The travelers became anxious.

A day passed. Gradually it was becoming clear that the passengers were not going to be allowed to leave the ship. Police boats circled the ship to make certain no one attempted to jump overboard. Other small boats carried relatives of the passengers, looking up longingly at their dear ones. Still nothing happened.

The passengers were close to panic. One man slashed his wrists in a suicide attempt. Captain Schroeder feared that mass suicides might occur if his ship were ordered back to Germany. He established suicide patrols. Groups of men moved throughout the ship to stop desperate passengers who might try to kill themselves.

The captain argued with officials on shore. He urged a German diplomat to try to get the Cuban government to accept the passengers. The diplomat replied, "These are Jews, Captain, feeling here is against them." Schroeder was furious. "They are also people," he snapped, "and I care about people."

The captain's efforts were unsuccessful. Cuban President Bru said, "The post that I occupy has painful duties, which oblige me to disregard the impulses of my heart and follow the stern dictates of duty." Apparently he saw his duty as upholding the decree and not accepting the illegal visas.

A U.S. diplomat sent a telegram to U.S. Secretary of State Cordell Hull asking what might be done. The reply was: "There appears to be no action that . . . could properly [be taken] at present."

Captain Schroeder received orders for the *St. Louis* to leave the harbor. The ship quivered as the big engines rumbled to a start. A group of screaming passengers rushed the gangway but were pushed back by Cuban police. The *St. Louis* steamed away.

The story of the *St. Louis* had made headlines in newspapers around the world. Eager readers had followed the complicated story. It had become a great opportunity for German propaganda. According to the Nazis, the treatment of passengers aboard the *St. Louis* was proof that no nation wanted Jewish refugees.

Captain Schroeder had not yet been ordered to return to Germany. He was permitted to cruise slowly while further efforts were made to find a haven for the passengers. The ship passed close to Miami, and hopeful eyes looked toward the United States for help.

One of President Roosevelt's advisors called Secretary Hull to see if something might be done. Hull said, "This is a matter primarily between the Cuban government and these people."

A committee of passengers had sent a cable to President Roosevelt asking for help. Involved in many other complicated political and economic matters, the president had not followed the *St. Louis* episode very closely. He chose not to overrule the opinion of the State Department. To this day no one knows for certain why the president, a man sympathetic to the plight of refugees, decided as he did.

Captain Schroeder finally received orders to return his ship to Germany. The captain was determined that his passengers should never have to face Nazi horrors again. He considered crashing the huge liner into the rocky shoreline of southern England with the hope that the passengers could be evacuated safely. Such a dangerous and drastic action was not needed.

The governments of England, France, Belgium, and Holland, after lengthy negotiations with refugee organizations, reluctantly agreed to accept the *St. Louis'* passengers. The anguish of the voyage had ended. The passengers were safe at last.

The refugees were finally safe, but their refuge did not necessarily last for long. When the German army swept through Europe during the early years of World War II, they brought with them Hitler's new policy of "the final solution." He was no longer forcing Jews to emigrate. They were now to be taken to death camps. Before the war was over, millions of Jews had been killed. No one is certain how many of the passengers of the *St. Louis* were victims of the war. According to one estimate, only 240 of the over 900 passengers survived.

The major sources for this story were:

Feingold, Henry L. *The Politics of Rescue: The Roosevelt Administration and the Holocaust.* New Brunswick, N.J.: Rutgers University Press, 1970.

Morse, Arthur D. *While Six Million Died: A Chronicle of American Apathy.* New York: Random House, 1967.

Thomas, Gordon, and Witts, Max M. *Voyage of the Damned.* New York: Stein and Day, 1974.

Wyman, David S. *Paper Walls: America and the Refugee Crisis, 1938-1941.* Amherst, Mass.: University of Massachusetts Press, 1968.

ACTIVITIES FOR "YEARNING TO BREATHE FREE"

Write all answers on a separate sheet of paper.

Historical Understanding

Answer briefly:

1. Identify three ways the Nazi government discriminated against Jews during the 1930s.

2. What were the major provisions of the 1924 National Origins Immigration Act?

3. Define the following terms: *isolationist, nativist, anti-Semite,* and *restrictionist.*

Reviewing the Facts of the Case

Answer briefly:

1. Approximately how many Germans could legally immigrate to the United States each year during the 1930s?

2. What action did President Roosevelt take after hearing of *Kristall-nacht*?

3. Why were the Cuban visas invalidated?

4. How did the Nazi government make use of the voyage of the *St. Louis* for propaganda purposes?

5. What was the official position of the U.S. Department of State regarding the refugee passengers?

6. What was Hitler's "final solution"?

Analyzing Ethical Issues

There are a number of incidents in this story involving the following values:

AUTHORITY: a value concerning what rules or people should be obeyed and the consequences for disobedience

LIFE: a value concerning when, if ever, it is justifiable to take or threaten the life of another

For each of the two values above, write a sentence describing an event in the story involving that value. For example:

The value of authority was involved when President Bru decided to invalidate the visas.

Expressing Your Reasoning

1. Should President Roosevelt have admitted the passengers aboard the *St. Louis* into the United States?

2. Some people believe that President Roosevelt should have taken direct action to help the passengers on the *St. Louis*; other people believe he was right in what he did. Below are some arguments on each side of the issue. For both positions indicate which reason you find most persuasive and why.

President Roosevelt should have taken direct action to help because:
   a. As the U.S. president he had an obligation to set an example for the rest of the world.
   b. He should have placed the lives of the passengers over the law or any other problem.
   c. Most of the refugees would legally have been allowed into the United States in a few years.
   d. People fleeing from governments that violate their rights are refugees and should not be treated the same as other immigrants.
   e. He had often expressed his sympathy for the refugees from Nazi Germany.

President Roosevelt should not have taken direct action to help because:
   a. The United States was not at war with Germany and should not risk angering Hitler.
   b. U.S. law limited the number of immigrants allowed into the United States each year. He should not make an exception for the *St. Louis* passengers.
   c. Some Americans believed Jews had too much power in the

United States. Permitting the passengers to enter the United States might lead to more anti-Semitism.

d. The majority of Americans did not want any more immigrants than allowed by law.

e. Secretary Hull was correct. The problem was between the passengers and the Cuban government.

3. It is difficult to decide how many people should be allowed to enter the United States each year. It is also difficult to decide which people should be allowed to enter. What policy should there be regarding who may enter and who may not enter the United States? Write a proposed immigration policy. In your policy refer to the following considerations:

a. Whether the person can speak English.

b. The age of the person.

c. The physical or mental health of the person.

d. Whether the person has relatives in this country.

e. Whether the person is likely to be able to get a job.

f. Whether the person has ever been in trouble with the law.

g. The person's race or nationality.

h. The political opinions or beliefs of the person.

4. *Seeking Additional Information.* In making decisions about such questions as those above, we often feel we need more information before we are satisfied with our judgments. Choose one of the above questions about which you would want more information than is presented in the story. What additional information would you like? Why would that information help you make a more satisfactory decision?

PART 3

Hot and Cold War
(1941-1960)

A Loaded Weapon

JAPANESE RELOCATION

(*Courtesy of the Library of Congress*)

Japanese-Americans Being Evacuated, March 1942

President Franklin Roosevelt called it "a date which will live in infamy." Early Sunday morning, December 7, 1941, Japanese bombs fell on Pearl Harbor, the U.S. naval base in Hawaii. It was a scene of nearly total destruction. Two thousand Americans were killed and an equal number wounded. America's offensive naval power in the Pacific had been wiped out. The surprise attack meant war between the Empire of Japan and the United States.

The attack on Pearl Harbor was a tremendous shock to all Americans. Its aftermath was especially dreaded by Americans of Japanese ancestry. They feared that in the panic following the attack, hostility toward them might grow. They might be linked to the Japanese enemy abroad. There was good reason for them to feel alarmed. Prejudice against Japanese-Americans had been widespread, especially on the West Coast, for one half-century before Pearl Harbor.

Soon after Commodore Matthew Perry opened contact with Japan in 1854, some Japanese were issued passports for travel to the United States. Immigration from Japan to the United States remained a trickle until 1891. In that year the number of Japanese entering the United States reached 1,000 for the first time. The new immigrants were largely young, poor, single men. Many came expecting to return to Japan once they earned enough money to buy land there. Unable to save the necessary amount, some became permanent residents in the United States. The 1920 census reported 110,010 Japanese in the U.S. mainland.

The young Japanese males who settled in the United States were prevented by law and custom from marrying white women. Instead they took "picture brides." Often on the basis of only a photograph, their marriages were arranged by matchmakers in Japan. The young brides-to-be sailed to meet their prospective husbands, sight unseen.

The *Issei*, first generation Japanese-American immigrants, settled mostly in California, Oregon, and Washington. The majority worked in fruit orchards, vineyards, and farms. Others found jobs laboring for the railroads, in canneries, logging, and meat-packing.

At first the Issei were welcomed by the local residents. There was a high demand for their labor. Industrious and willing to work for low wages, they did not complain about their working conditions.

The ambitious Issei soon became unpopular. Unions regarded them as unwelcome competitors for jobs. Local farmers often resented the Issei success at growing citrus fruits, potatoes, and rice. The value of Issei farm crops grew from $6 million in 1909 to $67 million just ten years later.

Anti-Japanese feeling grew along the West Coast. Some of it stemmed from racial prejudice. Many white Americans would not accept nonwhites as equals.

Some California newspapers began writing about a *yellow peril.* This notion suggested that waves of Japanese immigrants would gradually engulf the state. The immigrants were portrayed as tricky, inscrutable, deceitful, and treacherous.

Official actions were taken against the Japanese. In 1906 the San Francisco school board established separate schools for Japanese children. Pressure exerted on President Theodore Roosevelt to stop Japanese immigration led to the "Gentlemen's Agreement" with Japan in 1907. As part of the agreement the Japanese government agreed to reduce immigration to the United States. In exchange, the United States promised not to adopt laws that discriminated against the Japanese. In 1907, 30,824 Japanese entered the United States. The year following the agreement, immigration from Japan dropped to 3,275.

In 1922 the U.S. Supreme Court declared that Japanese immigrants (Issei) were "aliens ineligible to citizenship." The basis for this denial was a 1790 act of Congress that limited citizenship to "free white persons." After the Civil War the law was expanded to include persons of African descent. The effect of the Supreme Court decision was that white immigrants from Europe and blacks from Africa could become naturalized U.S. citizens, but Asians could not. The children of the Issei, called *Nisei,* were, however, legally U.S. citizens. According to the Constitution anyone born in the United States is a citizen.

The goal of halting Japanese immigration to the United States was accomplished in 1924. That year, while admitting immigrants from other parts of the world, Congress excluded all immigration from Asiatic countries. The action infuriated the Japanese government, which claimed the United States had violated the Gentlemen's Agreement.

There were other ways, though not enforced by law, that Americans of Japanese origin were branded with a badge of inferiority. For example, they were often refused housing in white neighborhoods. A California billboard of the period read: "Japs, don't let the sun shine on you here. Keep moving."

It is no wonder that the Issei and their Nisei children dreaded what might be done to them after Pearl Harbor. In the aftermath of the sneak attack, well-publicized remarks by some prominent Americans stirred the panic. For example, a columnist for the *San Francisco Examiner* said:

> Everywhere the Japanese have attacked to date, the Japanese population has risen to aid the attackers. . . . I am for the immediate removal of every Japanese on the West Coast to a point deep in the interior. Herd 'em up, pack 'em off and give 'em the inside room in the Badlands. Let 'em be pinched, hurt, hungry, and dead up against it.

U.S. Army General John DeWitt, military commander of the newly created Western Defense Command, envisioned immediate dangers on the West Coast. He expected naval attacks and air raids. Adding to the danger, the general believed, was the likelihood that Japanese living along the West Coast would commit acts of *sabotage* (destruction of property by enemy agents) and *espionage* (spying to obtain government secrets). In a report to the secretary of war, General DeWitt said:

> In the war in which we are now engaged racial affinities are not severed by migration. The Japanese race is an enemy race and while many second and third generation Japanese born on United States soil, possessed of United States citizenship, have become "Americanized," the racial strains are undiluted. . . . It therefore follows that along the vital Pacific Coast over 112,000 potential enemies of Japanese extraction are alive today.

In January 1942, Earl Warren, then attorney general of California, declared that Japanese-Americans had "infiltrated . . . every strategic spot" in California. He added, "I have come to the conclusion that the Japanese situation as it exists in this state today, may well be the Achilles heel of the entire civilian defense effort. Unless something is done it may bring about a repetition of Pearl Harbor."

The remark that most fueled public hostility was a widely reported one made by secretary of the navy, Frank Knox. After inspecting the extensive damage at Pearl Harbor, he held a press conference in Los Angeles. There he said that the Japanese attack had been accompanied

by "the most effective fifth column work that's come out of this war."
The term *fifth column* refers to secret organizations within a country
that aid an invading enemy.

Rumors circulated about Japanese-Americans pointing the way for
Japanese pilots at Pearl Harbor or aiding the enemy in other ways.
These rumors were false. Not a single act of sabotage or espionage by a
Japanese-American in Hawaii was ever proven. Nonetheless, the scare
stories were widely believed.

Contributing to public anxiety during early months of the war was
grim news from the South Pacific. Japanese military forces were
making swift progress there. Allied defeats at Manila, Guam, Wake
Island, and Hong Kong weighed heavily on the hearts of Americans.
By February 1942, the military position of the United States in the
Pacific was perilous. It was a time of fear.

The war was moving closer to home. Japanese submarines attacked
shipping near the California coast. There were reports of signaling
from the Pacific Coast to enemy ships at sea, both by radio and by
flashing lights. Residents of the coastal states expected a Japanese
attack.

A growing sentiment for evacuation of Japanese-Americans soon
resulted in government action. In February 1942 President Roosevelt
issued Executive Order 9066. It gave the army authority to move
civilians out of western coastal states.

In March, Congress unanimously passed Public Law 503, which
provided for enforcement of the president's order in the courts. Under
the authority of the new law, the army began issuing civilian exclusion orders. The Pacific coastal strip was divided into exclusion areas.
About a week after orders were posted in an area, all Japanese,
whether citizens or not, were required to prepare to evacuate.

One member of each family was required to report for registration.
Within five days of registration all Japanese in an area were processed
for removal. On the day of departure they were given identification
tags and transported by bus or train to temporary assembly centers
along the West Coast. They were to remain there until permanent
inland relocation centers were ready for them. Over 120,000 Japanese,
two-thirds of them U.S. citizens, were evacuated. Although the United
States was at war with Germany and Italy, no German-Americans or
Italian-Americans were evicted from their homes.

The federal government argued that mass evacuation was a military

necessity. Several reasons were given to support this argument. Some
of the major ones were:

1. The Japanese-Americans posed a threat as enemy agents. Many of
   them lived around aircraft plants, ports, dams, bridges, power
   stations, and other strategic points.
2. Widespread distrust of the Japanese population lowered public
   morale on the West Coast. Evacuation would lift morale.
3. The Japanese themselves were in danger of attack by angry citizens.
   There had been several violent acts, including murders, committed
   against them. In relocation camps they would be safe.
4. Loyalty of Japanese-Americans to the United States was doubtful.
   There was no way to distinguish loyal U.S. citizens from those
   whose first loyalty was to Japan. All Americans of Japanese
   ancestry were considered citizens of Japan by the Japanese government. Some had sent their children to Japan for schooling. As a
   group, the Japanese in the United States had maintained their
   cultural traditions and had not blended into the mainstream of
   American life.
5. In total war, constitutional rights have to give way to drastic
   measures.

Yoshiko Uchida, in her book *Desert Exile*, describes what it was
like for her family to be uprooted from their home in 1942. At the
time of the evacuation, the Uchida family consisted of Yoshiko, a
college student, her older sister, Keiko, and their parents. The girls
were both Nisei. Their Issei parents had a strong devotion to their
adopted country. The family lived comfortably in a house on Stuart
Street in Berkeley, California. On national holidays Mr. Uchida hung
an enormous American flag on the front porch.

At five o'clock on Pearl Harbor Day, Yoshiko came home from the
library to find an FBI agent in the living room. Her father was gone.
As an executive of a Japanese business firm, he was one of many
aliens (noncitizen residents) considered especially dangerous by the
government. They were seized immediately after the Japanese attack
and sent to an internment camp in Montana.

In April 1942, Yoshiko, her mother, and her sister were ordered to
report to Tanforen Assembly Center. They had ten days to prepare.
They desperately tried to dispose of their household possessions. The

piano was left with one neighbor; other pieces of furniture with another. Like many others, they suffered financial losses in having to dispose of their property so quickly. Some had to sell their houses below market value. Others had to abandon their businesses or sell them at a loss.

On the day of departure the three women arrived at their church, the designated assembly point, carrying the few belongings they were permitted to bring. They were taken to a fenced-in camp that had been built at Tanforen racetrack. This was to be their temporary home until the government could construct inland camps far removed from the West Coast.

It had rained the day before their arrival. The grounds had become a mass of slippery mud. The girls helped their mother through the mud past tar-papered barracks until they reached Barrack 16, the one to which they had been assigned. It was a horse stable. Each stall was about ten feet by twenty feet, empty except for three folded army cots. The smell of horses hung in the air. The family stall was cold and dank and afforded little privacy.

Meals were served in a mess hall. Their first dinner at Tanforen consisted of two canned sausages, a boiled potato, and a piece of butterless bread. Meals improved but most of the time they were skimpy and starchy. Yoshiko and her sister were usually hungry.

Gradually the interned residents worked to improve conditions at Tanforen, a community of 8,000. A form of limited self-government was set up. Buddhist and Christian churches were established. A post office was opened. Education and recreation programs were organized. Yoshiko worked in the elementary school, for which she was paid $16 a month. Eventually her father was allowed to join the family in their stall at the temporary assembly center.

After five months at Tanforen the family was sent to Topaz, a relocation center in the Utah desert. They found a crude, incomplete, and ill-prepared camp. Yoshiko and her family felt depressed in the bleak desert camp. Military police patrolled the barbed wire perimeter of the camp. Swirling masses of sand in the air constantly coated their bodies and clothing. There were few comforts, and life at Topaz was only slightly better than it had been at Tanforen. The Uchida family adjusted to the routine hardships of camp life, but they missed their house on Stuart Street. Yoshiko, homesick, angry, and despairing, characterized her life at Topaz: "No matter what I did, I was still in an artificial government-sponsored community on the periphery of the real world. I was in a dismal, dreary camp surrounded by barbed wire in the middle of a stark, harsh landscape that offered nothing to refresh the eye or heal the spirit."

Some Japanese-Americans spent three years in one of ten government relocation centers like Topaz. The Uchida family spent just over a year in confinement. Upon their release they gradually returned to a comfortable life as Americans. The bitterness of their bondage lingered in their memories after the war.

The vast majority of Japanese-Americans, like the Uchida family, cooperated fully with government authorities during the relocation period. A dramatic demonstration of patriotism came from the men of the 442nd Regimental Combat Team. After Pearl Harbor, Americans of Japanese descent were excluded from the armed forces of the United States. In 1943 the government allowed Japanese-Americans to volunteer for the army. An all-Nisei combat team was established. The unit fought in Europe with extraordinary bravery. It was one of the most highly decorated U.S. combat units of the war. It suffered over 9,000 casualties, including 600 dead.

Not all Japanese-Americans declared loyalty to the U.S. government. At Tule Lake, one of the relocation centers, a militant minority was openly pro-Japan during the war. More than 5,000 members of this minority renounced their U.S. citizenship. Also, at the end of the war, 4,724 residents of relocation centers chose to return to Japan.

A small number of Japanese-Americans resisted the evacuation when it began. One of them, born and raised in the United States, was Fred Korematsu. After graduation from high school in Oakland, California, Fred worked in a shipyard as a welder. At the outbreak of the war his membership in the Boilermaker's Union was cancelled because of his race. He took a job as a gardener and fell in love with a white woman.

The evacuation orders disrupted the couple's plan to marry. In an effort to escape detention, Fred had plastic surgery done on his face, changed his name, and posed as a Spanish-Hawaiian. The ruse failed. While leaving a post office near Oakland, he was seized by FBI agents. In federal court Korematsu was found guilty of breaking the law.

Fred Korematsu appealed his conviction to the U.S. Supreme Court. In the case of *Korematsu* v. *United States* (1944), the high court was asked to decide whether the evacuation and relocation of Japanese-Americans violated their constitutional rights. The nine justices of the

Court voted 6 to 3 to uphold Korematsu's conviction. Speaking for the majority, Justice Hugo Black said:

> Korematsu was not excluded from the Military Area because of hostility to him or his race. He was excluded because we are at war with the Japanese Empire, because the properly constituted military authorities feared an invasion of our West Coast and felt constrained to take proper security measures, because they decided that the military urgency of the situation demanded that all citizens of Japanese ancestry be segregated from the West Coast temporarily, and finally, because Congress, reposing its confidence in this time of war in our military leaders—as inevitably it must—determined that they should have the power to do just this.

Three justices dissented from the majority opinion. Justice Owen J. Roberts argued that Korematsu was a loyal citizen of the nation. He added that it was a violation of constitutional rights to imprison a citizen solely because of his ancestry and without evidence of disloyalty.

Justice Frank Murphy added strong words in his dissenting opinion. He wrote that the order to exclude all persons of Japanese ancestry from the Pacific Coast "goes over the very brink of constitutional power and falls into the ugly abyss of racism." He continued:

> Being an obvious racial discrimination, the order deprives all those within its scope of the equal protection of the laws as guaranteed by the Fifth Amendment. It further deprives these individuals of their constitutional rights to live and work where they will, to establish a home where they choose and to move about freely.

"Racial discrimination in any form and in any degree," added Justice Murphy, "has no justifiable part whatsoever in our democratic way of life."

In the third dissenting opinion, Justice Robert H. Jackson agreed that it was unconstitutional to transplant Americans on the basis of their race. He wrote that by declaring the exclusion order constitutional, the Supreme Court was, for all time, accepting the principle of racial discrimination: "The principle then lies about like a loaded weapon ready for the hand of any authority that can bring forward a plausible claim of an urgent need."

The decision in the Korematsu case upheld the constitutionality of excluding Japanese-Americans from the Pacific Coast during the Second World War. In September 1945, two weeks after Japan surrendered, the exclusion orders were rescinded.

The major sources for this story were:

Grodzins, Morton. *Americans Betrayed: Politics and the Japanese Evacuation.* Chicago: University of Chicago Press, 1949.
Korematsu v. United States, 323 U.S. 214 (1944).
Myer, Dillon S. *Uprooted Americans.* Tucson, Ariz.: University of Arizona Press, 1971.
Personal Justice Denied: Report of the Commission on Wartime Relocation and Internment of Civilians, Washington, D.C.: U.S. Government Printing Office, 1982.
tenBroek, Jacobus, Barnhart, Edward N., and Matson, Floyd M. *Prejudice, War and the Constitution: Causes and Consequences of the Evacuation of the Japanese-Americans in World War II.* Berkeley: University of California Press, 1968.
Uchida, Yoshiko. *Desert Exile: The Uprooting of a Japanese American Family.* Seattle: University of Washington Press, 1982.
Wilson, Robert A., and Kosokawa, Bill. *East to America: A History of the Japanese in the United States.* New York: William Morrow, 1980.

ACTIVITIES FOR "A LOADED WEAPON"

Write all answers on a separate sheet of paper.

Historical Understanding

Answer briefly:

1. Why did Japanese-Americans become unpopular along the West Coast?

2. What were the major terms of the 1907 "Gentlemen's Agreement"?

3. Why were the Nisei citizens of the United States but not their parents?

4. What was meant by the phrase *yellow peril*?

5. Define the following terms: *espionage, sabotage,* and *fifth column.*

Reviewing the Facts of the Case

Answer briefly:

1. What were Executive Order 9066 and Public Law 503?

2. What reasons were given by the U.S. government for evacuating Japanese-Americans from the Pacific Coast?

3. Briefly summarize conditions at Tanforen and Topaz.

4. What was the majority decision in the case of *Korematsu* v. *United States*?

5. What do the three dissenting opinions in the Korematsu case have in common?

Analyzing Ethical Issues

Examining the value of equality. Justice Murphy claimed that Fred Korematsu had been denied "equal protection of the law." Equality, a value embodied in the Declaration of Independence and the Constitution, concerns the fairness of treating people differently.

Identify one specific incident from the story involving the value of equality. For that incident indicate the groups of people being treated differently, as illustrated in the following example:

INCIDENT INVOLVING EQUALITY	GROUPS TREATED DIFFERENTLY
Japanese-Americans were sent to relocation camps.	*Japanese-Americans, German-Americans, Italian-Americans*

Expressing Your Reasoning

1. Did the U.S. government do the right thing when it evacuated Americans of Japanese ancestry from the Pacific Coast during World War II? Why or why not?

2. Was Fred Korematsu wrong to resist the evacuation order? Why or why not? Present your position and reasons in a carefully written paragraph.

3. For each situation below, indicate whether or not you think *equal protection of the law* is being denied. Be prepared to state reasons for your judgments.
   a. A landlord refuses to rent an apartment to Vietnamese immigrants.
   b. Persons under age 18 are refused admittance to movie theaters showing X-rated films.
   c. A private club denies membership to blacks.

d. Because of their religion, high school–age Amish children are not required to comply with a state compulsory school attendance law.

e. Men are required to register for military service.

f. A commercial airline requires pilots to retire upon reaching age 50.

g. Auto insurance rates are higher for people who are young and unmarried.

h. In some states people under age 21 are not permitted to purchase alcoholic beverages.

i. A school district has separate schools for black and white students.

j. A state university reserves some places in its freshmen medical school class for minority students.

4. Some people argue that evacuation of Japanese-Americans was the right thing to do at the time, but that it seems wrong looking back from the present time. Can an action be both right and wrong depending upon when the judgment about it is made? Explain your thinking.

5. *Seeking Additional Information.* In making decisions about such questions as those above, we often feel we need more information before we are satisfied with our judgments. Choose one of the above questions about which you would want more information than is presented in the story. What additional information would you like? Why would that information help you make a more satisfactory decision?

About Face

GENERAL JOSEPH STILWELL

(*Courtesy of the Library of Congress*)

General Stilwell (center) Holding a Conference on a Jeep Tour of
the Burma Front

(*Courtesy of the Library of Congress*)

General Joseph Stilwell, 1945

In the 1930s, Germany and Japan began policies of expansion in Europe and Asia, respectively. Most Americans resented the actions of the aggressor nations but hoped the United States could avoid going to war. On Sunday morning, December 7, 1941, Japanese bombs destroyed the U.S. Navy at Pearl Harbor in Hawaii. American hopes for peace were also destroyed. Soon the United States was at war with both Germany and Japan.

Faced with war in Europe and Asia, the United States and its major ally, England, formulated a general strategy. The plan was first to win the war in Europe and then devote full attention to the war in Asia. For such a strategy to succeed, it was necessary for China to cooperate. It was hoped that China, which had been at war with Japan for a number of years, could keep the main Japanese army busy until the war in Europe ended.

The United States was not prepared for war and could not send U.S. troops to help China. In March 1941, Congress passed the Lend-Lease Act. According to that law, the president was permitted to provide military supplies to nations fighting enemies of the United States. Chinese leader Jiang Jie-shi (Chiang Kai-shek) was given these supplies to use in fighting the Japanese.

The Allied strategy became extraordinarily complicated in practice. Although Jiang had said that his armies would fight hard against the Japanese, the special political and cultural situation in China interfered. As Jiang once said to President Roosevelt: "You will appreciate the fact that military cooperation in its absolute sense must be built on the foundation of political cooperation."

The internal political foundation of China was shaky. Journalists sympathetic to Jiang had given Americans the impression that he was in firm control of China. In 1937, he and his popular wife appeared on the cover of *Time* magazine as "Man and Wife of the Year." Their great popularity in the United States was not shared throughout China. Jiang was constantly struggling to remain in power.

One of Jiang's major opponents was the Chinese Communist party, led by Mao Ze-dong (Mao Tse-tung) and Jou En-lai (Chou En-lai). Although Jiang and the Communists had once worked together, underlying political differences led to bloodshed. Jiang's forces had driven the Communists into the northwestern province of Shanxi (Shansi) in 1935. Many of Jiang's best troops were stationed along the border to contain the Communists. As a result, these troops were unavailable to help fight the Japanese.

The Communists were only one of Jiang's political concerns. He had political rivals in other parts of China. When distributing military supplies, Jiang was careful to see that they went only to commanders he believed loyal to him. As a result, skilled commanders in strategic areas might not receive proper supplies if Jiang questioned their personal loyalty. Jiang did not want to equip armies led by possible political enemies.

Other factors prevented the Chinese from being the effective fighting force desired by the United States and its allies. Traditionally, it was Chinese military strategy to avoid direct battles. According to one proverb, "A hundred victories in a hundred battles is not the best of the best; the best of the best is to subdue the enemy without fighting." In part because of such traditional thinking, Jiang and his commanders often held troops out of battle or retreated.

Jiang hoped that the allies would play the major role in defeating Japan. He often thought that the United States and England were not doing enough to win the war and he resented the "Europe First" strategy.

In Chinese culture it was vital to *save face*. One was always to be polite, dignified, and respectful. Criticisms and insults were avoided. As a result, Jiang found it difficult to accept criticism or, as leader, to take directions from anyone. As part of the tradition of politeness, Jiang would often seem to be agreeing with others when he really did not agree. Bad news was especially unwelcome. As one proverb said, "Forgetting evil and speaking only good helps to hold society together and preserve men's dignity with one another."

The complexities of Chinese politics and culture led to continual misunderstanding with the Allies. General Joseph ("Vinegar Joe") Stilwell experienced the intense frustrations that can occur when people from different cultures try to work together.

General Stilwell was in his late fifties when World War II began. A graduate of West Point, he had spent many years in China. During those years he became a fluent speaker of Chinese and witnessed the bloody turmoil that accompanied China's internal political struggles. Not one to stay away from the common people, he traveled extensively, often on foot, through much of the huge nation. Probably more than any other U.S. military leader he understood Chinese culture. He had seen death, disease, and starvation among the peasants and soldiers. He was convinced, however, that Chinese soldiers could be great fighters, although he was disgusted with the tactics and corruption of their leaders. As he wrote in one report: "The Chinese soldier is excellent material, wasted and betrayed by stupid leadership." Vinegar Joe always said what he meant but was not careful about how he said it.

Stilwell was deeply patriotic and devoted to the United States. He was considered by many to be the best military leader and trainer of soldiers in the entire army. He despised snobbishness and self-importance and was uninterested in the privileges and awards that came with his high rank. Often he was seen out of uniform standing in meal lines with the regular soldiers. Because of his direct, often biting manner, he had been given his nickname. In a letter he described himself as "unreasonable, impatient, . . . sullen, mad, hard, profane, vulgar." He was also one of the most talented military leaders in the U.S. Army.

A few years before Pearl Harbor, Stilwell had considered retiring. After the war began, he told his superiors he would serve wherever he was needed. He would soon become a leading actor in the military drama unfolding in China.

As the war progressed, Japanese armies gained control of more and more of China. Jiang was forced to move his government to Chongqing (Chungking), deep in western China. U.S. leaders feared that China might be defeated or that Jiang might be forced to make peace with Japan. A worried President Roosevelt said to one of his sons: "If China goes under, how many divisions of Japanese troops do you think will be freed—to do what? Take Australia, take India—and it's as ripe as a plum for the picking. Move straight on to the Middle East . . . a giant pincer movement by the Japanese and Nazis, meeting somewhere in the Near East." The president believed it was essential to keep China in the war.

To keep China fighting, Roosevelt knew that Jiang would have to be treated as an ally the equal of England's Churchill. The president also had a postwar vision of a powerful China, led by Jiang, which would help keep peace in Asia. In addition, there was a racial reason for wanting to treat Jiang as an equal. Pearl Buck, a novelist with long experience in China, had informed the president: "The battles in the Pacific are already being made to appear a war between the white and yellow races." She argued that it should not appear as if Roosevelt and Churchill were fighting for white supremacy.

Jiang continually asked the United States for supplies. Because the Japanese controlled the Chinese ports, the major route for supplies was through Burma, up the Burma Road. If the Japanese could close that route, supplies would have to be flown in over the dangerous Himalaya Mountains—over "The Hump." Such a hazardous airlift would restrict the amount of supplies going to Jiang.

The Japanese began to threaten the Burma Road. Jiang and Roosevelt agreed that a U.S. general should be sent to protect the supply line. Jiang said he would supply troops for the general to command. They would work with the British troops in Burma. General Stilwell was chosen to be the U.S. general in China and Burma.

When Stilwell arrived early in 1942, the situation in Burma seemed hopeless. The Japanese were making strong advances. Jiang did provide some Chinese troops for Stilwell to command. Frequently, however, Stilwell's plans were undercut by secret orders from Jiang to the Chinese commanders.

The Japanese advance was brutal. In the midst of the disaster, as Stilwell and his men retreated through the jungle, the general received an order from Jiang in distant Chong-qing. Jiang said a watermelon should be provided for every four men! Stilwell was outraged by the absurdity of the order. In his notes he began using insulting nicknames when referring to Jiang. Frequently he called him the Peanut.

A plane flew into Burma to take Stilwell to safety. He refused to fly out. He intended to lead his troops westward to India and wanted to be with them. Most of the Chinese troops had abandoned him. Yet he was determined, despite heat and mud and without adequate supplies, to lead out his remaining troops. He told his men, "By the time we get out of here many of you will hate my guts but I'll tell you one thing: you'll all get out." He was correct.

In May 1942, they reached India. The 59-year-old Stilwell, thin to begin with, had lost 20 pounds. Even as he retreated, Stilwell was formulating a plan to retake Burma and open the road. As part of the plan he wanted to train a few Chinese units to follow his orders and use the weapons supplied by the United States.

Privately Jiang blamed Stilwell for the loss of Burma. In meetings, however, he treated him with the traditional Chinese politeness. Stilwell knew of the Chinese value for saving face. He had once instructed U.S. officers, "In dealing with Chinese don't take their face from them unless you want to humiliate them and unless you do not care if you make enemies." In spite of this, Stilwell believed he had to shock Jiang into taking action to reform the army. Bluntly he told him of the incompetence and corruption of many of the Chinese commanders. He spoke of soldiers dying of disease and starvation while their officers sold supplies to enrich themselves. Bluntly he told Jiang of changes needed to make the Chinese army an effective fighting force.

Telling the Chinese leader of the failings of his army was gravely insulting to Jiang. As Stilwell wrote later, however: "NO ONE else dares to tell him, so it's up to me all the more." Jiang was shocked but remained cool and avoided a direct discussion of the topic. The frustrated Stilwell wrote: "Why doesn't the little dummy realize that his only hope is the . . . creation of a separate, efficient, well-equipped, and well-trained force?"

Jiang was in a difficult position. He needed U.S. supplies to help maintain his power. If the United States believed he was avoiding building a strong army, supplies might be withheld. In fact Jiang did not want a strong army of the type Stilwell proposed. In the complicated Chinese political situation some of the officers might turn against him and drive him from office.

Late in 1942, Jiang agreed to allow Stilwell to train some Chinese troops at a base in India. He also agreed to Stilwell's plan for retaking northern Burma. According to the plan, the X-Force, troops trained by Stilwell, would move from India into Burma. Other Chinese troops, the Y-Force, would move into Burma from the north. Together the two forces should be able to drive back the Japanese and reopen the Burma Road.

At a meeting with Churchill and Roosevelt at Cairo, plans for the Burma campaign were settled. Jiang insisted that the Allies launch a sea invasion of southern Burma at the same time the northern action began. Promises were made, but when the time came for the sea invasion it was called off. Jiang was told that the forces were needed elsewhere because of Allied setbacks in North Africa. Jiang believed a promise had been broken and refused to move the Y-Force.

Stilwell was angry. He was convinced Jiang wanted to avoid direct fighting with the Japanese. Jiang avoided giving that impression to others. When U.S. observers came to China they were treated royally by Jiang. Often visitors were taken to the front to see how the war was progressing. It was something of a false front, however. Visitors were shown Japanese prisoners and captured weapons. Reportedly, the same prisoners and weapons were moved to different parts of China to make it appear that Jiang's forces were effective in many areas.

Stilwell was disgusted with Jiang's delays and broken promises. He knew that the promises were part of the Chinese tradition of trying always to please others in face-to-face meetings. Nonetheless, to Stilwell, promises were made to be kept. He understood Chinese ways but could not always accept them.

President Roosevelt, aware of Japanese advances, was determined to keep China and Jiang in the war. He frequently praised Jiang as a fine leader. In 1943, he decided to award Jiang the Legion of Merit. It was the highest award the United States could give to a foreigner. Stilwell was ordered to make the presentation. He protested that Jiang did not deserve it. The president insisted. Stilwell wrote to his wife that presenting the award "will make me want to throw up." Despite his revulsion, the general finally consented and presented the award at a public ceremony. A few days later Jiang agreed to move the Y-Force into the Burma campaign.

Stilwell's troop training project in India was progressing. He was impressed with the Chinese peasants' ability to learn quickly. Often the general himself was down in the dust giving instructions on how to fire complicated weapons. There was discord between U.S. instructors and Chinese officers. Stilwell ordered his instructors not to interfere with traditional Chinese methods of discipline. At one point the Americans were shocked to see a Chinese soldier beaten with a pole. The soldier's flesh was cut to the bone. He was being punished for losing his blanket.

The Burma campaign began. Stilwell led his X-Force into the steamy jungles. The fighting was fierce, but progress was made. Early in 1944, it became strategically vital for the Y-Force to move into Burma, but Jiang held back. Stilwell was furious again: "I have been ignored, slighted, blocked, delayed, double-crossed, lied to and about."

Roosevelt was also becoming impatient with Jiang. He urged him to move the troops and reminded him that U.S. supplies could be cut off. Slowly, the Y-Force began to move.

In China the military situation had worsened. Japanese armies advanced steadily and were on the verge of taking U.S. air bases. Some Chinese officers were plotting the overthrow of Jiang and his government. U.S. military leaders became convinced that the situation could only be saved if Stilwell was given command of the entire Chinese army.

President Roosevelt realized that asking Jiang to turn over his armies to a foreigner would be taken as a profound insult. He also knew that Stilwell's relations with Jiang were strained. Nonetheless, the situation was becoming desperate. In a letter to Jiang the president said the future of Asia was at stake and that drastic measures were needed. He urged Jiang to appoint Stilwell as commander of all Chinese armies because: "I know of no other man who has the ability, the force, and the determination to offset the disaster which now threatens China." The president had written a strong message. He did not, however, say that he would cut off U.S. supplies if Jiang refused his plea. Stilwell delivered the president's message to Jiang.

Jiang agreed to appoint Stilwell, but there was little chance he would carry out his agreement. It was not simply a matter of personality conflict. Roosevelt had often urged Jiang to use the well-trained Communist troops against the Japanese. The Communists had proven effective fighters against the Japanese and had said they would fight under Stilwell's command. Jiang had no intention of allowing the Communists to become part of the regular Chinese fighting forces. From his point of view it would be political suicide to strengthen their armies.

The president sent a special representative, Patrick Hurley, to Chong-qing. He hoped the diplomatic Hurley could smooth relations between Jiang and Vinegar Joe. Hurley soon learned of Jiang's opinion of Stilwell. According to Jiang, "Stilwell had no intention of cooperating with me, but believed that he was in fact being appointed to command me. . . . If, ignoring reason and experience, I were to appoint General Stilwell as Field Commander, I would knowingly court inevitable disaster."

In autumn 1944, Hurley wrote to the president describing the situation. Jiang had insisted that Stilwell be recalled from China and returned to the United States. Hurley told the president he would now have to choose between Jiang and Stilwell.

The major sources for this story were:

Elsey, George M. *Roosevelt and China: The White House Story*. Wilmington, Del.: Glazier, 1979.

Feis, Herbert. *The China Triangle*. New York: Atheneum, 1965.

Tuchman, Barbara W. *Stilwell and the American Experience in China 1911-1945*. New York: Macmillan, 1971.

ACTIVITIES FOR "ABOUT FACE"

Write all answers on a separate sheet of paper.

Historical Understanding

Answer briefly:

1. What was the general strategy of the United States at the beginning of World War II?

2. Why did President Roosevelt want to keep China in the war?

3. What was the Lend-Lease Act?

4. Identify a political and a cultural factor that kept Jiang Jie-shi from pursuing the war in the way preferred by the United States.

Reviewing the Facts of the Case

Answer briefly:

1. What is meant by the Chinese tradition of *saving face*?

2. What was the difference between Stilwell's opinion of Chinese soldiers and their officers?

3. Why was the Burma Road militarily important?

4. Stilwell recommended reforms to strengthen the Chinese army. Why did Jiang reject Stilwell's ideas?

5. Why did President Roosevelt want to give Jiang the Legion of Merit?

6. Why did Jiang reject Roosevelt's request that Stilwell be made commander of the Chinese army?

Analyzing Ethical Issues

Considering the understanding and justification of actions. One of the themes in this story is the difference between *understanding* people's actions and *justifying* them. When we seek justification, we try to decide whether the way people act is right or wrong, good or bad, fair or unfair. Sometimes we can understand why a person does something but disagree over whether the action is justified. For example:

> *Stilwell understood why Jiang kept supplies from commanders whose personal loyalty he questioned. Although he understood Jiang's policy, Stilwell thought it was wrong because he himself believed military skill, not simply loyalty, should determine who received supplies.*

Write down one other example from this story in which Stilwell understood Jiang's actions but did not think they were justified.

Expressing Your Reasoning

1. Should President Roosevelt have recalled Stilwell from China? Why or why not?

2. Various cultures have different customs and traditions. Try to explain how each of the following cultural practices may have come about. Then decide whether or not each is justifiable. Give reasons for your decisions.

   a. A thief in Arabia is convicted for the second time and has his hand chopped off as punishment.

   b. In a harsh arctic climate, an old woman, who can no longer contribute to the survival of the tribe, is left on the ice to die.

   c. On a tiny Pacific island stealing is customary. A person will pretend to be friendly with someone and then take his or her possessions when the opportunity arises.

   d. People in one culture worship cattle as sacred. Even if they are starving they will not kill the cattle for food.

   e. In some cultures people cannot marry whom they choose. Parents decide whom their children must marry.

3. Many people believe that each culture should decide for itself what is right and wrong. Others believe standards of right and wrong should be universal—the same for all cultures. What is your view? Is it justifiable to judge the rightness or wrongness of practices in other cultures? Explain your position in a short essay.

4. *Seeking Additional Information.* In making decisions about such questions as those above, we often feel we need more information before we are satisfied with our judgments. Choose one of the above questions about which you would want more information than is presented in the story. What additional information would you like? Why would that information help you make a more satisfactory decision?

The Unluckiest Kid

PRIVATE EDDIE SLOVIK

(Photo by Hertz, courtesy of the Office of the Chief of Public Affairs, Department of the Army)

Two American Soldiers on Guard During the Battle of the Bulge

It seems . . . that ever since I was born I've had hard luck. I
spent five years in jail, got out when I was 22, got married when I
was 22, lived 15 months with my darling wife and was so happy
with her, and now they break up my happiness, put me in the
army, and try to kill us both and take everything we've got. . . .
We didn't do anything to anyone did we?

So wrote Private Eddie Slovik to his wife Antoinette in July of
1944. Years later she would say, "He was the unluckiest poor kid who
ever lived."

Born in 1920, Eddie Slovik spent his early years in poverty. The
economy of Detroit, Michigan, suffered greatly during the Depression and Eddie suffered along with it. Money was hard to come by
and life was difficult.

Young Eddie was often in trouble. After dropping out of school at
the age of 15, he and his friends committed a variety of minor crimes.
Eddie was able to avoid jail for a few years. Then, in 1937, he was
convicted of stealing about sixty dollars from the drug store where he
had been working for a few months. Eddie was sent to prison.

In September the next year Eddie was let out on parole. A few
months later he was in trouble again. He and some buddies stole a car
and crashed it. Eddie was returned to prison.

A prison supervisor, Harry Dimmick, worked hard to help Eddie
straighten out his life. Dimmick saw Eddie was a frightened, weak
kid. In Dimmick's opinion, Eddie would be all right if he stayed away
from his trouble-making friends and found a wife who would settle
him down. Those were Dimmick's hopes for Eddie when he was
released from prison at the age of 22.

Dramatic events had occurred in the world during Eddie's term in
prison. Hitler's invading armies had plunged Europe into war. The
Japanese had attacked Americans at Pearl Harbor. The United States
was now engaged in a deadly and destructive world war.

The United States was not well prepared for war. Weapons had to
be produced and fighting forces trained. General George S. Patton,
Jr., was worried that the United States might not be able to raise a
good fighting army: "We've pampered and confused our youth. We've
talked too much about rights and not enough about duties. . . .
Many a brave soldier will lose his life unnecessarily because the man
next to him turned yellow."

Slovik did not know of General Patton's worries. The horrors of war were distant to him. In a way, the war was at first helpful to Eddie. The production of war materials had helped the economy prosper. Eddie got a job with a plumbing company.

He also fell in love. Antoinette Wisniewski was the kind of woman Harry Dimmick had in mind for Eddie. Eddie worked hard to impress her and was successful. On November 7, 1942, they were married. Eddie got a good paying job at the DeSoto factory. He and Antoinette bought a car and began furnishing an apartment. Eddie had never been happier.

On their first anniversary, the happy couple moved into a new, more spacious apartment. That same day Eddie received a letter. The U.S. Army wanted him. He and Antoinette cried. Their dream life seemed to be ending.

In January 1944, Eddie left Detroit for military training in Texas. Whenever he could, he wrote to his wife—sometimes three or four letters a day.

Army training is rough for most beginning soldiers. Eddie's letters show he took it unusually hard: "Honest, honey, I feel like crying every time I sit down to write you a letter. . . . I am so unlucky." For Eddie the army was "just like being in jail. Only in jail it isn't this bad."

Eddie may have preferred jail to military service. When he was released from prison, he was required to make a monthly report to a parole officer. If he failed to report, he could be returned to jail for six months. After he was drafted, he failed to report to the parole officer but no action was taken. He wrote Antoinette of his hopes for jail: "They may still throw me in jail; I hope they do."

Eddie next tried legal ways to get released from army duty. His wife was ill and could not work steadily. Some of their possessions had to be sold to meet her expenses. Nonetheless, the army would not grant Eddie a hardship discharge. Like many other Americans, Eddie and his wife would have to sacrifice for the war effort.

Eddie sadly continued his training. He brooded about being away from his wife. In a letter to her he said: "We haven't done anything to anyone to have to be separated like this." Later he wrote: "Now I can just lie here and see my dreams go up in smoke, and I want to cry. Why do they make us suffer so? Why do they hate us?" For him military service was more a punishment than a duty. He could not understand why the army wanted him.

The army needed soldiers. On June 6, 1944, Allied forces, led by

General Dwight D. Eisenhower, landed on the beaches of Normandy, France. It was known as D day and was the beginning of the costly campaign to push the German army out of France and end the war. Thousands of men would die. More men were needed to replace them. Private Eddie Slovik was to be a replacement.

On August 7, 1944, Eddie and a few thousand others boarded a ship and sailed for Europe. He was to join the 109th Infantry Regiment of the 28th Division of the U.S. Army. The men he was to join were already engaged in battle.

For the day that Eddie sailed, the military history of the 28th Division reads: "On this date . . . the division has fought its bloodiest battle of the Northern France campaign. In the initial phase of the attack the 109th was hit extremely hard. . . . The 109th took very heavy casualties, beat off the German tanks and prevented a greater disaster."

The 28th became known as the "hard luck division" because it seemed to get involved in the fiercest battles of the war.

Aboard ship Eddie became friendly with Private John Tankey, also from Detroit. One night, as he was cleaning his rifle, Eddie said he never intended to fire it. John warned him: "You better be careful. You can get in trouble talking that way." John could not have known how right he was.

On August 25, Tankey and Slovik were on a truck with ten other men being driven inland to join the 109th. Along the way they saw the charred remains of war—wrecked buildings, equipment, and human bodies. Suddenly they came under attack. The men dug foxholes and jumped into them. They waited through a frightening night.

When Slovik and Tankey emerged from their foxholes, their fellow soldiers were gone. Perhaps the two privates had not heard the orders to move out; perhaps they were too scared to move; perhaps they just decided to stay behind. One fact was clear—they were now separated from the others.

Slovik and Tankey met a group of Canadian soldiers. The Canadians' job was to follow combat units and inform local citizens of the rules of military law governing the area. The two Americans made themselves useful, and the Canadians allowed them to stay with them for a time.

On October 5, Slovik and Tankey rejoined U.S. troops. It was believed they had accidentally been separated from their division. Eddie was assigned to a rifle platoon.

While with the Canadians, Eddie had quit carrying bullets in his ammunition belt. Instead he carried stationery for writing letters to his wife. Eddie was determined not to have to fire his rifle. He told his commander that he was too scared to fight. He asked, "If I leave now, will it be desertion?" The answer was yes. Eddie knew that desertion was one of the most serious of military crimes. Despite this he ran away. John tried to stop him, but Eddie said he knew what he was doing.

The following day, October 9, Eddie returned. He had written a note to one of the officers. In the note Eddie said that he had been a deserter while with the Canadians and that he had also deserted on the eighth. In bold letters he said he would run away again if ordered to join the rifle platoon.

An officer told Eddie that desertion was bad enough but writing a confession would make it even worse for him. He urged Eddie to tear up the note. Eddie refused and was placed in the *stockade* (a military jail).

Eddie may have had a plan. During the war thousands of soldiers deserted their units. The maximum penalty for desertion was death. Since the Civil War, however, no U.S. soldier had been executed for desertion. Typically deserters were imprisoned and eventually released. Occasionally they would receive the death sentence, but it was not carried out. Eddie had often said he preferred jail to combat. Perhaps he thought that he would be jailed for a few years and could then return to Antoinette.

While Slovik awaited his trial, other soldiers, including Private Tankey, fought the enemy in the cold of winter. Eddie wrote his wife: "The only luck I had in my life was when I married you. I knew it wouldn't last because I was too happy. I knew they wouldn't let me be happy." He begged her to wait for him.

Eddie was given another chance to return to his platoon. If he did, there would be no trial. Eddie refused. He then asked to be reassigned to a noncombat unit. His request was denied. He was told that the army could not move soldiers out of combat simply because they did not want to fight. It would be difficult to carry forth the war if soldiers were allowed to quit fighting whenever they wanted.

Eddie was brought to trial. A psychiatrist examined him and concluded: "I consider him sane and responsible for his actions." Eddie would not be able to claim insanity.

His *court-martial* (military trial) began on the morning of November 11, 1944. The court comprised nine officers who would make the judgment. Eddie was charged with desertion to avoid dangerous duty. He pleaded not guilty.

The trial did not last long. A few witnesses described the facts of the case. Eddie chose to remain silent. The court found Eddie guilty as charged.

The court had to determine Eddie's sentence. The officers voted by secret ballot. The presiding officer reminded the others that they would have to live with their decision for the rest of their lives. The vote was unanimous. Eddie Slovik was sentenced to death by firing squad.

Eddie was shocked but still hopeful. Others had been sentenced to death but were never executed. According to military law, the court's decision had to be reviewed by the other officers. Perhaps Eddie would still only go to jail.

Reviewers upheld the sentence of the court-martial. They agreed that Eddie had deserted with the hope of going to jail.

General Eisenhower had to give final approval for the death sentence. It was a hectic time for the general because U.S. troops were engaged in bloody combat with the Germans at the Battle of the Bulge.

Eisenhower's legal advisors reviewed the Slovik case. In their report they referred to Eddie's written confession and concluded:

> There can be no doubt that he deliberately sought the safety and comparative comfort of the guardhouse. . . . He had directly challenged the authority of the government, and future discipline depends upon a resolute reply to this challenge. If the death penalty is ever to be imposed for desertion it should be imposed in this case . . . to maintain that discipline upon which alone an army can succeed against the enemy.

General Eisenhower agreed with his advisors' recommendation. On January 31, 1945, in the snowy courtyard of a building in France, Private Eddie Slovik was executed by a firing squad.

The commander of the 109th Infantry Regiment sent the following message to his men: "I pray that this man's death will be a lesson to each of us who have any doubt at any time about the price we must pay to win this war. The person that is not willing to fight and die, if need be, for his country has no right to life."

The major source for this story was:

Huie, William B. *The Execution of Private Slovik*. New York: Duell, Sloan and Pearce, 1954.

ACTIVITIES FOR "THE UNLUCKIEST KID"

Write all answers on a separate sheet of paper.

Historical Understanding

Answer briefly:

1. What was General Patton's worry as the country prepared for war?

2. How did war contribute to Detroit's economy?

3. What was D day?

Reviewing the Facts of the Case

Answer briefly:

1. What did Harry Dimmick believe Eddie Slovik had to do in order to avoid trouble in his life?

2. What was the 28th Division's nickname? Why was it given?

3. Briefly describe the details of Eddie's two desertions.

4. How were deserters usually punished?

5. What advice did General Eisenhower receive about Eddie's case?

6. What message did the commander of the 109th Infantry give his men after Eddie's execution?

Analyzing Ethical Issues

Considering rights and duties. General Patton mentioned rights and duties. Another general, Norman Cota, commanded the 28th Division. He once said that he tried to get his men to understand the importance of duty by telling them: "Men, for every *right* that you enjoy there is a *duty* that you must assume. You've heard a lot of talk about *rights*; now you'll hear a lot about *duty*." Many people who think about ethical issues agree that for each right that we have, we also have a duty.

The rights listed below are guaranteed by the Constitution. Identify a duty associated with each right, as illustrated in this example:

RIGHT	DUTY
To freedom of speech.	*To respect others' right to speak.*

1. To vote.

2. To free exercise of religion.

3. To trial by jury.

In addition to constitutional rights, people often claim other rights. For each of the following rights that might be claimed, identify a duty associated with it, using the same form as in the example above.

1. To drive a car.

2. To live where one chooses.

3. To use public parks.

Expressing Your Reasoning

1. Was it wrong to execute Private Slovik? Why or why not?

2. Choose one of the following opinions about the execution of Eddie Slovik that you disagree with, and write a short essay responding to it.

   a. *Private Tankey:* "He was a poor kid who had had a raw deal. It's wrong to kill a man like that."

   b. *Private Morrison:* "I'm just sorry that others like him don't get the same treatment. If everybody had acted like he did, we'd be living under Hitler today."

   c. *General Cota:* "I was privileged to lead thirty-six thousand Americans into battle, and I saw many of them die for the principles in which we believe. . . . I thought it was my duty to this country to approve that sentence. If I hadn't approved it . . . then I don't know how I could have gone up to the line and looked a good soldier in the face."

   d. *Anonymous:* "It was wrong. No other deserters had been shot. He should not have been singled out."

3. *Seeking Additional Information.* In making decisions about such questions as those above, we often feel we need more information before we are satisfied with our judgments. Choose one of the

above questions about which you would want more information than is presented in the story. What additional information would you like? Why would that information help you make a more satisfactory decision?

Atomic Falling-out

J. ROBERT OPPENHEIMER

J. Robert Oppenheimer (right) Being Awarded a Medal of Merit by
Secretary of War, Robert Patterson

On August 7, 1945, Haakon Chevalier wrote a letter that began: "You are probably the most famous man in the world today, and yet I am not sure that this letter will reach you." The letter ended: "Meanwhile our pride and our love go out to you. You will not have much time to think of us. But when you do, remember that we are what we were, though bearing within us the marks of what has happened in the world."

The man to whom the letter was written was J. Robert Oppenheimer. The day before the letter was written an atomic bomb had been dropped on Hiroshima, Japan. Never before had such death and destruction been caused by a single weapon. On August 9, a second atomic bomb fell on Nagasaki. In the face of such destructive horror, Japan surrendered, and World War II came to an end. Oppenheimer had a leading role in the creation of the bomb and was now world famous as "the father of the atomic bomb." He was also Haakon Chevalier's best friend.

The two men met in 1937 at the University of California at Berkeley. Chevalier was an instructor in the French department and Oppenheimer a professor of physics. Oppenheimer was not yet known to the general public, but top scientists around the world were aware of his great intellectual powers.

Oppenheimer's brilliance showed early. As a small boy he became fascinated with art, music, literature, and science. The depth of his knowledge and understanding was unusual. At one point he became interested in geology. A few years later, at the age of 12, he was invited to give a scholarly lecture at the New York Mineralogical Club. The members were surprised to see a slender young boy who had to stand on a box so that he could be seen behind the speaker's desk. The intelligence of his speech made a deep impression on the audience.

Robert's interests and abilities made him stand out from others his age. Classmates often teased him for being different. The teasing hurt the sensitive youngster, but he would not give up his study and research. His parents and others became convinced he was a genius. By the time he graduated from high school he could read and speak five languages and had done college level work in math, physics, chemistry, Greek, and Latin.

Oppenheimer's early brilliance did not fade. He attended Harvard and was a spectacular success. Although he took many more courses than were required, he graduated in only three years and was number one in his class.

He maintained an active interest in many topics, but physics became his specialty. He was absorbed by the ground-breaking theory and research in the relatively new area of nuclear physics. Few U.S. scientists were experts in nuclear physics, so Oppenheimer went to Europe for further study. There the great experts in nuclear physics were amazed at his remarkable ability. He returned with a doctoral degree and was hired, at the age of 25, as a professor at the University of California.

He rapidly gained a reputation for the brilliance of his intellect. Top students came to study the complexities of theoretical nuclear physics with him. Oppenheimer had a sharp tongue and was often impatient with those who could not understand him. On the other hand, he was noted for charm and generosity toward those who became his friends. Many people became devoted to him.

The year Oppenheimer began teaching, 1929, was also the year of the stock market crash that ushered in the Great Depression. Oppenheimer was so involved in his work that he was unaware of the crash until long after it had happened. In time, however, the turmoil of the 1930s attracted his attention and concern.

Oppenheimer had substantial personal wealth, but it did not keep him from seeing the human suffering brought on by the Depression. Tens of thousands of banks and businesses failed. Millions of people lost their jobs and homes. Masses of people wandered about homeless, hungry, and heartbroken.

The hardships of the Depression led many to wonder if there was something wrong with the U.S. system of capitalism. Under capitalism, businesses and people are free to compete for profit by taking risks in open competition, without extensive government regulation. There had been depressions in the past but none so severe as that of the 1930s. Something had gone wrong in the United States. Was capitalism to blame? The communists answered yes.

In the 1930s, a small minority of Americans were attracted to some communist ideas. Some actually joined the American Communist party. Others, while unwilling to join the party, supported some of its policies and causes by speaking in their favor or donating money to support them. Nonmembers who supported communist causes were known as *fellow travelers*. For a time, J. Robert Oppenheimer was a fellow traveler.

By the 1950s, communism was regarded as a major threat to the United States. In the 1930s, however, it did not seem so threatening.

During the Depression years, some prominent Americans discussed communism and openly supported some of its ideas. Oppenheimer, for example, donated money to such communist causes as aid for migrant workers and victims of the Spanish civil war. He associated freely with Communists and fellow travelers.

Haakon Chevalier and his wife worked with and supported many of the same causes as did Oppenheimer. Together, the three had long discussions of world problems and what should be done to solve them. Soon they became close friends, often sharing dinner and going to parties together.

In 1939, Robert met Katherine ("Kitty") Harrison. They fell in love, and were married the following year. She had once been a member of the Communist party. She too enjoyed the Chevaliers, and the two couples were together frequently.

Oppenheimer continued his work in physics and his reputation for brilliance grew. He had a genius for solving problems that baffled other scientists.

More and more it seemed likely that a second world war was near. Japanese armies were on the march in Asia. In Europe, Hitler's Nazi forces were spreading their terror.

As war neared, many Americans who had once supported or sympathized with communism changed their minds. For a time it had seemed that the Soviet Union was the only nation prepared to take a strong stand against Hitler. In 1939, however, Soviet leader Stalin signed a nonaggression treaty with Hitler. It appeared that the Soviet Union was giving in to Nazism. There was also disturbing news of Stalin's brutal treatment of Soviet citizens. Soviet communism was rapidly losing its appeal to people like Oppenheimer. Hitler eventually broke the treaty and invaded Russia.

The bombing of Pearl Harbor brought the United States into war against Japan. Soon Americans were fighting in Europe and in the Pacific with the Soviet Union as an ally. The winning of the war required more than courageous soldiers. Modern tanks, ships, airplanes, and other advanced weapons were needed.

Top physicists thought they had the key to a new weapon of enormous destructive power. In theory it was possible to create an atomic bomb. No one could be certain, however, that a practical version could be made in time for use in the war. Governmental leaders decided that an all-out effort to create the bomb should be made.

Work on the bomb required the services of top scientists from around the nation. The press of time and secrecy made the job even more urgent. It was believed that Hitler's scientists were also at work on such a weapon. It was vital that the United States be the first to succeed. Complete secrecy had to surround the project. Leaks of information might help the enemy. Some governmental leaders believed that, in the long run, the Soviet Union would become America's most dangerous enemy. Atomic secrets were to be kept from the Russians as well as the immediate enemy.

General Leslie Groves was chosen to coordinate work on the bomb—code named the Manhattan Project. The tough, conservative military man was not a scientist but was skilled at organizing. One of his jobs was to see that necessary materials were obtained quickly; another was to make sure that no atomic secrets were leaked.

Groves could handle some aspects of the project, but a top level physicist was needed to recruit and work with the hundreds of scientists to be involved. What was needed was someone who understood the complexities of nuclear science and who could also solve problems of practical production. A person respected by other scientists was sought. It had to be someone who was loyal to the United States and who also could keep secrets.

Many candidates for top scientist were considered: J. Robert Oppenheimer was chosen. There was concern about his association with Communists and communist causes, and there were questions about his loyalty to the United States. General Groves was strongly anticommunist but was convinced that Oppenheimer was the best man for the job.

Groves and Oppenheimer decided that the project would have a greater chance of success if the scientists could work in one place rather than in laboratories scattered around the nation. They selected a desert area near Los Alamos, New Mexico, as the site for a secret atomic laboratory.

Oppenheimer traveled throughout the nation urging top scientists to come to Los Alamos. Many were reluctant to leave their homes and laboratories to work in the bleak desert, in buildings surrounded by fences and guarded by the military. Also, there would be little privacy. To maintain security, all incoming and outgoing mail would be read by security officials and telephone calls would be tapped. Oppenheimer, however, was respected highly and had an unusual ability to persuade and inspire. The scientists needed for the job went to Los Alamos.

Because of the need for security, Oppenheimer could not tell his friend Chevalier about the project. Chevalier knew, however, that Oppenheimer was involved in a top-secret war project. On one of their return visits to Berkeley, the Oppenheimers invited the Chevaliers for dinner. A brief but fateful conversation took place in the kitchen.

Chevalier said that a British-born engineer, George Eltenton, had approached him. Eltenton knew that Oppenheimer was involved in a war project and that Chevalier was a close friend. Eltenton said that he had ways of getting secret information to the Russians. When Chevalier finished speaking, Oppenheimer said he would have no part in any such activity. Apparently neither would Chevalier. In later years he said that he, like Oppenheimer, was disgusted with Eltenton's suggestion. Chevalier said he was trying to warn his friend about Eltenton and was in no way trying to get Oppenheimer involved in giving secret information.

After the short kitchen conversation the topic was dropped and the men returned to the dinner party. At the time, neither man thought their talk of much importance. It would, however, haunt them for the rest of their lives.

Oppenheimer continued to pour his energies into the Manhattan Project. As the work progressed, governmental concern with maintaining secrecy grew. Security officers followed Oppenheimer and others. Careful records were kept of where they went and whom they met.

Occasionally Oppenheimer was interviewed about security matters. He told one official that he had heard from an acquaintance that George Eltenton was interested in getting information to the Russians. He said that his acquaintance had contacted three people involved in the bomb project. He was pressed to give the name of the acquaintance but would not do so. He said he was quite sure his acquaintance was no threat to security and that to name him would cause unnecessary trouble. The acquaintance was Haakon Chevalier. Oppenheimer was the only person contacted, but, for some reason, he made up the story about three other scientists. Perhaps he was confused under the pressure of the interview and the complex demands of his work. No one knows why he failed to tell the truth to the security officer.

Groves was informed of the interview and met to discuss it with Oppenheimer. Oppenheimer said he would only reveal the name of the acquaintance if he was ordered to do so by the general. Groves did not insist. After all, Oppenheimer had volunteered Eltenton's name. If pressured too much, Oppenheimer might be unwilling to volunteer other information in the future. Also, Groves knew that Oppenheimer was vital to the project. The general had confidence in Oppenheimer's loyalty.

Security officials did not share Groves' confidence. They continued to investigate and interview Oppenheimer. Oppenheimer gave the names of many people he had known as Communists or communist sympathizers but would not name his secret acquaintance. He said it would be a "low trick" to name someone he was convinced was innocent of any wrongdoing.

The security officials continued to press Groves with their suspicions. Some wanted Oppenheimer removed from his position at Los Alamos. Groves would not remove Oppenheimer but did give in to demands that he find out the name of the acquaintance. In December 1943, Groves ordered Oppenheimer to name the acquaintance. Relutantly, Oppenheimer uttered the name—Haakon Chevalier.

Work at Los Alamos continued. The strain on the scientists was intense, both mentally and physically. Oppenheimer was six feet tall and his weight dropped to a mere 115 pounds. Questions emerged as the time for testing the bomb grew near. Would it work? Would the countless hours of theorizing, calculating, and creating end in failure? And, if it was a success, should its great force be used?

Oppenheimer was called to Washington to discuss with President Truman's advisers what to do if the bomb passed its upcoming test. Many issues were discussed. One was whether to hold a demonstration, in some isolated place, of the power of the new weapon. If the Japanese could see the terrible destructive force of the bomb, perhaps they would surrender lest it be used against them. Oppenheimer was not convinced that such a demonstration would be spectacular enough to bring surrender. If it were not, the Japanese would, in effect, be given advance warning that it would be used. The element of surprise would be lost, and Japan might devise some way to defend against the bomb. The advisers recommended that the bomb, if successfully tested, be used against Japan without warning.

On July 16, 1945, the atomic device was exploded in the desert. The thunderous roar and the glare of a huge fireball stunned the observers. It was the equivalent of 20,000 tons of explosives! The words of an ancient Hindu poem came to Oppenheimer: "I am become death; the shatterer of worlds."

President Truman directed that the bomb be dropped on Japan. On August 6, the flaming fury hit Hiroshima. Over one hundred thousand people were immediately killed or injured. Still others yet unborn would suffer the effects of radiation. The bomb destroyed over half of the city.

Oppenheimer was a national hero. The war was over. American lives would not have to be sacrificed in an invasion of Japan. Oppenheimer felt personal satisfaction over the scientific achievement represented by the bomb. Like many other scientists who had worked on the project, he also felt distressed about the terrible force that had been unleashed.

In his letter, Chevalier sympathized with his friend: "There is a weight in such a venture which few men in history have had to bear. I know that with your love of men, it is no light thing to have had a part, and a great part, in a diabolical contrivance for destroying them."

President Truman was not so sympathetic. In a conversation with the president, Oppenheimer suddenly said: "Mr. President, I have blood on my hands." Later, Truman told an adviser: "Don't you bring that fellow around again. After all, all he did was make the bomb. I'm the guy who fired it off."

The war was over, but concern for security became greater than ever. Leaders of the Soviet Union had broken wartime promises, and Soviet armies occupied many Eastern European nations. Nations that were supposed to be free after the war were now dominated by the Soviet Union. As some governmental leaders had predicted, the Soviet Union had become America's chief adversary. Fears of communism and Communist agents reached new heights in the United States.

Having been identified by Oppenheimer, Chevalier's name appeared in growing files of people who might be a threat to the United States. Chevalier was interviewed, followed, and secretly investigated. He told Oppenheimer about the interviews. Chevalier could not understand why he was under investigation. On hearing of this, Oppenheimer became upset. He did not, however, tell Chevalier that he had given his name to the security officials during the war.

Oppenheimer became highly influential after the war. He served on many governmental advisory groups dealing with questions of nuclear policy. He had access to top-secret information about U.S. nuclear research. President Truman ordered a major secret effort be made to create a hydrogen bomb. This new weapon, known as the *super*, would be many times more powerful than the atomic bomb.

Oppenheimer was not enthusiastic about trying to create the super. He preferred that major efforts be placed in developing a defense system for the United States rather than in creating a more powerful nuclear bomb. He knew the Soviet Union was making progress in the creation of a hydrogen bomb, but he feared for the future of the world if such weapons were ever used. Of the two powers he said: "We may be likened to two scorpions in a bottle, each capable of killing the other, but only at the risk of its own life." Some people believed that Oppenheimer's coolness toward the hydrogen bomb caused delays in progress toward its completion.

In 1953, with fear of communism at a new high, a former government official sent a letter to the FBI. The letter charged that Oppenheimer was a Soviet agent. A special secret hearing was held to investigate the accusation.

Oppenheimer's security files had been reviewed often in the past. Now the old information was to be used anew. One item in his files was that he had initially lied when questioned about his friend Chevalier. During the hearings, Oppenheimer was asked why he had lied. The only answer he could give was: "Because I was an idiot."

General Groves was asked about his reaction to Oppenheimer's withholding of information about Chevalier. Groves said that he had no doubts about Oppenheimer's loyalty to the United States. He had dismissed Oppenheimer's reluctance to name Chevalier as "the typical American school boy attitude that there is something wicked about telling on a friend."

After the lengthy investigation, the hearing board concluded that Oppenheimer was a loyal American. The board also said that he had "an unusual ability to keep to himself vital secrets." Nonetheless the board said that Oppenheimer's past associations with Communists and fellow travelers, his lack of enthusiasm for the hydrogen bomb, and his delays in telling the truth about Chevalier made him a security risk. By a vote of 2 to 1, the board recommended that Oppenheimer no longer have access to secrets and that he be barred from future government employment.

The results of the hearing made headline news around the world. Haakon Chevalier heard about it in Paris, where he had moved after having difficulty getting a job in the United States. An expected promotion at the University of California had been mysteriously blocked as had other opportunities. Chevalier was shocked that his famous friend would be so treated by the United States. Chevalier was soon to receive an even greater shock.

As details of the hearing became public, Chevalier found the answer to a question he had long pondered. Oppenheimer had given his name to security officials during the war. Because of Oppenheimer he had been followed and investigated, and perhaps kept from getting satisfactory jobs. Oppenheimer's statements left the impression that Chevalier might be trying to deliver secret information to the Russians.

Chevalier wrote to Oppenheimer. Even though letters were exchanged, Chevalier could never get a clear answer to the question: "Why had my dearest friend invented that damaging story about me?" The falling-out between them was never mended.

The major sources for this story were:

Chevalier, Haakon M. *Oppenheimer: The Story of a Friendship*. New York: George Braziller, 1965.

Michelmore, Peter. *The Swift Years: The Robert Oppenheimer Story*. New York: Dodd, Mead, 1969.

Stern, Philip M. (with Green, Harold P.). *The Oppenheimer Case: Security on Trial*. New York: Harper & Row, 1969.

ACTIVITIES FOR "ATOMIC FALLING-OUT"

Write all answers on a separate sheet of paper.

Historical Understanding

Answer briefly:

1. What was meant by the term *fellow traveler*?

2. What was the Manhattan Project?

3. What was one thing that Soviet leader Stalin did that led some Americans to turn away from their interest in communism?

Reviewing the Facts of the Case

Answer briefly:

1. What did Chevalier tell Oppenheimer in their famous kitchen conversation?

2. What lie did Oppenheimer tell to security officials?

3. Why were security officials suspicious of Oppenheimer?

4. After Hiroshima, what did Oppenheimer say to President Truman? How did the president react?

5. What was the *super*?

6. What were three reasons Oppenheimer was judged to be a security risk?

7. What shocked Chevalier when he heard the details of Oppenheimer's security hearing?

Analyzing Ethical Issues

There is agreement about the answer to some questions. For other questions there is disagreement or uncertainty about the correct answer. We call these questions issues. Issues can be categorized as factual or ethical. A factual issue asks whether something is true or false, accurate or inaccurate. An ethical issue asks whether something is right or wrong, fair or unfair. Factual issues ask what *is*; ethical issues ask what *ought to be*. For example:

> Could the atomic bomb have been created without Oppenheimer's involvement? *Factual.*
>
> Should Chevalier have forgiven Oppenheimer for mentioning his name? *Ethical.*

For each of the following questions, decide whether the issue is factual or ethical.

1. Are people who sympathize with communism likely to give secrets to the Soviet Union?

2. Would Japan have surrendered if a demonstration nuclear blast were set off?

3. Was it right for Oppenheimer to withhold Chevalier's name from security officials?

4. Did Chevalier lose important jobs because of Oppenheimer?

Expressing Your Reasoning

1. Should Oppenheimer have revealed Chevalier's name when first asked to name the acquaintance who told him about Eltenton? Why or why not?

2. There are many arguments that can be made in favor of or against Oppenheimer's initial withholding of Chevalier's name. Evaluate each of the following arguments, and indicate whether you think it is strong or weak. Explain the reasons for your judgments.
   a. Oppenheimer should have given the name, because the officials had an important job to do.
   b. Oppenheimer should have given the name, because withholding it would look suspicious, and he could have gotten in trouble.
   c. Oppenheimer should not have given the name, because Chevalier was his friend.
   d. Oppenheimer should not have given the name, because he did not think Chevalier was any threat to security.
   e. Oppenheimer should have given the name, becuase Chevalier did not ask him to keep their kitchen conversation confidential.
   f. Oppenheimer should have given the name, because loyalty to his country is more important than loyalty to his friend.
   g. Oppenheimer should not have given the name, because investigators would probably spy on Chevalier.
   h. Oppenheimer should not have given the name, because investigators who interviewed Chevalier might find out that Oppenheimer had lied about the three scientists who had been contacted.

3. Oppenheimer was called to Washington to meet with President Truman's advisors. They had to make a recommendation about how, if at all, the atomic bomb should be used. Many points of view were considered. Below are some arguments that were used to oppose the use of the bomb and some used to favor its use. (Most of these arguments were considered at the meetings; others are added here for purposes of discussion.)

The bomb should not be used because:
a. It is too horrible and the United States should not be the first to use such a weapon in warfare.
b. Japanese civilians would die, and civilians should not be attacked.
c. The Allies have been demanding that Japan surrender unconditionally. The surrender terms are too severe; Japan might surrender, without the bomb, if the terms were softened.
d. A demonstration of the bomb's power should be made so that Japan can surrender before the bomb is dropped.

The bomb should be used because:

a. A conventional invasion of Japan would lead to the loss of U.S. soldiers. Dropping the bomb would save American lives.

b. The Soviet Union seems interested in expanding its power in Europe and Asia. Dropping the bomb on Japan would demonstrate U.S. power to the Soviets and might deter their expansion.

c. The Japanese have made a surprise attack on Pearl Harbor and their armies in Asia have been brutal. Dropping the bomb would be a way of getting back at them.

d. A demonstration of the bomb's power would allow the Japanese to plan some kind of defense, and it would eliminate the element of surprise.

Oppenheimer decided to recommend that the bomb be used without warning. Was he right in making that recommendation? Why or why not? Present your position in a short essay of a few paragraphs. In your essay refer to some of the arguments above.

4. Oppenheimer did not tell Chevalier that he had given his name to security officials. Did Oppenheimer have any obligation to tell Chevalier what he had done? Why or why not?

5. *Seeking Additional Information.* In making decisions about such questions as those above, we often feel we need more information before we are satisfied with our judgments. Choose one of the above questions about which you would want more information than is presented in the story. What additional information would you like? Why would that information help you make a more satisfactory decision?

Pink Lady

HELEN GAHAGAN DOUGLAS

(*Western History Collections, University of Oklahoma Library*)

Helen Gahagan Douglas on a Mobile Campaign Platform During the
1950 Election Campaign

She was once described by a dazzled critic as "ten of the twelve most beautiful women in the world." In her twenties she was a brilliant Broadway actress. During her thirties she became an accomplished opera singer. Next she chose a career in politics. Her third career ended with what one historian called the ugliest campaign of U.S. political history.

Helen Gahagan was born in New Jersey, a child of privilege, in 1900. As a young girl she dreamed of a theatrical career. Her father, a successful engineer, was dismayed by her dreams. He insisted that she buckle down and forget about acting. Schooling, he insisted, was her only safeguard against a life without purpose or interests. He told her she must go to college and learn to think so that she would not become a slave to emotion.

In college, Helen joined the drama society. She was steadfast in her ambition to pursue a career on the stage. By age 22 she was acting on Broadway. Her performances received critical acclaim, and she quickly rose to stardom.

While in her late twenties, Helen took voice lessons and discovered that she also had a singing talent. She gave up her successful acting career to become an operatic soprano. Singing in French, German, and Italian, she added dramatic flair to the starring roles of many operas, including *Tosca* and *Aïda*. Critics in the musical capitals of Europe praised her talent highly.

In 1931, Helen married Melvyn Douglas, her leading man in a Broadway play. The couple moved to California. Melvyn soon became one of the most popular Hollywood movie stars of the period.

In California, Helen Douglas was lured away from the opera stage by politics. She sympathized with the plight of industrial workers who were suffering because of unemployment during the Great Depression. Grim conditions faced by migrant farm workers seeking refuge from the dust bowl horrified her.

A long-standing Republican, Helen Douglas was drawn to the Democratic party by President Roosevelt's New Deal. She became a personal friend of the first lady, Eleanor Roosevelt. Franklin Roosevelt appointed Mrs. Douglas to the National Advisory Committee of the Works Progress Administration (WPA). The WPA was a federal job creation program designed to reduce the record-breaking unemployment of the Depression.

In 1944, following several years of work with the California Democratic party, Douglas was elected to Congress from the Fourteenth

District in Los Angeles. During her three terms in the House of Representatives, she avidly supported Roosevelt's domestic policies and those of his successor, Harry Truman.

Helen Douglas acquired a reputation for integrity. She was admired as courageous and able, even by her political enemies. She took what were considered liberal positions on major domestic issues of the day. For example, she supported federal funding for cancer research, civilian control of atomic energy in the United States, slum clearance, public housing, expanded social security benefits, and public ownership of power utilities. Her support for federal control of California's vast oil tidelands made her unpopular with California oil interests. Many oil producers thought they would have easier access to oil if the off-shore oil deposits were owned by the state.

Douglas also worked to provide civil rights for minorities. Her devotion to this cause was symbolized by admission of her black secretary to the House cafeteria. Blacks had previously been excluded. The ban was lifted in response to pressure from Douglas.

As a member of the House Committee on Foreign Affairs, Douglas usually supported the foreign policies of the Truman administration. She stood firmly behind the *Marshall Plan*, which provided U.S. aid for the rebuilding of western European economies following World War II. She also played a significant role in legislation to fund the *North Atlantic Treaty Organization* (NATO). The NATO military alliance was America's commitment to join western European countries in resisting Soviet expansion in Europe during the late 1940s.

In foreign affairs, Douglas' most enthusiastic support was for the infant United Nations. That cause twice set off clashes between her and the Truman administration. The first conflict came over the *United Nations Relief and Rehabilitation Administration* (UNRRA). Established to provide food, medicine, and other essentials to countries ravaged by World War II, UNRRA received half its funding from the United States. In 1946, the United States decided to pull out of UNRRA because much of its aid was going to countries where communists were gaining strength.

Douglas had been appointed a member of the U.S. delegation to the United Nations. At a meeting of the delegation, she urged her fellow delegates to oppose the State Department directive to withdraw the United States from UNRRA. In the midst of her remarks a phone call suddenly came for Douglas. It was from Secretary of State Dean Acheson. He icily informed Douglas that she was not a free agent. "You're at the United Nations as a delegate charged with the responsibility of carrying out U.S. policy. You can agree or disagree with that policy in Congress but not when you're at the UN. I order you to drop this campaign of yours to keep us in UNNRA." Douglas complied but considered the pullout a disgraceful abandonment of the needy in Europe.

The second clash with Truman's foreign policy stemmed from Douglas' belief that the United States was undermining the authority of the newly formed United Nations. This time the conflict involved what was called the *Truman Doctrine*, a bill to provide military aid to Greece and Turkey. The Soviet Union was threatening both countries, and the United States wanted to prevent Soviet expansion. Douglas agreed that the Russians should be blocked, but not by the United States acting alone. She wanted the Russian military buildup on Turkey's border to be handled by the United Nations. Her vote in Congress to oppose the Truman Doctrine was not a popular one.

The years Douglas spent in Congress coincided with the emergence of the *cold war*. This term refers to combat without open fighting between the two postwar superpowers, the Soviet Union and the United States. The Russians tried to increase the number of pro-Soviet communist regimes in the world. They supported military coercion and subversion by local communists of existing governments. The United States was determined to stop communist advances by giving aid to anticommunist governments.

In the United States, the cold war brought not only dread of the Soviets abroad, but also fear that communists within the country were infiltrating the government. The *House Un-American Activities Committee* (HUAC) began investigating suspected communists. Douglas, a member of HUAC, spoke out against the emerging uproar over communism in a House speech:

> The spreading of this fear is in fact propaganda for communism. I am nauseated and sick to death of the vicious and deliberate way the word "communist" has been forged into a weapon and used against those who organize and raise their voices in defense of democratic ideas. . . . Communism could successfully invade only a weakened democracy. A vigorous democracy—a democracy in which there are freedom from want, freedom from fear, freedom of religion, and freedom of speech—would never succumb to communism or any other ism.

Fear of what some orators called the "red menace" continued to spread in the United States. The Soviet Union had defied wartime agreements by expanding into Poland and Bulgaria. Hungary, Romania, East Germany, and Czechoslovakia soon fell into the Soviet orbit. England's wartime leader, Winston Churchill, was to say that an "iron curtain" had descended upon Europe. When the Soviets threatened Greece and Turkey, Western leaders became alarmed.

Then, in 1949, three events produced near panic in the United States. Representative Richard Nixon, a member of HUAC, charged that Alger Hiss, former presidential advisor and respected diplomat, had lied about providing government secrets to communist agents. In September of that year, the Soviet Union exploded its first atomic bomb, years before U.S. experts had expected. The following month, Chinese Communists took control of mainland China.

Several politicians began to exploit alarm over the spread of communism. Joseph McCarthy, Republican Senator from Wisconsin, charged that the government was infested with communist agents working to destroy democracy. Many people were terrorized by fear that they might be named communists. The careers of some were damaged by such accusations.

In 1950, amid the growing furor over communist influence in the United States, Douglas decided to run for the U.S. Senate from California. She defeated the incumbent in the Democratic primary because of her extraordinary personal popularity. One of her supporters was Ronald Reagan, then a Democrat and later to become a Republican president.

Her Republican opponent, also a member of the House, was Richard Nixon. In an era dominated by fear of communists, Nixon was an attractive candidate. As the key figure in the Alger Hiss case, Nixon had received nationwide publicity. He had a reputation as a leading anticommunist.

Nixon was first elected to Congress in 1946 by suggesting that his Democratic opponent was linked to communists. The 1950 elections, said Nixon, would allow Americans "the choice between freedom and state socialism." He referred to Truman administration programs as "creeping communism." "Call it planned economy, the Fair Deal, or social welfare," he said, "but it is still the same old socialist baloney any way you slice it."

As a liberal, Douglas was vulnerable to such remarks by the

conservative Mr. Nixon. The country was shifting away from the liberal policies of the New Deal. Primary elections in the spring of 1950 offered a preview of the theme that would dominate the campaign in California. A respected New Deal senator from Florida, Claude Pepper, was defeated in the Democratic primary by an opponent who called him "Red Pepper." A North Carolina senator lost to an opponent who accused him of taking the country down the road to socialism.

Suggesting that political opponents were sympathetic to communism became known as *red-baiting*, red being the color of the communist revolutionary banner. This practice of recklessly accusing people of being communists later became known as *McCarthyism*, after the Wisconsin senator. Red-baiters used the terms socialism and communism interchangeably. Both were portrayed as left-wing evils that threatened U.S. democracy.

On June 25, 1950, Communist North Korea invaded South Korea. The United Nations sent an army to stop the invaders. U.S. troops, fighting under the blue flag of the United Nations, lost their first engagements. Americans were horrified. It seemed that communists were advancing upon them from all sides. The panic was greatest in California, the state closest to the hostilities on the far side of the Pacific. FBI director J. Edgar Hoover claimed there were almost seven thousand communists working underground in California. The movie industry, it was said, was riddled with traitors.

Members of Congress were eager to prove they were not soft on communism. The McCarran Internal Security Bill was introduced. It was based on a similar bill offered earlier by Richard Nixon. The new bill, among other things, required suspected communists or "communist-front" organizations to register with the attorney general. These included groups that were not communist but that were suspected of having some communists among their members. Under the bill, groups designated by the attorney general would be required to provide membership lists and financial statements to the government. In case of an internal-security emergency, the bill gave the president sweeping power to detain anyone who it was believed might possibly be a spy. President Truman said the McCarran Bill was worse than the Sedition Act of 1798 and that it took a "long step toward totalitarianism."

Douglas agreed with the president's opinion of the bill. She added

that it endangered the freedoms of speech, press, and assembly protected by the First Amendment. The Senate passed the bill, and it
went to the House.

There was tense silence on the House floor as the roll call vote was
taken. When the clerk began calling names, Douglas was approached
by a fellow California Congressman. "Helen," he whispered, "don't
vote against this bill." Surprised, Douglas asked, "You're voting
against it, aren't you?"

"Yes, but I'm not running for the Senate against Richard Nixon.
You won't be able to get around the state fast enough to explain why
you voted against the bill after he gets through telling voters that you
did it because you're soft on Reds. He'll beat your brains in."

Other California Representatives approached Douglas and pleaded
with her not to vote against the bill. One warned, "It'll cost you!"
Another remarked, "Why jeopardize your campaign? This bill is
going to pass overwhelmingly. Your vote won't matter. Anyway,
Truman will veto it."

Douglas realized that a no vote would give Nixon ammunition to
accuse her of being a communist. The clerk called, "Douglas of
California."

"No."

Election strategy, the congresswoman later maintained, "wasn't a
compelling reason to vote against conscience on a bill that struck at
the heart of the First Amendment of the Bill of Rights." Only 24 others
voted with Douglas, and the McCarran Bill passed the House. Douglas
remembered that when she cast her vote against the bill, she happened
to catch Nixon's eye. "He was grinning broadly. I knew that he would
twist the issue so that my vote against the abuse of civil rights in the
bill would be presented as a vote for communism." Her hunch was
correct.

In California, Nixon forces ran a smear campaign against Douglas.
She was accused of being soft on communism and doubt was cast
upon her loyalty to the country.

It was a campaign carefully calculated to pin the Red label on
Douglas. Anonymous telephone calls were made to tell voters Douglas
was a communist. Nixon implied that his opponent was a shade of
red. At one whistlestop during his energetic campaign, he said Douglas
was "pink right down to her underwear." Later, Nixon asked of
Douglas, "Why has she followed the communist line so many times?"

Nixon also charged that Douglas "gave comfort to Soviet tyranny." During the campaign the pairing of Helen Douglas with communism came almost daily and was widely reported in California newspapers.

The most damaging tactic by the Nixon campaign was the release in August of the "pink sheet," a flyer printed on pink paper. It falsely implied that Helen Douglas had formed a partnership with Vito Marcantonio, "the notorious Communist party-line Congressman from New York." The flyer stated that Douglas, as a member of the House, had voted with the leftist Marcantonio a great number of times while Nixon had voted opposite them. The pink sheet went on to say: "How can Helen Douglas, capable actress that she is, take up so strange a role as a foe of communism? And why does she when she has so deservedly earned the title of 'the pink lady'?"

The Nixon campaign had defamed Douglas by innuendo. It was guilt by association with Marcantonio, the only member of the House who belonged to the procommunist American Labor party. The charge that Douglas was his ally was deliberately misleading. In fact, a majority of House Democrats had also voted with Marcantonio on key votes. Nixon himself voted with him 112 times. Douglas tried in vain to shed the image of her created by the pink sheet. The "pink lady" label stuck, and Nixon won the Senate seat with 56 percent of the vote.

In response to the attacks of her opponent during the campaign, Douglas coined the phrase *Tricky Dick*. The label was to haunt Richard Nixon throughout his political career as senator and vice-president. It was revived at the time of his resignation from the presidency in 1974 as a result of involvement in the Watergate scandal.

The defeat in California sent Douglas into political obscurity. In her later years she said, "There's not much to say about the 1950 campaign except that a man ran for the Senate who wanted to get there, and didn't care how."

The major sources for this story were:

Brodie, Fawn M. *Richard Nixon: The Shaping of His Character*. New York: W. W. Norton, 1981.
Douglas, Helen G. *A Full Life*. New York: Doubleday, 1982.
Mankiewicz, Frank. *Perfectly Clear: Nixon from Whittier to Watergate*. New York: Quadrangle/ The New York Times, 1973.
Nixon, Richard M. *The Memoirs of Richard Nixon*. Vol. 1. New York: Warner, 1978.

ACTIVITIES FOR "PINK LADY"

Write all answers on a separate sheet of paper.

Historical Understanding

Answer briefly:

1. Identify the following: The Marshall Plan, NATO, HUAC, and the Truman Doctrine.

2. What was the *cold war*?

3. What three events in 1949 heightened fear of communism in the United States?

4. What was *McCarthyism*?

Reviewing the Facts of the Case

Answer briefly:

1. Cite three positions taken by Douglas that earned her a reputation as a liberal.

2. Why was there conflict between Douglas and the Truman administration over UNRRA?

3. Why did Douglas vote against the Truman Doctrine?

4. For what reason did Douglas oppose the McCarran Internal Security Bill? Why did some of her colleagues in the House urge her to vote for the bill?

5. How was the "pink sheet" used during the 1950 U.S. Senate campaign in California?

Analyzing Ethical Issues

Comparing liberal and conservative views of values. The 1950 U.S. Senate race in California was regarded by many as a pitched battle between a liberal (Mrs. Douglas) and a conservative (Mr. Nixon). Generally, liberals tend to favor social reforms and new changes in government, whereas conservatives tend to favor preservation of the

existing order. Sometimes liberals are placed to the left of center on a
political spectrum and conservatives to the right of center:

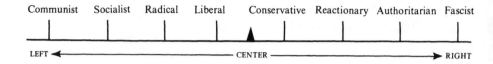

The meaning of these political labels can be confusing. One way to
distinguish liberals and conservatives from each other is to compare
their views on issues involving the following values:

AUTHORITY: a value concerning what rules or people should be
    obeyed and the consequences for disobedience
    A liberal orientation: Major changes in society should be
        initiated and carried out by the federal government.
    A conservative orientation: Government power should be
        decentralized; control should be at the state and local level,
        without interference from Washington.
LIBERTY: a value concerning what freedoms people should have
    and the limits that may be justifiably placed upon them
    A liberal orientation: Freedom to express one's views should
        be expanded, and those who dissent should be tolerated
        whatever their opinions.
    A conservative orientation: Limits should be placed on in-
        appropriate expression; criticism of established traditions
        should not be encouraged.
PROPERTY: a value concerning what people should be allowed to
    own and how they should be allowed to use it
    A liberal orientation: Government should distribute wealth
        more evenly so as to narrow the gap between rich and
        poor.
    A conservative orientation: The greater one's achievements,
        the more material rewards that person deserves. Those
        who do not earn should not receive benefits from those
        who do.

Three issues from Douglas' political career are presented in the list
below. Each issue involved the value of authority, liberty, or property.
As shown in the following example, indicate which value(s) is (are)

involved in each issue, and indicate which of the positions stated for each issue is a liberal one and which is a conservative one.

Should health insurance for the elderly be tax supported? *Property*

a. Individuals should plan for possible hardships and not expect their misfortunes to be paid for by others.   *conservative*

b. Everyone should contribute to the costs of health care for the aged, because old people have higher medical expenses and often can't afford to pay them.   *liberal*

1. Under whose control should the California oil tidelands be placed?
   a. Federal control of off-shore oil deposits is necessary to ensure that energy wealth is shared by all people in the country.
   b. State governments know best how to manage resources within their boundaries.

2. Should the Communist party be outlawed in the United States?
   a. Communists intend to destroy democracy, and the United States should not tolerate forces bent on the destruction of its government.
   b. In a democracy all are entitled to join the political party of their choosing, however unpopular its doctrines.

3. Should the government pay for construction of public housing for poor people in slums?
   a. Some people can't afford the cost of good housing, but they still deserve a decent place to live. Those who can afford it should be taxed to help those in need.
   b. People are responsible for housing themselves according to what they can afford to purchase. It is unfair to tax one person to pay someone else's rent.

Expressing Your Reasoning

1. Should Helen Douglas have voted yes on the McCarran Internal Security Bill? Why or why not?

2. One of Richard Nixon's political advisors told the candidate that politicians must be willing and able to "shoot a little dirty pool." Was Nixon wrong to try to win the Senate seat in California by

convincing voters that Helen Douglas was a communist sympathizer? Write a paragraph supporting your position.

3. Whether the candidates were truthful became a major issue during the 1950 Senate race in California. There are many other situations in which the issue of truth-telling arises. Each of the situations below involves the value of telling the truth. Indicate for each whether the truth ought to be told, and state a reason for your position.

   a. Should a student tell the teacher about a classmate's cheating on the final exam?

   b. Should an intelligence agent tell a reporter about an assassination plot against a foreign official?

   c. Should a friend tell of plans for a surprise party when asked about them by the one to be surprised?

   d. During a trial, a lawyer discovers that her client committed the crime as charged. Should she tell the jury?

   e. Should a paid informant tell the police about a crime committed by his friend?

   f. Should a middle-aged movie star tell the truth about her age?

   g. When asked, should a relative tell a terminally ill patient about his diagnosis?

   h. Should a spy reveal his true identity when questioned by enemy officials?

   i. Should a friend tell his buddy that his girlfriend was seen on a date with someone else?

   j. A young man dislikes his girlfriend's expensive new shoes. Should he admit it if she asks his opinion?

4. *Seeking Additional Information.* In making decisions about such questions as those above, we often feel we need more information before we are satisfied with our judgments. Choose one of the above questions about which you would want more information than is presented in the story. What additional information would you like? Why would that information help you make a more satisfactory decision?

A Clash of Symbols

PAUL ROBESON

(*Photograph by Gordon Parks. Courtesy of the Library of Congress*)

Paul Robeson

Early in September 1949, thousands of people gathered in a park near Peekskill, New York. They were there to hear an outdoor concert by one of the world's most famous singers and actors. A helicopter whirred overhead, the chattering of its motor often interfering with the music. After the concert, cars and buses carrying the audience inched along an exit road. Suddenly there were screams as rocks and bricks were hurled through the air. An angry mob, filled with hate and fear, attacked the departing audience. Many people were injured.

The ugly clash at Peekskill made headline news. The audience had come to hear the rich deep voice of Paul Robeson. The big black man was more than a highly talented entertainer. To the audience he was a symbol for free expression and racial equality in the United States. To the swarm of protesters he was a symbol of communistic forces trying to undermine the United States. Paul Robeson was one man seen in two drastically different ways.

The concert at Peekskill was one scene in the drama of Paul Robeson's life. From opening act to final curtain, his life story tells much of the promises and problems of the United States during the first half of the twentieth century.

Robeson's father had once been a slave. By the time of Paul's birth in 1898, his father was a minister in New Jersey. Although the family was poor, Paul was urged to walk with pride and work hard at getting a good education. Paul's mother died of burns suffered in a home accident. His father's burdens increased, but he still spent much time with Paul. It was a close, loving relationship.

Throughout the United States black people often faced discrimination. Many restaurants and hotels refused to admit black customers. When traveling by train, blacks often had to ride in cars separate from those for whites. Sometimes blacks were openly insulted when walking down the street. Paul's older brother, Reed, would not tolerate racial insults. He was frequently in trouble with the law for getting into fist fights with people who called him names. He told Paul, "Stand up to them and hit back harder than they hit you!"

Paul's father opposed physical violence. He said that to succeed Paul should always appear grateful to white people and avoid doing anything that might frighten them. He also told Paul that to be accepted as an equal, a black must be superior in his or her accomplishments. Paul was taught to achieve to his greatest ability. In schoolwork, for example, his father was not satisfied unless Paul got the highest possible grades.

He was one of only two or three blacks in his high school, but stood out for other reasons as well. He was at the top of his class in almost every subject. In addition he was an outstanding athlete, a top debater, and the star singer in the glee club. He graduated number one in his class.

Paul was popular among his classmates, but his color was sometimes a barrier. For example, he could not go on his class trip to Washington, D.C., when, at the last minute, it was discovered their hotel would not accept any black guests.

Paul learned that Rutgers University was offering a four-year scholarship to whoever achieved the top score on a special examination. With his family's help, Paul put in long hours of study for the examination. The hard work paid off. He received the highest score in New Jersey and won the scholarship.

As the only black in his Rutgers class, Paul knew he would face problems. Nonetheless, his brilliant showing on the examination encouraged him. He thought: "Equality might be denied, but I *knew* I was not inferior."

Paul did face problems but overcame them. The football coach wanted Robeson, who was 6 foot 3 inches tall and weighed over 200 pounds, to play but some of the white players resented the idea. Several times Paul was brutally beaten during practice sessions. He fought back with courage and was soon accepted. He became a major star and, in 1917 and 1918, was named an all-American player. He also starred in track, basketball, and baseball.

His athletic success was matched by his academic success. He was a top student and earned membership in the highest honor societies. He was valedictorian of his class.

Upon graduation a banquet was given in his honor. His father had died the year before. In his banquet speech, Paul said: "I want my life work to be a memorial to my father's training and to be not for my own self but to help my people to a higher life." Paul was determined to eliminate discrimination against blacks.

Robeson had been accepted at both the Harvard and Columbia law schools. He chose Columbia in part so he could live in the Harlem section of New York City, a section almost totally populated by blacks.

In many ways, Harlem was the capital of black America. In the early 1920s it experienced what some have called the Harlem Renaissance. Many black artists, writers, musicians, and intellectuals lived and worked in Harlem. Their influence spread throughout the nation and the world. The talented Robeson became friendly with leading figures in Harlem.

Robeson completed law school, occasionally playing professional football to help pay expenses. While at Columbia, he met Eslanda Goode, then a student completing advanced study in chemistry. They fell in love and were married in 1921. Six years later, their only child, Paul Jr., was born.

The practice of law did not appeal to Robeson. He found singing and acting more rewarding. His powerful singing and speaking voice thrilled listeners. In 1924 he was hired to play the leading role in Eugene O'Neill's play *All God's Chillun Got Wings*. News that he had been hired brought immediate controversy.

In the play Robeson's character is married to a white woman. In the United States interracial marriage was generally frowned upon and against the law in over half of the states. Some people lashed out at the play, claiming O'Neill was trying to promote interracial marriage. Threats of violence were made but none were carried out.

Robeson continued acting and singing. His artistry drew wider and wider attention. Both his fame and income grew. Soon he was performing in London and throughout the European continent. He was a smashing success both on and off the stage. Audiences flocked to see and hear him. Wealthy Europeans invited him to parties and other social gatherings.

Robeson became an international celebrity, making frequent trips between the United States and Europe. In London he starred in Shakespeare's *Othello*, as he did years later in New York. In the United States he was acclaimed for his performance in the musical *Showboat*, especially for his singing of "Ol' Man River." He appeared in motion pictures both in the United States and Europe.

Robeson became a living symbol. To many blacks he was a hero, not only for his personal achievements, but also because he had shown that blacks could succeed in a white-dominated world. Robeson was also popular among whites. Some believed he represented the freedom in the United States that allowed talented people to rise regardless of their race. One publication stated a view held by many— that Paul Robeson was "America's most distinguished living Negro."

The glitter of stardom never blinded Robeson's vision of racial equality. For example, he tried to avoid playing any parts in movies or dramas that represented blacks in undignified ways. He continued to be offended deeply by all instances of discrimination against blacks anywhere in the world.

Robeson's long stays in Europe had a strong effect on him. He and his family faced virtually no racial prejudice. They could travel first class and be served in the finest restaurants and hotels. Robeson contrasted his treatment in Europe to that in the United States where he frequently met with discrimination. In later years Europe would have its share of racial hatred, but at that time the Robesons faced very little.

Robeson's stay in Europe influenced his ideas about racial issues. He became interested in the richness of African culture. Promises of racial equality made by Communists and the Soviet Union also affected him.

In London Robeson met students from British colonies in Africa. They challenged images of Africa as a vast, dark continent populated by ignorant, primitive people. Robeson learned that such images were inaccurate. African history and culture were rich and complex. Robeson became convinced that if American blacks learned about their African roots, they would find a proud heritage. He also hoped that if white Americans learned more about African history and culture, there would be greater respect for black people.

Robeson had heard that the Communist leaders of the Soviet Union preached complete equality for all people regardless of race or sex. He was eager to see if such equality existed in practice. In the mid-1930s he was invited to visit the Soviet Union with his family.

On their way to Moscow, the Robesons passed through Germany. Hitler and his Nazis had come to power. They claimed that certain white Germans formed a master race. All others were inferior. At one train station, the Robesons got a hint of the terror that was to befall Germany and much of Europe in coming years. A group of tough Nazi storm troopers approached the Robesons as they awaited their train. Paul expected to be attacked, but he and his family boarded the train quickly and escaped violence.

In contrast to the tense moments at the German railroad station, the Robesons received a friendly welcome in the Soviet Union. Paul's artistry was known and appreciated by many Russians. He was greeted warmly wherever he went. To the Robesons it appeared that there actually was racial equality in the Soviet Union. Paul told a Russian host: "I feel like a human being for the first time since I grew up." In future years he would make more visits to the Soviet Union.

As World War II approached, Robeson began to act on his personal beliefs. In England he gave concerts to raise money for Jewish victims of the Nazis. He helped raise money for those who opposed the fascists in the Spanish civil war. Some people criticized him, saying that performers should stick to entertainment and stay out of political matters. Robeson disagreed. He said: "The artist must elect to fight for Freedom or for Slavery. I have made my choice. I had no alternative."

In September 1939, the Robesons returned to the United States. Paul's popularity as an entertainer was greater than ever. He bought a large house in Enfield, Connecticut. Nicknamed "The Beeches," the house had a swimming pool, tennis court, and bowling alley. It was an excellent place for Robeson to relax between performing tours.

Robeson's concern for equality and freedom extended to all people he believed were treated unfairly. He opposed the policies of nations that had colonies in Africa and elsewhere. He was distressed by the poverty and difficult conditions faced by many workers in the United States and abroad.

Although Robeson had made famous a patriotic song, "The Ballad for Americans," some doubted his loyalty to the United States. When the Soviet Union attacked Finland, most Americans were disgusted. Robeson would not criticize the Soviet action. He was asked to perform at a benefit to raise money for Finnish war victims, but refused.

Throughout World War II Robeson used his artistry to help the United States and its allies. He traveled widely entertaining troops as well as workers in war industries. He helped raise money to support the war effort. After the war he went to Europe and entertained the victorious Allied armies.

Robeson had hoped that the victory would help bring equality for American blacks and freedom for many colonial nations. From his point of view, however, there was little change. Returning American black soldiers still faced discrimination. England and other colonial powers seemed unwilling to grant independence to their colonies. Also, it was becoming clear that the United States and the Soviet Union, although allies during the war, were becoming enemies.

The Soviets were doing all they could to spread communism

throughout Eastern Europe. They broke agreements they had made during the war. They used brutal methods to establish communist governments in countries such as Poland and Czechoslovakia. In these nations, opponents of Soviet expansion were often terrorized by police and many were put to death. Soviet dictator Stalin had used such tactics in establishing his power. The Soviets were now using them to gain control of Eastern Europe. Robeson would not speak out against Soviet expansion. He was more concerned with U.S. policy at home and colonial policy abroad.

Believing the war had failed to achieve noble purposes, Robeson spoke out. His political views were unpopular with the majority of Americans, and his business advisor urged him to remain silent. Robeson's feelings were strong, however, and he would not hold them back. In one speech he even said the United States was taking over the role of Hitler in the world. He also said the Soviet Union should be given America's atomic secrets.

Some people were convinced Paul Robeson was a member of the Communist party. At that time governmental investigating committees tried to determine the extent of communist influence in the United States. In California, Robeson was called before one such committee. He was questioned and, under oath, swore that he was not a member of the Communist party.

Although Robeson had denied party membership, he did work with organizations that had communists as members and with other organizations that were suspected of being communist-dominated. More and more he faced resentment. Some concerts were cancelled when local people objected to his political views. His great popularity as an entertainer began to fade because of his association with what were regarded as radical political causes.

Robeson had admired President Roosevelt but was unhappy with the policies of President Truman. The president had announced the Truman Doctrine. According to this policy, the United States would provide aid to countries threatened by communist revolutions supported by the Soviet Union. Robeson's affection for the Soviet Union was strong as ever. He believed American fears of the Soviets were extreme and unwarranted.

Robeson also believed the president was failing to take a strong stand for racial justice. In some parts of the country extremist white mobs tortured and lynched blacks. In a meeting with Truman, Robeson asked the president to take action against such violence. The president said he personally opposed the violence, but the mood of the country made it politically impossible for him to do anything about it.

Robeson continued to speak out and continued to be associated with communism. It was not illegal to be associated with communists, communist ideas, or even to be a member of a Communist party. Nonetheless, people who expressed affection for the Soviet Union or for communist ideas were widely seen as threats to the United States. Such feelings increased when it was discovered Soviet spies were working to get American secrets, including atomic secrets.

In Washington, the House Un-American Activities Committee was busy investigating communism in the United States. The committee often proceeded in a reckless manner, making it appear that some people who refused to answer certain questions were actually Communists. The reputations of some people were ruined when they were unfairly charged with being threats to the United States. Witnesses who refused to answer questions about whether they were Communists could be charged with contempt of Congress and sent to jail.

In 1948, a congressional committee was considering a law that came close to outlawing the Communist party. Among other things, the law would have made it illegal for Communists to be employed by the federal government or to be given passports for foreign travel.

Robeson testified against the proposed law before the congressional committee. He said it was un-American to punish people for their political beliefs. He was asked if he was a member of the Communist party. He replied: "The question has become the very basis of the struggle for civil liberties . . . men are about to go to jail for refusing to answer it. I am prepared to join them. I refuse to answer it." He was also asked if he would fight for the United States if there was a war against the Soviet Union. Robeson said it would depend on the circumstances.

Robeson was not charged with contempt, and the proposed law, although it had passed the House of Representatives, was not voted on by the Senate.

The following year, Paul Robeson became more controversial than ever. In April 1949, Robeson was in Paris to speak before a large meeting of the World Congress of Peace. As part of his speech he said: "It is unthinkable that American Negroes could go to war on behalf of those who have oppressed us for generations against the Soviet Union which in one generation has raised our people to full dignity."

Robeson said many things in his speech, but what made news in the United States was the idea that American blacks should not fight in a war against the Soviet Union. Reactions to his remarks were mixed. Most Americans, both black and white, condemned Robeson's ideas. Some defended him. Some said they disagreed with him, but he had a right to say what he believed.

In the aftermath of the Paris speech, Robeson was scorned in various ways. In some places his recordings were banned. The president of a black college that had awarded Robeson an honorary degree said he wished it had not been awarded. A football publication omitted his name from its listing of all-Americans. A Connecticut official even tried, unsuccessfully, to get the state police to keep the Robesons from returning to their home. In the midst of these reactions the Peekskill incident occurred.

Peekskill was a popular summer camping and resort area for people from nearby New York City. Some of the visitors were regarded as Communists by local residents.

In the past Robeson had given well-attended concerts in the area. When, in 1949, it was announced that he would give another concert, there was immediate public dispute. Supporters of Robeson saw him as a champion of free speech and thought, a fighter for freedom and equality. Those who opposed him saw him as a representative of communism; of forces working to divide and destroy the American way of life. This split of opinion, symbolized by Paul Robeson, would clash violently at Peekskill.

The concert was intended to raise money for a New York organization many believed was communistic. The leader of a local patriotic organization sent a letter to the newspaper urging that people who attended the concert be shown "that they are unwelcome around here either now or in the future."

The letter had not directly urged violence, but violence occurred. On the evening of August 27, arriving concert-goers were met by a crowd of protesters. Fighting broke out. People were beaten, cars overturned, and the stage destroyed. By the time police arrived the damage had been done. There would be no concert that evening.

Some were delighted that the concert had been shut down. Others condemned the violent action. A group of Robeson supporters invited him to return for another concert as a way of standing up to the protesters.

If Robeson returned it seemed likely there would be more violence. He had to decide what to do. At a rally in Harlem he announced his decision: "Yes, I will sing wherever the people want to hear me. I sing of peace and freedom and of life. . . . If the State Troopers do not protect us, we shall have forces enough to protect ourselves."

On September 4, over twenty thousand people came to Peekskill for the concert. More than two thousand served as guards, some carrying baseball bats, to protect the rest. Almost a thousand state police were also there. Protesters near the entrance to the concert grounds screamed insults at the arriving audience. The concert went on. It was followed by violence.

The departing audience was attacked as their cars and buses traveled along the exit road. Many were badly hurt. Robeson escaped uninjured.

When the Korean War began, Robeson objected to U.S. involvement. He said troops should be sent to fight the Ku Klux Klan in the American South rather than to Korea. The State Department revoked Robeson's passport. He was no longer permitted to travel outside the United States. A major European tour had to be cancelled.

Officials at the State Department said that Robeson's travels and speeches were not in the best interests of the United States. Robeson said the government had no right to prevent private citizens from saying what they wanted when traveling abroad. The officials disagreed but said his passport would be returned if he signed a paper indicating whether he was or was not a Communist. Robeson refused.

Because of their declining income, the Robesons had to give up their big home in Connecticut. Eventually, in 1958, after lengthy legal actions, his passport was returned. Robeson resumed his world travels and performances.

Still popular in foreign countries, Paul Robeson was applauded almost everywhere he went. He was treated as a hero in the Soviet Union. A Soviet mountain peak was named in his honor, and he received other awards. Illness befell him, and he returned to the United States in 1963, where he died 13 years later.

The major sources for this story were:

Gilliam, Dorothy B. *Paul Robeson: All-American*. Washington, D.C.: The New Republic, 1976.
Hamilton, Virginia. *Paul Robeson: The Life and Times of a Free Black Man*. New York: Harper & Row, 1974.
Hoyt, Edwin P. *Paul Robeson: The American Othello*. Cleveland, World, 1967.
Robeson, Paul. *Here I Stand*. New York: Othello Associates, 1958.

ACTIVITIES FOR "A CLASH OF SYMBOLS"

Write all answers on a separate sheet of paper.

Historical Understanding

Answer briefly:

1. Identify two forms of discrimination faced by blacks during the first half of the twentieth century.

2. What was the Harlem Renaissance?

3. What was the Truman Doctrine?

Reviewing the Facts of the Case

Answer briefly:

1. When he was a little boy, what advice about dealing with white people did Paul receive from his brother Reed? from his father?

2. Why was Paul's role in O'Neill's play controversial?

3. What were two ways that Robeson's European travels influenced his thinking about racial issues?

4. Why wouldn't Robeson sing at the Finnish benefit?

5. How did Robeson help the Allies during the war?

6. What were two reasons Robeson was disappointed with President Truman?

7. What did Robeson say at the Paris meeting that caused controversy in the United States?

8. Why was Robeson's passport revoked?

Analyzing Ethical Issues

There are a number of incidents in this story in which the following values of liberty and loyalty are involved:

LIBERTY: a value concerning what freedoms people should have and the limits that may justifiably be placed upon them

LOYALTY: a value concerning obligations to the people, traditions, ideas, and organizations of importance in one's life

Explain how the values of liberty and loyalty both were involved in the incidents listed below. For example, in the passport incident both values were involved:

> The State Department revoked Robeson's passport after he spoke against the United States' involvement in the Korean War.
>
> *The values of liberty and loyalty were involved because Robeson's freedom to travel and speak was limited (liberty). The government believed he had an obligation to support U.S. policy (loyalty).*

1. Robeson refused to sing for the Finnish benefit.

2. When testifying before a committee in Washington, D.C., Robeson refused to answer the question of whether he was or was not a member of the Communist party.

Expressing Your Reasoning

1. Should Robeson have returned to Peekskill for the September concert? Why or why not?

2. While testifying before a committee in Washington, Robeson refused to answer the question of whether or not he was a Communist. Should he have answered the question? Why or why not?

3. In 1950, the State Department revoked Robeson's passport. Was it right for the department to revoke his passport? State your position in writing.

4. *Seeking Additional Information.* In making decisions about such questions as those above, we often feel we need more information before we are satisfied with our judgments. Choose one of the above questions about which you would want more information than is presented in the story. What additional information would you like? Why would that information help you make a more satisfactory decision?

Sky Wars

U-2 EPISODE

Nikita Khrushchev (center) Examining Pilot's Equipment
Found Among Wreckage of U-2 Plane Piloted by Francis Gary Powers

Americans of the 1950s seemed to be enjoying the happiest days of their lives. World War II had been won, and President Dwight D. Eisenhower had helped end the Korean War. The concern of many Americans was what to cook on their outdoor barbecues, what television shows to watch, and what flashy new car to buy. A new era of peace and prosperity had begun.

The popular president stirred hope and confidence. Throughout the world he was known as a great military hero but also as a man of peace. Time and time again he had spoken of the need for peace and justice. Often relaxing on the golf course, the war-hero president symbolized the ease of the postwar United States. Although Hitler's schemes for world conquest had been stopped, there was now a new fear. It was believed that members of the Communist party, directed by leaders of the Soviet Union, were determined to overthrow the democracies of the world.

Communist governments had been established by force in China and many eastern European countries. The new communist governments were hostile to U.S. interests. Communist revolutionary groups were reportedly at work in many other places. To hold back the spread of communism, the United States had established a policy known as *containment*. According to this policy the United States would provide military support for nations trying to resist communism.

There were fears that communists were secretly gaining a foothold within the United States government. In the early 1950s, Senator Joseph McCarthy began a series of investigations designed to expose communist influence. He was unable to prove his most serious charges, but many people continued to be suspicious about communists in government.

The development of nuclear bombs and missiles added to world tensions. Both the United States and the Soviet Union were capable of filling the skies with terrible new weapons that could destroy entire cities and kill millions of people.

This time of strained relations between the United States and the Soviet Union was known as the *cold war*. The threat of nuclear destruction, however, created fears that a hot war could break out at any time. President Eisenhower was willing to use nuclear weapons if necessary, but he hoped the necessity would never arise. He once said, "The one—and only—way to win World War III is to prevent it."

One hope for peace was to get the United States and the Soviet Union to agree to cut back or end the production of the frightening new weapons and to ban further nuclear testing. One problem was how to make sure the nations would live up to any such agreement. The president had a plan for solving the problem.

In July 1955, President Eisenhower met with Soviet leaders at Geneva, Switzerland. The president made a dramatic proposal. He said the two nations should exchange blueprints of their military bases and permit airplanes to fly over one another's countries. The planes would be allowed to take photographs that would show whether any unusual military preparations were being made. According to Eisenhower, this would reduce the "possibility of great surprise attack, thus lessening danger and relaxing tension." The proposal became known as the Open Skies Plan.

The Soviets were suspicious. One Russian leader, Nikita Khrushchev, said the plan was simply a way for the United States to spy on the Soviet Union. He told Eisenhower: "This is a very transparent espionage device. . . . You could hardly expect us to take this seriously." The Russians wanted to protect their secrets. They may also have believed their spies could operate effectively in the more open society of the United States. The Open Skies Plan never got off the ground.

One thing that did get off the ground was a remarkable U.S. spy plane known as the U–2. The U.S. Central Intelligence Agency (CIA) had long sought a way of getting information about military developments in the Soviet Union. The Soviet Union was a highly secretive nation. It was even difficult for outsiders to get road maps. Spies were limited in their ability to get information. The U–2 would solve that problem.

The U–2 was sometimes described as a jet-powered glider. Its power and light weight permitted it to fly high in the sky and over long distances. It could fly higher than any other airplane and would be out of the range of Soviet rockets or fighter planes. Special built-in cameras could take amazingly detailed close-up pictures of activity on the land below. It was believed that the plane could fly so high that Soviet radar would be unable to detect the flights. Production of the plane was approved by the president. The whole operation was top secret. Only a few people in government were allowed to know about it.

CIA Director Allen Dulles was impressed. President Eisenhower was also impressed—but a little nervous. He was worried about what might happen if the plane went down in the Soviet Union. If it were shown that the United States was violating Soviet air space for the purpose of spying, cold-war tensions might reach the breaking point. In one meeting the president said: "I'll tell you one thing. Some day one of these machines is going to be caught and then we're going to have a storm."

The president's advisors did not share his worry. Secretary of State John Foster Dulles, brother of the CIA director, argued that after a number of successful flights the Russians would be too embarrassed to admit they had not detected them. The Russians liked to brag about how advanced their weapons were. According to Dulles, "If the Soviets ever capture one of these planes, I'm sure they will never admit it."

Even if the plane went down, it seemed likely that the Soviets would learn nothing important about its true mission. Eisenhower was led to believe the U–2 could not survive a fall from over 70,000 feet. Also, each plane had a destruct button. The pilot could push the button and, after a short delay, an explosion would destroy the cameras and possibly the entire plane. Supposedly the pilot could parachute away, although he might be destroyed along with the plane. The president's advisors persuaded him that the spy flights could succeed, but he continued to worry that something might go wrong.

In 1956, U–2's began periodic flights over parts of the Soviet Union. The photographs were valuable. Many U.S. politicians feared the Soviets were building more bombers and missiles than the United States. There was talk of "bomber gaps" and "missile gaps." The president was urged to spend large amounts of money to close the gaps. Photographs from the U–2's helped the president judge how much money to spend. Critics said he was not spending enough money for U.S. defense, but the president held spending down to levels he thought correct. Of course, he could not tell people about the secret photographs that helped him make his decisions.

U.S. fears of Soviet superiority in the air increased in October 1957. The Russians announced the launching of the 184-pound *Sputnik*, the first earth-orbiting satellite. A month later a thousand-pound satellite containing a live dog was launched. In December, the United States attempted to launch a small satellite. The rocket exploded in a flaming failure. In the race for space the Russians were in the lead. Some feared the Soviet Communists might try to conquer the world with orbiting weapons aimed at the earth.

Although the Soviets were making progress in space, their missiles could not shoot down the U-2's. It was discovered, however, that Soviet radar was capable of tracking the flights. They were aware of the overflights but had not condemned them publicly. Perhaps Secretary Dulles' prediction was correct. The president continued to approve the flights.

In 1959, world hopes for an end to the cold-war tension received a boost. Premier Nikita Khrushchev was invited to visit the United States. Some months later, President Eisenhower would visit the Soviet Union. Khrushchev toured the United States and met with President Eisenhower for a few days after his trip. It was announced that a summit meeting would be held in Paris the following spring. Top leaders of the Soviet Union, England, France, and the United States would meet to try to solve some of the problems facing the world. Khrushchev and Eisenhower seemed to end their meetings cordially. Both men spoke of ending the cold war.

After Khrushchev's visit a British reporter had written: "Mr. Eisenhower brought honor to himself, dignity to his office, distinction to his nation, and hope to the cause of peace." Around the world people seemed to agree. Hundreds of thousands cheered him as he spoke for peace on an international tour.

The Paris summit was to begin on May 16, 1960. A few weeks earlier the president approved what might be the final U-2 overflight. Some believed Soviet missiles were improving and that the plane might be shot down. The president might cancel future flights because of the risk. Still there was probably time for one more.

Early in the morning, May 1, 1960, U-2 pilot Francis Gary Powers prepared for an overflight to the Soviet Union. In the pocket of his flight suit was a silver dollar that the pilots could carry if they chose. Hidden within the coin was a pin. On the end of the pin was a dark, sticky substance—curare. One prick of the pin and death followed almost immediately.

Powers was to fly from a secret air base in Pakistan to a base in Norway. He believed it was the first time a U-2 had flown all the way across the Soviet Union. Powers wondered what would happen if his plane were also the first U-2 to be shot down.

The U-2 zoomed into the skies and soon reached its altitude.

Powers began activating the cameras. Then there was an orange flash. The plane lurched forward. It went out of control and began rolling downward through space. The pilot struggled to free himself. As he left the cockpit of the spinning airplane he was unable to push the destruct switches. The plane continued on its collision course with earth. Powers' parachute opened and he floated downward. About to come down in the middle of the Soviet Union, he pulled out the poison pin and stared at it.

Later that day the president was told that the U-2 was missing and was probably down in the Soviet Union. No one knew for sure what had happened to the plane or the pilot. Maybe the Russians knew nothing about it. Eisenhower was soon to find out.

On May 5, an angry Khrushchev announced that the Russians had shot down a U.S. spy plane. He condemned the "bandit flight" and expressed his outrage at a U.S. act of aggression.

The president and his advisors met to decide how to respond to Khrushchev's speech. The Soviet premier had not given any details about the plane or the pilot. Perhaps they were both destroyed leaving no evidence of the spying equipment. After much discussion, the president agreed that the State Department should release a *cover story*, a story designed to hide the truth about the spy missions.

According to the story, the U-2 was a weather research plane. The pilot had probably blacked out from lack of oxygen and accidently drifted into Soviet airspace. The State Department spokesperson said the United States was not trying to mislead the world about what happened. He said, "There was absolutely NO—NO—NO deliberate attempt to violate Soviet air space, and there has never been."

In a few days, the crafty Soviet leader sprung his trap. It caught the United States in a major lie. On May 7, Khrushchev shocked the world. He announced that he had most of the parts of the airplane including the camera equipment and film. He showed photographs of the plane to prove his claims. Then the biggest surprise. He announced the pilot had been captured "alive and kicking." He showed the unused poison pin and a picture of Francis Gary Powers. With glee he said the pilot had made a full confession about his role in the spy missions.

In his speech Khrushchev wondered aloud if Eisenhower had approved the flights. It was possible, said the Russian, that some overly enthusiastic member of the CIA had ordered the flights without the president's knowledge. After a series of meetings, the State Department admitted that the U–2 flights were for the purpose of spying. In the statement it was suggested that the president had not been involved.

To relieve the president of personal responsibility, CIA Director Allen Dulles offered to resign and take the blame for the incident. Eisenhower, however, was not satisfied with creating the impression that he was unaware of the CIA's operations.

The president was faced with a difficult choice. If he let Dulles take responsibility, it would appear that the president was not in control of his own government. On the other hand, no world leader had ever admitted personal involvement in spying. Eisenhower decided to break with tradition.

The president publicly accepted full responsibility for ordering the U–2 flights. In a news conference he said the Soviet Union had become such a secret society that the U–2's were "a distasteful but vital necessity" for gathering information. He said the United States was trying to avoid war: "We are looking to our own security and our defense and we have no idea of promoting any kind of conflict or war." In later days the president reminded people that all nations engaged in spying. He said that there were hundreds, perhaps thousands, of Russian spies at work in the United States.

A few days after his news conference the president left for the Paris summit meeting. In spite of the U–2 episode, he hoped progress toward lasting peace could be made. His hopes were to be frustrated. At the beginning of the first Paris meeting, Khrushchev demanded to speak. He claimed that his "friend" Eisenhower had betrayed him. He insisted that the president publicly condemn the flights, order them stopped, and apologize for allowing them to occur. Unless the president did so, the Russians would not participate in the meetings.

The president announced that the flights had already been cancelled. He would not meet any of Khrushchev's Paris demands. Earlier the president had told friends that he would not "crawl on my knees to Khrushchev." He said the United States still wanted to work for peace and accused the Soviet leader of wanting to wreck the meetings before they even began.

Khrushchev would not budge. He called off plans for Eisenhower's visit to the Soviet Union. To reporters he announced: "Unless President Eisenhower apologizes and admits America made an aggressive action against the Soviet people, I will return home." Khrushchev returned home, ending the Paris conference.

Although the summit had failed, many Americans were proud that their president had stood up to Khrushchev. He was cheered by a huge crowd as he returned to the White House. A large banner with the words "Thank you, Mr. President" was waved.

Not all Americans approved of the president's handling of the U-2 episode and the Paris meeting. Senator J. William Fulbright was especially critical. He said that America's standing in world opinion had been lowered. According to Fulbright, the president should not have taken personal responsibility because "the orderly conduct of international affairs will quickly become impossible." He emphasized that diplomatic traditions should have been upheld.

Fulbright made another, more complicated, criticism. According to the senator, the United States had no right to engage in spying. He argued: "If a man is starving to death, and if he robs a grocery store, we can understand his action on the basis of need; but his need does not give him the right to become a burglar." Fulbright believed the president's reasoning was flawed because he claimed that the need for information gave the United States a right to spy. From Fulbright's point of view, the United States could not claim to be a moral leader if it defended its actions with faulty reasoning. In a way, Fulbright was putting the president's actions on trial before U.S. public opinion.

In the Soviet Union, Francis Gary Powers' actions were placed on trial before a Russian court. Powers was charged with the crime of espionage. The maximum penalty was death. Powers, of course, had already confessed his guilt. The Russians, however, were planning to make his trial a big show. They wanted to embarrass the United States further. The trial was held in a huge theater and hundreds of reporters and spectators were allowed to attend. It made headline news.

Powers was provided with a Russian defense lawyer. The lawyer made no effort to defend the U.S. pilot but told him how to behave if he wanted to avoid the maximum penalty. According to the lawyer, the downed pilot's best hope would be to tell the truth, cooperate with the Soviet questioners, admit his guilt, and publicly apologize for what he did.

Powers appeared cooperative. He seemed willing to answer all questions. Although he admitted his guilt, he would not condemn the United States for ordering the flights. When asked if he regretted what he did, he said, "I am profoundly sorry I had any part in it."

On August 19, 1960, his sentence was announced. He was to be sent to prison for ten years.

Many Americans were disgusted with Powers. Some thought he should not have given any information to the communists. Others said he should have used the poison pin. *Newsweek* magazine asked, "Should he, like Nathan Hale, have died for his country?"

Powers did not serve the full ten-year sentence. In 1962, he was exchanged for Rudolf Abel, a Soviet spy who had been captured in the United States.

On his return Powers was again criticized by many Americans. His behavior was investigated by a Senate committee. The committee concluded that Powers had not done anything wrong. The committee report said that he had been told by his superiors to cooperate with the Russians in the event he was downed. Powers also had avoided telling certain important secrets. It was also noted that he was under no orders to use the poison pin. Such a decision was his alone to make.

For a time Powers worked as a test pilot for Lockheed, the same company that had built the U-2. Later he took a job as a helicopter pilot reporting traffic conditions for a Los Angeles television station. In 1960, he had survived the downing of his plane over the Soviet Union. In 1977, his helicopter fell from the skies of southern California. This time he did not survive.

The major sources for this story were:

Ambrose, Stephen E., and Immerman, Richard H. *Ike's Spies: Eisenhower and the Espionage Establishment.* Garden City, N.Y.: Doubleday, 1981.

Branyan, Robert L., and Larsen, Lawrence H. *The Eisenhower Administration: A Documentary History.* New York: Random House, 1971.

Divine, Robert A. *Eisenhower and the Cold War.* New York: Oxford University Press, 1981.

Eisenhower, Dwight D. *Waging Peace: 1956-1961.* Garden City, N.Y.: Doubleday, 1965.

Goldman, Eric F. *The Crucial Decade—and After: America, 1945-1960.* New York: Vintage Books, 1960.

Lyon, Peter. *Eisenhower: Portrait of a Hero.* Boston: Little, Brown, 1974.

Parmet, Herbert S. *Eisenhower and the American Crusades.* New York: Macmillan, 1972.

Powers, Francis G. (with Gentry, Curt). *Operation Overflight: The U-2 Pilot Tells His Story for the First Time.* New York: Holt, Rinehart and Winston, 1970.

Wise, David, and Ross, Thomas B. *The U-2 Affair.* New York: Random House, 1962.

ACTIVITIES FOR "SKY WARS"

Write all answers on a separate sheet of paper.

Historical Understanding

Answer briefly:

1. Why did the United States pursue a policy of *containment*?

2. What does the term *cold war* mean?

3. Why did *Sputnik* cause concern among many Americans?

Reviewing the Facts of the Case

Answer briefly:

1. What did Eisenhower hope to accomplish by his Open Skies Plan?

2. How did John Foster Dulles respond to Eisenhower's worries about the U-2?

3. What was one way the U-2 photographs were valuable to the United States?

4. What cover story did the United States give after Khrushchev's first announcement of the downing of the U-2?

5. Why did Allen Dulles offer to resign?

6. What was one reason President Eisenhower took personal responsibility for the U-2 missions?

7. What were Khrushchev's demands of Eisenhower at Paris? How did the president respond?

8. What were two of Senator Fulbright's criticisms of the president?

9. What did Francis Gary Powers' lawyer tell him to do?

10. Why were many Americans critical of Powers?

Analyzing Ethical Issues

Distinguishing motives from actions. For purposes of this activity, *action* is defined as human behavior that we can observe. *Motives* are the forces or thoughts that lead people to take action. Motives are not as obvious as actions, and sometimes we have to infer, based on some evidence, why people behave the way they do. For example, consider this *action*:

> In 1959, Khrushchev accepted an invitation to visit the United States for personal talks with the president.

We cannot be certain of his *motives*, but some suggestions are:

> *Perhaps he just wanted to appear to be seeking world peace.*
>
> *Perhaps he really wanted to be friendly with the United States.*
>
> *Perhaps he was under pressure in Russia to make a peace gesture.*

Suggest one or two possible motives for the following actions (behaviors):

1. The State Department first claimed the downed U–2 was a weather plane.
2. President Eisenhower would not meet Khrushchev's demands at Paris.
3. Khrushchev made demands on Eisenhower at Paris.
4. Powers confessed to being a spy.
5. Senator Fulbright criticized the president.

Expressing Your Reasoning

1. President Eisenhower defended the U–2 missions and refused to apologize to Khrushchev at Paris. Should he have apologized? Why or why not?
2. President Eisenhower approved the release of a State Department story denying that the U–2 plane was on a spy mission. Should he have done that? Why or why not?
3. In a Senate speech, William Fulbright criticized the president's handling of the U–2 episode. Prepare a short speech indicating your opinion of Fulbright's criticisms.
4. *Newsweek* magazine raised the question of whether Powers should have used the poison pin. Write a letter to the editor indicating how you would answer the question about Powers.

5. *Seeking Additional Information.* In making decisions about such questions as those above, we often feel we need more information before we are satisfied with our judgments. Choose one of the above questions about which you would want more information than is presented in the story. What additional information would you like? Why would that information help you make a more satisfactory decision?

PART 4

Searching for
Consensus
(1961 to the Present)

Rock Smites Moses

ROBERT MOSES

(© *Arnold Newman*)

Robert Moses

Imagine having the power to shape and remodel a sprawling city. You could decide where and when to construct buildings, to build highways and bridges, and to lay out parks, beaches, pools, and playgrounds. You could do almost anything you wanted. People would praise you for improving their lives. One might dream of having such power, but it is almost impossible to believe it could really happen. It did happen, however, to a man named Robert Moses.

Handsome, intelligent, and athletic, young Robert Moses decided to devote his life to public service. The creation of public works in New York, both the state and city, would be the object of his seemingly limitless energy and imagination. By the end of his long, remarkable career he controlled the development of New York City in ways no one else had ever done.

Moses was filled with ideas for making public improvements, but he knew that ideas were not enough. As he once said, "The important thing is to get things done." To get things done he needed power. He learned how to get it.

Robert Moses learned his lessons about power in the tough world of New York politics. By the early 1900s, New York City had suffered at the hands of politicians who were more interested in getting elected than in serving the people. Once elected, such politicians helped secure their power through *patronage* (the practice of giving public jobs to friends and political supporters). The jobs were rewards for helping the politician get elected. Too often the people hired were unwilling or unable to do good work. It was once discovered, for example, that some lifeguards hired by the city did not even know how to swim!

In 1913, a mayor who wanted to clean up city politics was elected. Robert Moses was assigned the task of creating a plan to assure that city workers would be hired and promoted on the basis of their ability. Moses worked hard at the job and created a detailed plan. The mayor lost the next election, and the winning politicians threw out Moses' plan before it could become law. Political patronage continued to rule.

The idealistic Moses was hurt and discouraged, but he did not give up. He had learned that he needed political power in order to implement his ideas for public improvements.

A popular young city politician named Al Smith was on the rise. He and Robert Moses became close friends. Smith was impressed with Moses' ability. When Smith was elected governor, he made Moses his key advisor.

At Albany, the state capital, Moses became an expert on the laws that defined the powers of state agencies. He learned how laws could be written or revised to create new powers. Always one who knew what he wanted, he was now learning how to get it.

Moses' first steps to power were through the parks. The population of New York City was growing and the city was becoming crowded and noisy. People needed places outside of the city where they could go for a day of relaxation and enjoyment. Few places were available.

In Moses' eyes, nearby Long Island would be an ideal place for parks and beaches. There were two problems. For one, much of the land was privately owned. For another, there were no good highways leading from the city to the island. On hot summer days lines of automobiles jammed the few narrow roads leading to the island. Even if people were able to reach the island, there were few satisfactory places to spend the day.

For years Moses had made plans for huge beaches and parks on the island as well as plans for building highways so that people could get there easily. Using his new law writing skill, he drew up a plan for the Long Island Parks Commission. It was an organization with legal power to obtain land and develop it for parks and beaches. The state legislature passed the law that Moses had written. As a favor to his friend, Governor Smith appointed Moses head of the new park commission.

With his usual feverish energy, Moses went to work. He hired the best architects, engineers, and builders. His first major project was Jones Beach. Along the miles of beach he built two huge bathhouses, restaurants, walkways, and parking lots. He used the finest building materials and spent much more money than he had originally said would be needed. He believed that once the project got under way, government officials would continue to give enough money for its completion rather than let it sit half finished. He was right.

When Jones Beach opened in the late 1920s, Moses received national attention and praise. No one had ever seen anything like it. A park expert visiting from England announced: "This is the finest seashore playground ever given the public anywhere in the world." Robert Moses was a hero.

The popular Moses was soon appointed head of all New York City parks. Later he was selected head of all state parks. Hundreds of planners worked for him. They worked long, hard hours, but Moses worked even longer and harder. According to one employee, "Hours didn't mean anything to him. Days of the week didn't mean anything to him. When there was work to be done, you did it."

To the public it seemed Moses worked miracles. Swimming pools, playgrounds, parks, and athletic fields were built or improved. No one had ever done so much so quickly. Ceremonies were held when each new facility opened. Children and their parents cheered whenever Moses rose to speak.

Moses had the image of a man above dirty politics, of an unselfish man devoted to the public good. However, the public did not know what went on behind the scenes. They did not know how Moses got things done.

Millions of dollars were spent on Moses' projects, but elected officials feared trying to control his spending. If a powerful politician tried to stand in his way, Moses would threaten to resign. Public outcry would doom the political career of anyone seen as responsible for ousting the popular Moses.

Moses also had other ways of getting things done. Some of the people who worked for him were assigned to investigate the private lives of powerful people, seeking information about possible wrongdoing. Moses kept detailed secret files on these people. If a powerful politician tried to limit Moses' activities, Moses would threaten to reveal his secret information. Even if there had been no scandal, Moses could make it appear as if wrongdoing had occurred.

Moses was tough. In later years, one mayor said of him:

> I would never let him do anything for me in any way, shape, or form. I'd never ask him—or permit him—to do anything of a personal nature for me because—and I've seen it time and time again—a day will come when Bob will reach back in his file and throw this in your face, quietly if that will make you go along with him, publicly otherwise. And if he has to, he will destroy you with it.

The highways and bridges envisioned by Moses would take years of planning and construction. To succeed, Moses would need great amounts of money and a long-term position of power. He saw a way to get both.

One way in which a large public project, like a bridge, can be built is through what is known as an *authority* (an organization set up by the state to build a specific project). Money for the project is raised by selling bonds. People who buy bonds are, in effect, loaning their money to the authority. Over a period of years this money, plus interest, is repaid. Money to repay the bondholders can be raised from tolls charged for each car that passes over the completed bridge. As soon as the bonds are paid, the authority goes out of business.

Moses had been made head of the Triborough Bridge Authority. It had been set up to build the Triborough Bridge. In order to build other projects, he wanted the authority to remain in existence even after the bridge was paid for. He used his influence to persuade state legislators to accept changes in the laws governing the authority.

Under the new law, money from bridge tolls could be used to help pay for other projects, not just to pay off the Triborough Bridge bonds. The law also allowed the authority to issue new bonds for new projects. In this way Moses could have a continual supply of money to carry out his plans.

If laws can be changed once, Moses reasoned, they can be changed again. Because he did not want to take a chance that future legislators would change the law, he looked for a way to guarantee his power. He found it in the Constitution of the United States.

The Constitution prohibits states from overturning or interfering with contracts. A *contract* is a legal agreement made between persons or organizations. The terms of a contract cannot be changed unless both parties to the contract agree to the change. Moses realized that when a bond is sold, a legal contract is made between the buyer and seller. When new Triborough Bridge bonds were sold, he had it written into the agreement that the authority would stay in existence until the bonds were repaid. The terms of the agreement were a contract that the state could not overturn. Moses' Triborough Bridge Authority would stay as long as new bonds were issued.

In a quiet way Moses had obtained extraordinary power. He was so clever at getting laws changed that people did not notice how his power increased until long after the laws were passed. While praising Moses for one of his projects, a man said, "More power to you!" In fact, it would be hard to imagine Moses getting much more power than he had.

Moses did not seek personal wealth. He used his power to build. Among the achievements of his long career are huge bridges such as the Verrazano-Narrows Bridge, miles of highways such as the Cross-Bronx Expressway, hundreds of parks and playgrounds, and massive buildings, such as Lincoln Center, the United Nations Headquarters, and Shea Stadium. The list could go on and on.

Moses was appointed to many positions of power. At one time he held 12 important positions in state and city government. The money at his command helped secure his power. Whenever possible he made certain that money to build his projects went to builders and others who were politically powerful and would support his ideas. Also, New York City was often in debt and could not afford to build major public works. Mayors or other elected officials who wanted to get credit for improving parks or building playgrounds had to come to Moses—and they would have to do things his way.

As Moses' power increased, so did his insensitivity to the opinions of others. For example, his planned route for the Cross-Bronx Expressway cut through the heart of the neighborhood known as East Tremont. Residents of the area protested. They proposed a new route through an unpopulated area a few blocks away that would save their homes. Stubbornly Moses refused to change the route. Even the newly elected mayor could not influence him. Moses did things his way or not at all.

The completion of his projects was the most important thing to Moses. He seemed not to care what it took to get them done. When building in the heart of a crowded city, he said, "You have to hack your way with a meat ax." As he once said, "If the end doesn't justify the means, what does?"

Eventually his means for getting things done led him into trouble. In the mid-1950s, he planned to enlarge the often crowded parking lot of the Tavern-on-the-Green restaurant in Central Park. The owner of the restaurant was friendly with Moses and often hosted fancy parties for people Moses wanted to impress. To extend the parking lot, a pleasant little area of the park would have to be destroyed. The area was a favorite place of the wealthy families who lived nearby. Beneath huge shade trees, mothers and their children spent hours each day relaxing and playing on the cool grass. By accident they discovered Moses' plan.

One day a mother noticed a group of men in the little park area. After they had left, she found a large piece of paper. The mother examined it and realized it was a plan to build a parking lot on the beloved green spot.

Residents called Moses to protest. He was not interested. After all, he had moved thousands of families for his big projects. Here only about 25 families were protesting. None of them would be moved, only a bit of park would be paved over. As usual he moved quickly.

On the morning of April 26, 1956, area residents awoke to the roar of a bulldozer as it prepared to tear up the little park. Women rushed from their homes, many pushing baby carriages. They blocked the way of the workers and their machines. Construction for that day was halted.

In the past, families who objected to Moses' projects were often poor and without influence. This time the families were wealthy and knew how to get attention. Newspaper and television reporters had been called. That day's news was filled with pictures and stories about the "Battle of Central Park." The highly praised Moses looked like a bully pushing around women and children.

As always, Moses pushed ahead. After midnight, under cover of darkness, his workers quietly built a four-foot fence around the area. Silently a truck drove a big bulldozer into the enclosed area. By morning work had begun. As huge trees tumbled down the mothers again rushed out. This time squads of police held them back. Again reporters were there and it was a major news story. Pictures showed crying women being held back by the police.

The mothers were able to persuade a judge to order the construction halted until its legality could be determined. Moses, as head of city parks, was probably acting within his legal authority, but the bad publicity was hurting him.

New Yorkers loved Central Park. Few people could see any value in destroying even a small part of its greenery to extend the parking lot of a private restaurant. Moses, once known as the protector of parks, was now associated with a bulldozer trying to destroy them. Letters to newspapers condemned him: "So the great Moses had to stoop to pulling a sneak attack at night to outmaneuver the embattled Central Park mothers!" Moses' reputation was taking a beating.

Had he taken his case to court, Moses would probably have won. He decided, however, that the damage to his image would be too great. He withdrew from the battle and built a playground where his parking lot would have been.

Although his pure image had been stained, Moses continued to hold power and to build major projects. More and more, however, people began to question the wisdom of his plans for more bridges and highways.

There is little doubt that, over the years, Moses' bridges and highways provided important services to the people of New York City. The population was growing and more and more people owned automobiles. More highways and bridges were necessary to make travel easier. Nonetheless, problems arose. More cars and highways helped create *urban sprawl*, the expanding growth of suburbs around the central city.

Thousands of people moved out of the city to suburbs in Long Island and elsewhere. They continued to hold jobs in the city and each day rush hour meant massive traffic jams. Moses' solution to the problem of traffic jams was to build more highways. As each highway opened, however, it soon became congested with traffic. Many experts became convinced that what was needed was more and improved mass transportation in the form of trains, buses, and subways.

The City of New York could not afford to build or even properly maintain mass transportation. Existing subways were crowded and inefficient. Another major problem was the Long Island Railroad.

The Long Island Railroad was the major form of mass transportation for thousands of commuters from the island. It was in such bad shape that it became a national joke. The cars were shabby and poorly ventilated, and the trains frequently did not run on time, or at all. One day's report read: "Trains cancelled yesterday—one; commuters affected—1,000. Trains more than ten minutes late—187; total time lost—74 hours, 15 minutes; commuters affected—140,250."

Moses was not the man to provide better mass transportation for New Yorkers. He was only interested in highways and bridges, and he still had the money and power to do what he wanted. No one could persuade him to change his mind.

Moses continued rolling along until he ran into a rock in the form of Governor Nelson Rockefeller. The governor, nicknamed Rocky, had his own ideas of what New York needed. He wanted to build college campuses around the state, to renew the decaying inner city of the capital at Albany, and to improve mass transportation for New York City. He also knew that Moses would oppose him. Like Moses, the governor was a tough and clever man. He was determined to get his way.

According to state law, Moses, now over 65 years old, had reached the age of required retirement from many of his government jobs. The law, however, permitted governors to make exceptions for some people. Past governors had always made Moses an exception; Rockefeller would be different.

Rockefeller met with Moses in New York City. The governor wanted to appoint his brother Laurence head of state parks, one of the jobs held by Moses. Rockefeller said he would permit Moses to remain as head of the Long Island Park Commission if he resigned from the state post. Moses was furious. He was not interested in any deal. Angrily he marched out of the meeting.

In the past, Moses would threaten to resign if any politician attempted to remove him from an appointed job. Because of his popularity no politician wanted to risk being held responsible for Moses' resignation. Moses threatened again. He told Rockefeller that he would resign from all his state jobs and tell the public that the governor was just trying to get his brother a job. Moses believed Rockefeller would back down. He did not. To Moses' amazement, the governor accepted his resignations.

Moses was stunned. He still controlled the Triborough Authority but was out of all his state park positions, positions that he had helped make important. His announcement that the governor was simply trying to reward his brother caused some public criticism of Rockefeller. In general, however, the public did not rally to Moses' defense.

Rockefeller had reduced Moses' power but still needed his cooperation. The state could not afford to pay for all of the governor's building plans. Rockefeller needed to get control of the vast amount of money at the command of the Triborough Authority. The question was how to get it away from Moses.

The governor had proposed a new authority, the Metropolitan Transportation Authority (MTA). The MTA would be responsible for building and improving mass transportation for the city. As part of the plan, the Triborough Authority would be under the control of the MTA.

Not surprisingly, Moses opposed the idea. He called it absurd and said, "It just won't work. . . . They don't know what they are driving at." Moses was still regarded as a great expert on the construction of public works. His opposition to the plan was reported widely. By law, voters of the state had to approve Rockefeller's plan. Without Moses' support it might be voted down.

Even if Moses supported the MTA there was still the problem of the contract written into the Triborough bond sales. The contract guaranteed Triborough's existence for years to come. The voters might approve the MTA idea, but courts might rule the takeover of the Triborough Bridge Authority to be unconstitutional—a violation of contract. The terms of the contract could only be changed if both the bondholders and Robert Moses agreed to change them.

The Triborough bondholders were officially represented by the Chase Manhattan Bank. The bank was owned by the Rockefeller family, and the governor's brother, David, was president. Speaking for the bondholders, Rockefeller's bank had informed the governor that it would not object to allowing the MTA to take control of the Triborough Bridge Authority. Now the governor had to get Moses to go along.

In March 1967, Rockefeller met with Moses. Two days later Moses announced that the MTA was a great idea! Moses said he would work hard to persuade voters to approve the new authority. What had happened? Why did Moses suddenly change his opinion of the MTA?

It is difficult to determine exactly what happened. According to one source, "It was learned . . . that Governor Rockefeller had offered Robert Moses a seat [on the MTA board]." Friends of Moses have reported that he was confident that Rockefeller had promised him a position of power in the new organization.

Moses campaigned hard for the MTA and the state voters approved it. When Moses asked what job he would have in the new organization he was shocked at the answer. Moses would have no power. Officially he would be a paid consultant to be called upon if needed. He was crushed. Once one of the most powerful men in twentieth century New York, Robert Moses had been struck down.

The major source for this story was:

Caro, Robert A. *The Power Broker: Robert Moses and the Fall of New York.* New York: Vintage Books, 1975.

ACTIVITIES FOR "ROCK SMITES MOSES"

Write all answers on a separate sheet of paper.

Historical Understanding

Answer briefly:

1. What is *urban sprawl?*

2. What is *patronage?*

3. How are bonds used to finance major public projects?

Reviewing the Facts of the Case

Answer briefly:

1. Why did Robert Moses become a public hero?

2. What were three of the ways Moses obtained power?

3. What was the Triborough Bridge Authority? Name one way it raised money for projects.

4. In what way did Moses use the Constitution to maintain his power?

5. What was the "Battle of Central Park"? How did it affect Moses' reputation?

6. Why did Governor Nelson Rockefeller want to strip Moses of his power?

7. What promise is it believed Governor Rockefeller made to Moses in order to gain his support for the MTA?

Analyzing Ethical Issues

Considering ends and means. Robert Moses often spoke of the ends justifying the means. By this he meant that if one is trying to accomplish something good, it does not make much difference what you do in order to accomplish it. In the next section you will be asked to evaluate this general idea. First, however, it is useful to clarify the meaning of ends and means. We define an *end* as a goal; what it is that one is trying to accomplish. A *means* is the method or methods one uses to achieve the goal.

Decide whether you consider each of the statements in the list below as illustrating an end or a means, and explain your reasoning. For example:

Moses often said that projects would cost less money than they actually did.

Means. He said this as a way to achieve the goal of getting his projects started.

1. Robert Moses learned how to get laws passed.

2. Moses built the Triborough Bridge.

3. Moses had special terms written into the Triborough bond agreements.

4. Governor Nelson Rockefeller expanded the state university system in New York.

5. Moses tried to extend the parking lot of a restaurant in Central Park.

6. Moses tried to eliminate political patronage from public employment in New York City.

Expressing Your Reasoning

1. It appears that Governor Nelson Rockefeller promised Robert Moses a position of power in order to get his support for the MTA. After the MTA was approved, Rockefeller refused Moses a position of power. Would it have been right for the governor to have broken his promise? Why or why not?

2. Robert Moses once said that when trying to make public improvements "the important thing is to get things done." He also asked, "If the end doesn't justify the means, what does?" He usually acted on the basis of these beliefs although some people objected to the means he used for his ends. The following are some means that he used. Indicate whether each was justified and explain why or why not.

   a. He often threatened to resign if powerful politicians stood in his way.
   b. He kept files of information about powerful people and said he

would publicize embarrassing information if these people opposed him.

   c. He used bond agreements to assure the continuation of the
Triborough Bridge Authority.

   d. At some points, in order to raise money, he said that a proposed
project would cost much less than it actually would. He believed
that once a project got started, political leaders would give him
the money to complete it, rather than let the project stand half-
built.

   e. When possible he made certain that money for his projects
went to builders and other contractors who had political influence and who would support his ideas.

3. How would you answer Moses' question: "If the end doesn't justify
the means, what does?" In a short essay of two or three paragraphs,
explain your answer. Try to give an example to support your point
of view.

4. *Seeking Additional Information.* In making decisions about such
questions as those above, we often feel we need more information
before we are satisfied with our judgments. Choose one of the
above questions about which you would want more information
than is presented in the story. What additional information would
you like? Why would that information help you make a more
satisfactory decision?

What a Waste

MY LAI, VIETNAM

Lt. William Calley (center) Being Escorted to the Stockade
After Being Found Guilty of the Premeditated Murder of
Vietnamese Civilians

Vietnam, March 16, 1968. An important military achievement is reported. U.S. soldiers have killed 128 enemy Vietcong in the hamlet of My Lai, part of the village of Song My. The battle makes headline news in the United States. The commander of U.S. troops in Vietnam sends a letter congratulating the soldiers for their success and the high body count of the enemy dead.

The reported military success at My Lai was one event in the long, costly, and controversial war in Vietnam. By the end of the war approximately fifty-five thousand Americans had been killed, three hundred thousand had been wounded, and billions of dollars had been spent.

U.S. involvement with Vietnam began after World War II. The French, attempting to regain control of their former colony, were opposed by military forces of the Communist leader, Ho Chi Minh. U.S. leaders, fearing the spread of communism in Southeast Asia, provided military aid to the French. The French efforts failed. In 1954, after losing a major battle at Dien Bien Phu, the French realized they could not win in Vietnam.

At the peace conference following the war, Vietnam was divided, supposedly temporarily, at the 17th parallel. Ho Chi Minh's military forces took control north of the line. In the south, a U.S.-supported anticommunist government headed by Ngo Dinh Diem was established. Although the fighting with the French was over, bloodshed did not end. The military struggle for control of Vietnam continued.

Diem's government was unable to secure firm control of South Vietnam. He and other government officials were accused of bribery and other forms of corruption. People suspected of opposing Diem were often imprisoned. Many were tortured and killed. Most Americans were unaware of the corruption and brutality of Diem's regime. In the United States, Diem was pictured as a courageous fighter against communism.

It was U.S. policy to try to halt the advance of communism. Over the years, top officials endorsed what has been called the *domino theory*. According to this view, if one nation fell to communism, neighboring nations would soon topple like dominoes. President John Kennedy, for example, was reported to have said: "Burma, Thailand, India, Japan, the Philippines, and obviously Laos and Cambodia are among those whose security would be threatened if the red tide of Communism overflowed into Vietnam."

Within South Vietnam, opposition to Diem's government intensified. Guerrilla warfare began in the mountains, jungles, and rice paddies. Government officials and troops came under attack from the guerrillas.

The major military opposition to the Diem government came from the *National Liberation Front* (NLF). Formed in 1960, the NLF, with increasing aid from North Vietnam, was determined to overthrow the government of South Vietnam.

NLF guerrillas, known to Americans as the Vietcong or VC, used violence to create political instability in South Vietnam. Public buildings were bombed, government officials murdered, and government troops attacked. The guerrillas frequently struck at night and seemed to disappear during the day. Government forces could not stop them.

By the early 1960s Americans were aware of the problems with Diem's rule. In South Vietnam there was a military coup in 1963. Diem was overthrown and killed. American officials had been aware of the planning for the coup but did not oppose it. Afterward, the United States supported the succession of military leaders who took control of the government.

Initially, aid from the United States was in the form of money and military supplies. Then U.S. military men went to Vietnam as advisors to the army. Some American soldiers actually engaged in direct combat with the Vietcong. Early in the presidency of Lyndon Johnson, tens of thousands of U.S. soldiers entered the war as combat troops.

In the summer of 1964, a patrolling U.S. naval vessel briefly exchanged gunfire with North Vietnamese vessels in the Gulf of Tonkin off the coast of North Vietnam. On August 7, at President Johnson's request, the Congress passed the *Gulf of Tonkin Resolution*. It was not an official declaration of war, but it allowed the president to take virtually any military action he wished in order to help South Vietnam or to defend U.S. troops who might be attacked. Saying he would not be the first U.S. president to lose a war, President Johnson took massive action.

In 1965, extensive bombing of North Vietnam began. It was hoped that Ho Chi Minh, as a result of the bombing, would try to persuade the NLF to seek peace. He would not.

By the end of the year about two hundred thousand Americans were in Vietnam and many more were to come. Soldiers of the North Vietnamese regular army also began entering South Vietnam in large numbers.

In the United States, opposition to increased U.S. involvement in the war was growing. Demonstrations against the war occurred in city streets and on college campuses. Occasionally there were bloody clashes between demonstrators and police. Thousands of young men, believing the war was wrong, refused to serve in the military. Some fled the country to avoid the military draft; others went to prison for refusing to obey the draft laws. The war dragged on.

Conventional military strategy was ineffective in Vietnam. No clear lines of battle were established as they had been in Europe during the world wars. Instead, fighting flared up at various points around the country.

It was especially difficult to take control of rural areas. Many villagers had no respect for South Vietnamese government officials. Many supported the NLF, sometimes from fear of the Vietcong.

One tactic of the Vietcong was to avoid large scale military combat. Using hit-and-run attacks and sniper fire, they battled the U.S. and South Vietnamese troops. When U.S. troops pursued the Vietcong into nearby villages they would often find only women, children, and old men. In many villages the guerrillas had elaborated systems of tunnels and underground rooms for escaping and hiding supplies and weapons.

The guerrillas were also effective at laying mines and booby traps. U.S. soldiers were killed and wounded, sometimes without ever seeing their enemy.

In their effort to combat the Vietcong, military leaders created *free-fire zones* and sent soldiers on *search-and-destroy missions*. Free-fire zones were areas in which civilian villagers were removed. It was then presumed that any Vietnamese in the area must be the enemy and troops were free to shoot them. In search-and-destroy missions, soldiers swept through rural areas seeking Vietcong and attempting to kill them or to take them prisoner.

Although efforts were made to protect civilians from harm, such efforts were often not successful. Traditionally, Vietnamese have a powerful spiritual attachment to their villages. Often they were reluctant to leave them even if the area had been declared a free-fire zone.

Civilians were also endangered because U.S. troops could not easily tell who was an innocent civilian and who was an enemy. The Vietcong were native Vietnamese as were the villagers.

Some villagers carried weapons and supplies for the guerrillas, informed them of U.S. troop movements, helped set booby traps, and provided other forms of assistance. U.S. troops often failed to distinguish between villagers who aided the Vietcong and those who did not.

It is impossible to know accurately how many civilians were killed during the war. According to one estimate, five hundred thousand were killed and over a million wounded by the actions of U.S., South Vietnamese, Vietcong, and North Vietnamese troops.

According to international law, civilians are supposed to be protected during war. In all wars, however, there are instances of civilians being killed. One such instance occurred at My Lai on March 16, 1968. It involved the men of Charlie Company, a unit of the American Division.

The American Division had come to Vietnam about four months earlier. Many of its soldiers were assigned search-and-destroy missions in free-fire zones. By this time in the war, because clear battle lines could not be established, military success was determined by the number of enemy soldiers killed—the body count. Units with high body counts received praise from their officers who, in turn, received praise from their superior officers.

The men of the American Division soon saw some of the more brutal aspects of the war. They saw civilians suspected of being Vietcong or supporters of the Vietcong beaten, tortured, or even killed. They saw their buddies maimed by booby traps and snipers. Some came to hate all Vietnamese. One member of Charlie Company said, "Why shouldn't I? They were the enemy." Another soldier, frustrated and angry, said: "I hope they kill everybody over there."

The commanding officer of Charlie Company, Captain Ernest Medina, was regarded by his men as a tough leader. Born in poverty, Medina hoped to make the military his career. The leader of one of Medina's platoons was 24-year-old Lieutenant William Calley. Calley admired Medina and, like him, wanted a career in the military.

Charlie Company was assigned to an area believed to be a Vietcong stronghold. For weeks they saw little combat action but some of the men were ripped apart by mines. Many soldiers were convinced that local villagers had helped in the placement of mines. Although the Americans had no direct evidence of the villagers' involvement, they noted it was rare for a local resident to step on a mine.

On February 25, 1968, six men of Charlie Company were killed by mines and twelve were wounded. On March 14, one man was killed and another lost both eyes, an arm, and a leg. The next day, after an emotional funeral service, Captain Medina gave his men their orders for the following day.

Medina's commanding officer had ordered the company to move into the hamlet of My Lai. It was said that about two hundred

Vietcong were there. Medina was told by his superiors that the women and children would be out of the village by early morning. The company was to burn the village, blow up escape tunnels, and kill all animals to disrupt the Vietcong's food supply. Stiff resistance was to be expected from the Vietcong in and around the hamlet.

The men of the company later disagreed about whether or not Medina ordered them to kill everyone who was in the village. Medina denied that he gave such orders. Lieutenant Calley may have thought those were the orders for, the next day, he would direct his men to "waste" the village.

On Saturday morning, March 16, the attack began. Artillery shells were fired into the hamlet. Helicopters brought in the combat-ready troops. Lieutenant Calley and his men leaped from the helicopters firing their weapons. It was a time of noise, danger, and uncertainty.

The crackling of gunfire that filled the air was all from U.S. weapons. No return gunfire came from the enemy. Cautiously the soldiers entered the hamlet. They saw women, children, and old men. It was quiet. Some were sitting in front of their houses preparing morning rice.

The soldiers began rounding up the people. Then, without warning, it happened! Some soldiers began killing the people. Calley joined in and, according to the testimony of witnesses, ordered others to do the same.

Not all obeyed the orders to kill the villagers, but most did. One helicopter pilot, horrified by what he saw, landed and flew some of the Vietnamese to safety.

In a few hours it was over. Hundreds of old men, women, and children lay dead or dying. According to some later investigations, five hundred or more were killed. The official report for that day's action at My Lai said that 128 Vietcong had been killed.

The reported success at My Lai was front page news in the *New York Times*. According to the story, the My Lai battle was part of "another American offensive to clear enemy pockets still threatening the cities." It would be a long time before the truth about My Lai was known to the public.

According to military law it is wrong to kill civilians during war, it is wrong for officers to order such killings, and wrong for soldiers to obey those orders. In addition, witnesses to wrongful acts must report them to superior officers, and those officers must investigate the charges and punish those who are guilty.

Although the military law is quite clear, during wartime there are pressures not to follow it. Some will not report crimes for fear of being called troublemakers or of having their promotions held up. Some officers are reluctant to investigate or punish possible crimes for fear the publicity would make their units look bad, affect their careers, or lessen public support of the war effort.

Some top-level officers, hearing bits of information about My Lai, made a partial investigation but did not make an extensive effort to determine what happened. A combat photographer, and a military reporter, both at My Lai, claimed that any efforts they might have made to get the truth passed up through military channels would have failed. They did not try.

Eventually, however, the truth about My Lai became known. A young helicopter door gunner, Ronald Ridenhour, was not at My Lai but heard the details of what happened from some men who were. He was deeply distressed. He became convinced that those involved should be investigated and punished, saying, "I wanted to get those people." Later he said, "As far as I was concerned, it was a reflection on me, on every American, on the ideals that we supposedly represent."

When he returned to the United States, Ridenhour told friends what he had heard about My Lai, and that he wanted to report what he knew. Most of his friends urged him not to report it. They said he should not turn in his fellow soldiers. One friend said, "Forget about it if you know what's good for you and America."

Ridenhour could not forget about it. He had always wanted to be a writer and he considered trying to sell his story to a news magazine. He discussed the matter with one of his former teachers. The teacher advised Ridenhour to report his information to government authorities. Ridenhour agreed.

In April 1969, Ridenhour sent letters to military officials, members of Congress, and President Nixon. Ridenhour described in detail what he had heard about My Lai and gave the names of soldiers that he was told were involved. Some who received the letter wondered about its accuracy and why it had been sent. One military man said: "I can't believe a guy who did not participate in something, that his conscience would bother him a year later more than the men involved." In spite of the doubts of some officials, a military investigation quietly began.

The news of what happened at My Lai began to reach the public.

On a national television show, one soldier who had been there described what had gone on. Combat photographs of the gory scene were published. The story of My Lai and the name of Lieutenant Calley became internationally known.

Many Americans condemned the massacre. Others reacted differently. Some refused to believe it really had happened. They could not believe U.S. soldiers would do such things. Some defended the soldiers. A worker in Boston said, "What do they give soldiers bullets for—to put in their pockets?" A woman in Cleveland said, "It sounds terrible to say we ought to kill kids, but many of our boys being killed over there are just kids, too."

Supporters of the soldiers and Lieutenant Calley reminded the public of the many instances of civilians being killed by the Vietcong and North Vietnamese. They said such things happen during wartime. Some said Calley should not be blamed because he was only following the orders of superior officers.

Those who blamed Calley and the others said that wrongdoing must be punished even if it occurs during the stress of combat. General Westmoreland, former commander of U.S. troops in Vietnam, stated that incidents like My Lai are "the actions of a pitiful few. Certainly the Army cannot and will not condone improper conduct or criminal acts."

The investigation led to formal charges and military trials. Lieutenant Calley, Captain Medina, and some others were charged with murder. Many of their superior officers, including the commander of the American Division, were charged with violations of military regulations involving the investigation and reporting of military crimes.

Of all those charged with wrongdoing, only Lieutenant Calley was convicted of murder. He was sentenced to life imprisonment. Later his sentence was reduced to 20 years. Calley never went to prison. He was allowed to serve his time at a military base. Convicted in March 1970, he was paroled and returned to civilian life a few years later.

Many U.S. soldiers in Vietnam fought with courage and dignity in what was probably the most unpopular war in the history of the United States. Events such as those at My Lai tainted their image and restrained public recognition of their bravery.

The major sources for this story were:

Fitzgerald, Frances. *Fire in the Lake.* Boston: Little, Brown, and Company, 1972.
Hersh, Seymour M. *Cover-Up.* New York: Random House, 1972.
Hersh, Seymour M. *My Lai 4.* New York: Random House, 1970.
Lawson, Don. *The United States in the Vietnam War.* New York: Thomas Y. Crowell, 1981.
———. *Vietnam: A Teacher's Guide.* New York: The Asia Society, 1983.

ACTIVITIES FOR "WHAT A WASTE"

Write all answers on a separate sheet of paper.

Historical Understanding

Answer briefly:

1. How was the *domino theory* applied to Southeast Asia?

2. What was the *NLF*?

3. What was the *Gulf of Tonkin Resolution*?

4. Why did the body count of enemy dead become a measure of the success of the war effort?

Reviewing the Facts of the Case

Answer briefly:

1. What is a *free-fire zone*? What is a *search-and-destroy mission*?

2. Identify three causes of danger to rural civilians during the war.

3. What orders was Captain Ernest Medina said to have given to his soldiers?

4. Describe the official military report of the results of My Lai.

5. What are three provisions of military law regarding the treatment of civilians during wartime?

6. Why were military men sometimes reluctant to report or investigate war crimes?

7. What did Ronald Ridenhour's friends advise him about reporting what he knew about My Lai? What reasons did Ridenhour give for his reporting?

8. Of what crime was Lieutenant William Calley convicted?

Analyzing Ethical Issues

There is agreement on the answer to some questions. For other questions there is disagreement about the answer. We call these questions issues. Issues can be categorized as factual or ethical. A factual issue asks whether something is true or false, accurate or inaccurate. An ethical issue asks whether something is right or wrong, fair or unfair. Factual issues ask what *is;* ethical issues ask what *ought to be.* For example:

> How many civilians were killed during the Vietnamese War? *Factual.*
>
> Should top-level commanders be punished for war crimes committed by their soldiers? *Ethical.*

For each of the following questions, decide whether the issue is factual or ethical.

1. Did most Americans support the war?

2. Could Ho Chi Minh have persuaded the NLF to seek peace?

3. Was it right to place William Calley on trial for murder?

4. Did Captain Ernest Medina order his troops to kill villagers?

5. Should the United States have provided aid to the French?

6. Was President Lyndon Johnson right in sending more troops to Vietnam?

7. Would a North Vietnamese victory cause neighboring countries to become communist?

8. Did most South Vietnamese support the NLF?

Expressing Your Reasoning

1. Americans disagreed about whether Lieutenant William Calley and others should have been brought to trial for what happened at My Lai. Should Calley have been tried? Why or why not?

2. Ronald Ridenhour heard about what happened at My Lai. He decided to report what happened. Was he right in what he did? Write a paragraph expressing your answer to this question. Give reasons for your opinion.

3. *Seeking Additional Information.* In making decisions about such questions as those above, we often feel we need more information before we are satisfied with our judgments. Choose one of the

above questions about which you would want more information than is presented in the story. What additional information would you like? Why would that information help you make a more satisfactory decision?

Fingerprince

ROBERT LEUCI AND POLICE CORRUPTION

(Courtesy of John Dominis, Life *Magazine. © 1972, Time Inc.)*

Nicholas Scoppetta (facing) and Robert Leuci Discussing
Police Corruption

To many people, New York is one of the most exciting and glamorous cities in the world. The sparkle of Broadway shows, the elegance of fine restaurants, and the swirl of high fashion combine to create one glittering image of the city.

There is another image of the city, one in striking contrast to that of a shiny entertainment center. The city has its dark, dangerous underworld of crime, drug addiction, and violence. Robert Leuci knew this underworld well—perhaps too well.

Leuci was a police detective, a member of the Special Investigating Unit (SIU). The purpose of the SIU was to capture big-time drug dealers. It had been created in the early 1960s after the famous French Connection case. In that case, a few smart and courageous detectives had broken a crime ring that was bringing huge amounts of heroin into New York from France. Soon afterward, authorities decided a small group of highly skilled detectives might be the best way to combat the growing drug traffic.

Fewer than one hundred of the thousands of law enforcement officers in New York were selected to work in the SIU. Members of the unit had almost complete freedom to work the way they chose. As long as they arrested major drug dealers they did not have to worry about commanding officers overseeing their every move. The SIU detectives were an elite group, envied and admired by other members of the police force. They became known as the Princes of the City.

SIU detectives worked in teams of three or four men. Together they patiently and cleverly tracked down criminals. Often they had drug addict informants who would give information that was helpful in capturing drug dealers. Time and again they would burst into an apartment or hotel to capture dealers and their supply of drugs.

It was dangerous work. The detectives frequently risked their lives to make arrests or to protect one another. The friendship, respect, and trust among the team members was extraordinary. The danger of their work helped bring them as close together as family members.

Robert Leuci was one of the best of the Princes of the City, although he was only in his early thirties. He had contacts with the Mafia, one of the biggest organized crime groups then dealing with drugs. He knew a great deal about the operations of organized crime.

Leuci also knew of the horrors of drug addiction. His own brother had become a heroin addict. He was sickened at the sight of his brother's desperate crying and begging for drugs.

The SIU detectives were unusually skilled at investigating crimes.

They knew how to pose as drug dealers or buyers so that they could work their way into the hazardous secret world of big-time drug dealing. They knew how to wear tiny recording devices to collect evidence of criminals making their deals. As a result of their undercover work the detectives made many major drug arrests.

The arrests pleased government officials. They were not pleased, however, by frequent stories of police corruption. More and more there were rumors that arrested drug dealers would offer bribes to be set free. It was said that some police officers accepted these bribes. Tens of thousands of dollars were supposedly involved. It was even said that some police officers were making money by selling captured drugs!

Law enforcement officials were determined to find out if stories of police corruption were true. The fight against drugs could not succeed if some dealers were able to buy their way out of arrests.

It was extremely difficult to get direct evidence of police corruption. Some dealers or addicts might say that a police officer took money, but few people, especially juries at a trial, would take the word of a sleazy criminal over that of the police. Also, it was virtually impossible to get one police officer to testify against another. The police were deeply loyal to one another. One of their strongest rules was never to disclose wrongdoing by another officer. They simply would not "put the finger" on one of their own.

An investigation into police corruption and drug dealing was begun. One of the government officials assigned to investigate was Nicholas Scoppetta. He had heard that Robert Leuci knew about illegal behavior on the part of some police officers. Perhaps Leuci could be persuaded to cooperate in the investigation. In February 1971, Scoppetta arranged a meeting with the young detective.

At the meeting, Scoppetta noticed that Leuci seemed tense and troubled. Scoppetta named some detectives who were rumored to be corrupt. Leuci said he knew the men and that they were great detectives. He said nothing else.

The two men began to meet frequently and a friendship developed. Robert, however, had no interest in cooperating in the investigation. He said Nicholas did not understand the risks and dangers faced by the police when trying to capture drug dealers. A detective put his life on the line every day. He accused Scoppetta of being out to get the police. Angrily he said that everybody was against the police and only police cared for one another. Emotionally, Leuci asked Scoppetta if he understood that the police force was the only barrier between decent society and the jungle. Scoppetta did not answer.

Later Leuci admitted that police officers did illegal things. He admitted that he had been involved in three illegal acts. However, according to Leuci, the real problem was not with the few police involved but with some district attorneys, even judges, who would accept bribes. If Scoppetta would be willing to investigate the real problem, Leuci might be willing to help. Scoppetta was interested.

Robert told his wife, Gina, about his talks with Scoppetta. Gina was worried that the government people might force Leuci to turn against his partners. She said, "Do you think they will allow you to do whatever you choose to do?" Robert said he would never hurt any of his friends. Gina disagreed: "They will force you to hurt your friends, people who have done no harm to you, only good. . . . How are you going to live with that?" Robert thought deeply about his wife's warnings.

Guilt for past wrongdoings troubled Leuci. Perhaps if he worked with Scoppetta he could get over the bad feelings about himself. He talked with Scoppetta and told him he would not work against his partners and friends. Scoppetta said, "Please believe that we will never force you to do something that you can't live with." Leuci believed him.

The two men made a deal. Robert would investigate suspects by wearing hidden recording equipment to get evidence of bribes being offered. He would risk his life for the investigation. In return, Nicholas agreed that, while some police officers might have to be investigated, Robert would not have to work against his partners and friends.

Scoppetta was excited. Other investigations of corruption had not been successful. Now, with Leuci's help as an undercover agent, major arrests might be made.

The dangerous work began. Leuci's 1971 Pontiac was equipped with hidden recording devices. The detective was also fitted with a tiny transmitter which was taped to his body. The first case involved a Mafia drug leader and reputed murderer named Mickey Coco.

Coco knew that federal drug agents were investigating him. He had heard there was a detective who was willing to sell secret information about the investigation. Coco was willing to buy it.

Even though Leuci was a police officer, Coco had long been friendly with him. Now he called on Leuci and asked him to arrange a meeting with the corrupt detective who was willing to sell information. Leuci arranged the meeting—and tape recorded it with his hidden equipment.

Scoppetta was thrilled with the recordings of the criminal deal. Leuci had misgivings. Coco had always trusted him and been friendly. Now Leuci had turned on him. Scoppetta said: "That's why you are so important, Bob. That's why you are about to make such a meaningful contribution to society. No ordinary undercover cop could get involved in this at the level you can." He reminded Leuci that Coco was a killer and major drug dealer. "He lives in a world that we've got to get rid of." Still, Leuci said he would prefer to investigate people he did not know personally.

Leuci's skill and courage, as well as his underworld contacts, made him extraordinarily valuable to government investigators. His secret tape recordings could put many criminals in jail. As he continued his work, federal investigators came to New York City to work with him in preparing cases against criminal suspects.

Although the investigations were secret, rumors circulated through the underworld that Leuci could not be trusted. Scoppetta began to fear for Leuci's safety. Were it known for certain that he was making tape recordings, there was little doubt that Leuci would be killed. In two frightening instances he narrowly escaped being murdered by suspicious mobsters.

For over a year Leuci gathered tape recordings of criminal actions. Finally, government investigators decided it was too dangerous for him to continue. According to one story, there were underground plans to put a bomb in Leuci's car. Strange automobiles had been seen driving past Leuci's house. His family was probably in danger.

Leuci's family was moved from New York City to a house in the Catskill Mountains. Officers guarded the house around the clock. In the city, Leuci was placed under guard in a military barracks on Governor's Island. Each day he and government lawyers carefully listened to his tape recordings and began preparing cases for court.

Pressure on Robert mounted. He was concerned for his family's well-being. He also faced the stress of the courtroom. He would be subject to intense questioning by the defense lawyers of the accused criminals. If juries did not believe his answers, the criminals would go free. Leuci had to appear as an honest man who told the truth.

The star witness faced a dilemma. Before he had begun his undercover work, he had admitted to three acts of wrongdoing. In fact there had been more than three but he had always denied it. He knew that defense lawyers would question him about possible past corruption. If he admitted to all of his wrongdoings, he would be admitting that he had lied when he said there had only been three. This evidence of lying might persuade juries that his word could not be trusted. On the other hand, if he denied having committed more than three wrongdoings he would be lying. In court he had to take an oath that he was telling the truth. To lie under oath is *perjury*. Perjury is a serious crime, and Leuci could face years in jail if his lying were discovered.

The first trial began. The defense lawyer looked Leuci in the eye and asked if he had ever committed more than three illegal acts. There was tension in the courtroom. Leuci answered, "No." The lawyer pushed on. Had Leuci ever given heroin to addicts in trade for information? Leuci answered, "No, never." He was lying but the jury believed him. The accused criminals were found guilty.

The pressure on Leuci increased. His friend Scoppetta had been promoted to a new job. New government officials now worked with Leuci. Also, the investigations had widened. Some investigators were looking into new stories of police corruption. Among those being investigated were former partners of Leuci. He was questioned about his friends' past conduct. Leuci would only say that they were great detectives. The officials doubted Leuci and thought that he was just covering up for his friends. The officials also suspected that Leuci had been involved in many illegal acts, but they had no evidence. Leuci felt the strain. At times he would begin weeping for no apparent reason.

Although police officers like Leuci were almost fearless when dealing with dangerous criminals, they shared one deep fear—the fear of being *indicted* (officially accused of wrongdoing). After indictment, the accused faces a jury trial. Even if the jury found the accused not guilty, the police department could, under its special rules, take disciplinary action. Often an indicted police officer, after an internal investigation by the police department, would be fired. It was almost impossible to find another job. Few people would be interested in hiring a police officer who had been charged with committing crimes.

The SIU detectives especially dreaded indictment. They were the Princes of the City and were admired by other police officers and by their friends and neighbors. They had great pride in themselves. They made the big-time drug arrests and did things their way. Occasionally they would take money from dealers or give drugs to addict informers.

Even though these were illegal actions, they had become routine, even customary. Now, however, with investigations of police corruption, the Princes were in danger.

One of the best ways for investigators to learn about corrupt police officers was from other officers. The bonds of loyalty and silence among the police made this difficult to do. Investigators tried to break those bonds. Intense pressure was put on individual SIU detectives suspected of wrongdoing. They were constantly questioned and threatened with indictment. It was suggested, but not promised, that a detective who put the finger on other detectives would not be indicted.

Panic grew among the SIU detectives. One of them, Joe Nunziata, was arrested for taking a bribe. The popular detective had made some of the biggest drug arrests in SIU history. He had also saved Leuci's life during a violent riot. To avoid going to jail, Nunziata was asked to give evidence against other detectives. He would not do it. Instead, Joe Nunziata committed suicide.

The death of Nunziata brought enormous grief to SIU detectives. The already tormented Leuci came close to an emotional breakdown. Later, in despair, he said to a friend: "We're policemen, and we can't cope with being criminals. When was the last time a Mafia guy committed suicide because he got in trouble? It isn't criminals who kill themselves, it's cops."

Many detectives believed that Leuci had been cooperating in the investigations of police corruption. Some thought he was responsible for Nunziata's downfall. In fact, despite the pressure, Leuci refused to inform on his friends and former partners.

Another arrested detective broke under the strain. Carl Aguiluz admitted that he and his partners had given drugs to informants, had taken money from some dealers, and had committed *perjury* (lying under oath). He knew these were illegal acts but claimed that many of the laws were senseless and that some interfered with police work. Aguiluz said it was necessary to reward addict informants with drugs. Also, he argued, taking money from dealers kept them from using the money to bribe their way out of jail. Furthermore, he said it was sometimes necessary to lie in court to get juries to convict criminals and that his perjury had never sent an innocent person to jail. Aguiluz had not been a partner of Leuci's, but he said that he knew Leuci had been involved in many similar illegal acts.

Investigators continued to push Leuci to admit to illegal acts committed by him and his partners. Scoppetta had agreed that Leuci would not have to inform on his friends, but Scoppetta was no longer involved in the investigations. Now, what should Leuci do? If he told the truth he would be violating the code of loyalty and silence. If he told the truth his partners might go to jail, lose their jobs, or even commit suicide. If he told the truth he might get indicted and sent to jail.

Leuci also thought of reasons for telling the truth. One of his partners might break and put the finger on him. Then he almost certainly would be indicted. If he told the truth now, he might be able to avoid indictment.

The heat of the investigation reached the boiling point. Leuci was threatened with indictment if he did not tell the truth. He met with a government lawyer with whom he had become friendly. The lawyer urged him to tell the truth. The desperate Leuci cried: "You are asking me to put to death my best friends. . . . They wouldn't do it to me."

The lawyer disagreed. He said Leuci's partners would probably tell all if they were in his place. Maybe Leuci should not have agreed to work with Scoppetta in the first place, the laywer added, but Leuci had made that decision. The lawyer argued that when Leuci had agreed to work with the government he had, in effect, agreed to play by the government's rules. He said, "The side you are on is the side where you have got to tell the truth."

Leuci was in great distress. He considered suicide. Finally, after long hours of thought, he made his decision. He would tell the entire truth. At a meeting with government investigators, Leuci detailed the illegal acts he and his partners had committed. They were the same kinds of offenses that Aguiluz and his partners had committed. After the meeting, the weary Leuci wondered if he had done the right thing.

Some investigators wanted to indict Leuci, because they believed he should be punished for his crimes. After all, they had indicted some others who had committed lesser crimes. In addition, they said, indicting Leuci would show the public that the government did not use witnesses who committed perjury. Future juries would have faith that government witnesses told the truth.

Other officials argued that Leuci should not be indicted. They pointed out that Leuci had performed heroic services for the government. He had helped put many criminals in jail and had risked his life to do so. One man said it was wrong for Leuci to have committed perjury, but it was understandable that he would try to protect his partners. Considering all that Leuci had gone through, he concluded it would be unfair to indict Leuci.

By late in the 1970s, after the long investigations, the SIU had been closed down. Over fifty of the approximately seventy detectives who had worked there were indicted. Many went to jail. Robert Leuci was not one of them. The government officials decided not to indict him.

The major sources for this story were:

Daley, Robert. *Prince of the City: The True Story of a Cop Who Knew Too Much.* Boston: Houghton Mifflin, 1978.
Wainwright, Loudon. "Sonny's Secret World." *Life* 73 (August 4, 1972): 44B–54.

ACTIVITIES FOR "FINGERPRINCE"

Write all answers on a separate sheet of paper.

Historical Understanding

Answer briefly:

1. What was the French Connection case?

2. What is an *indictment*?

3. What is *perjury*?

Reviewing the Facts of the Case

Answer briefly:

1. Why were SIU detectives known as the Princes of the City?

2. Why was it difficult for government investigators to get proof of police corruption?

3. What deal did Nicholas Scoppetta make with Robert Leuci?

4. What did Gina Leuci tell Robert when he was thinking about working with Scoppetta?

5. Why was Leuci's family moved away from New York City?

6. What perjury did Leuci commit? What was one reason he did it?

7. What did Carl Aguiluz tell government investigators?

8. What were two reasons it was difficult for Leuci to tell the truth to government investigators?

Analyzing Ethical Issues

Difficult decisions are often a mix of factual and ethical issues. A factual issue is a question that asks what *is* or might be. Factual issues are concerned with what is true or false, accurate or inaccurate. An ethical issue is a question that asks what *ought to be*. Ethical issues are concerned with what is right or wrong, fair or unfair. One difficult decision that Robert Leuci had to make was whether or not he should work with Nicholas Scoppetta. He had to consider both factual and ethical issues. For example:

DECISION: *Should Leuci work with Scoppetta?*

FACTUAL ISSUE: *Would his feelings of guilt lessen if he worked with Scoppetta?*

ETHICAL ISSUE: *Would it be right to make secret tape recordings of police officers involved in illegal acts?*

Find another instance in this story in which a difficult decision had to be made. Identify the decision and one factual and one ethical issue involved.

Expressing Your Reasoning

1. Should Robert Leuci have told the truth about illegal activities in which he and his partners engaged? Why or why not?

2. After Leuci's confession, government lawyers had to decide whether to indict him. Write a short essay of two or three paragraphs explaining whether you think he should have been indicted. Be sure to give reasons for your decision.

3. Electronic eavesdropping was often used by SIU officers. For each of the following situations indicate whether it would be right for a police officer to make a secret recording. Present reasons for your positions.

    a. In the hope of discovering evidence of criminal activity, an officer makes tape recordings whenever possible.

    b. A friend is about to confess a crime during a telephone conversation with an officer.

    c. An officer bugs a personal enemy in the hope of discovering evidence of wrongdoing.

    d. An officer conceals a microphone because he has reasonable suspicion that criminal activity is about to be revealed at a meeting.

4. *Seeking Additional Information.* In making decisions about such questions as those above, we often feel we need more information before we are satisfied with our judgments. Choose one of the above questions about which you would want more information than is presented in the story. What additional information would you like? Why would that information help you make a more satisfactory decision?

Cover-up Uncovered

JOHN DEAN AND WATERGATE

(Courtesy of Wide World Photos)

John Dean III Being Sworn in by the Senate Watergate Committee

June 17, 1972, was a quiet Sunday morning in Washington, D.C. Five men broke into the elegant Watergate building. They entered the headquarters of the Democratic party's National Committee. The men were wearing rubber gloves and carrying cameras, a walkie-talkie, and special electronic equipment to be used to "bug" the offices. Before the men carried out their mission, police arrived and they were arrested.

Who were these burglars? Why were they breaking into the head-quarters of the Democratic party? Were they acting on their own or following the orders of others? The answers to these questions would stun the nation. The efforts of powerful men to prevent the answers from becoming public would shake the foundations of U.S. government.

Soon after the arrests, reporters discovered some curious information. The name E. Howard Hunt appeared on papers in the pockets of two of the burglars. It was known that Hunt once worked as a consultant for one of President Richard Nixon's advisors. Was it possible there was a White House connection to the break-in? Another question arose. One of the burglars had been employed by the Committee to Re-elect the President (CRP). The CRP was organized to direct President Nixon's reelection campaign. Could it be that the break-in was somehow connected to the committee?

The idea that the burglars might have a connection to the president or his campaign organization was quickly denied. John Mitchell, the head of the CRP and former attorney general in the Nixon administration, announced that the burglars "were not operating on either our behalf or with our consent. There is no place in our campaign or in the electoral process for this type of activity, and we will not permit or condone it." The president himself denied any White House connection. At a press conference he said, "The White House has had no involvement whatsoever in this particular incident."

The president of the United States is one of the most powerful people in the world, possibly the most powerful. A president's decisions can affect the lives of people around the globe.

Presidents rarely make decisions alone. Close advisors have a strong influence in presidential decision making. Because of this, the advisors share the president's great power. They also share the honor and prestige that surround the presidency. Two of the president's closest advisors were H. R. Haldeman and John Ehrlichman.

Many people in Washington wished that they could be part of the tight circle of advisors who helped the president. Few would ever get the chance. One person who did was a bright young lawyer named John W. Dean.

In mid-1970, H. R. Haldeman called Dean to a meeting. He offered Dean an important job—counsel to the president. The counsel was the chief legal advisor for the president and his staff. Haldeman asked if Dean could be completely loyal to the president. Dean replied that he was certain he could be.

Sometime after the meeting with Haldeman, Dean was told that, in addition to being loyal, he must never tell others what the president spoke about in private meetings. As Dean later wrote, "I learned to keep my mouth shut."

Although he was counsel to the president, Dean rarely met with the president. He received his directions from either Haldeman or Ehrlichman. John Dean, however, was determined to get close to the president. To do so he realized he must work hard and not make mistakes. To gain the president's confidence, Dean and his staff needed to develop a reputation for doing excellent work. That reputation did develop, and soon more and more responsibility was given to John Dean.

In addition to offering legal advice, Dean's office was also asked to conduct investigations. For example, authors who wrote critical or insulting articles about the president were investigated to see if there was information that could be used against them. Dean was also asked to obtain information that might be used against people actively protesting U.S. action in the Vietnamese War. John Dean was a busy man.

In addition to trying to end the war in Vietnam, the president faced other delicate and complex foreign policy problems. He was trying to establish a friendly relationship with Communist China. At the same time, he was also trying to reduce the tensions between the United States and the Soviet Union. Furthermore, the president was working to prevent war between Israel and the neighboring Arab states in the Mideast.

To be effective, a president needs the support of the American people. Without such support a president will appear weak and have difficulty carrying out his policies when dealing with other powerful leaders. In the 1968 election, President Nixon had barely won. The

American people had not given him overwhelming support. The president wanted a landslide victory in 1972 so that he would have a strong hand in both national and international politics.

John Mitchell's CRP was officially in charge of President Nixon's campaign. Key political decisions, however, had to be discussed with and approved by the powers at the White House. All agreed it was important for Republican campaign officials to get inside information about Democratic party strategy and about Democratic presidential candidates. Such information could be used to defeat the Democrats.

A lawyer named G. Gordon Liddy, in part on John Dean's recommendation, was hired by the CRP. Liddy's main job was to set up a plan for getting the inside information on the Democrats.

Early in 1972, Dean and Mitchell attended a meeting with Liddy. Liddy presented an elaborate plan for gathering information about the Democrats and for disrupting their campaign. His plan would cost about one million dollars. It included hiring spies to work for Democratic candidates and wiretapping the telephones and offices of Democratic leaders. Liddy even spoke of plans to kidnap the leaders of anti-Republican demonstrations who might try to cause trouble at the Republican convention.

Mitchell quietly suggested that Liddy revise his plans, in part because of their expense. Dean was amazed at Liddy's ideas and knew that many of them would violate laws. He did not, however, argue against Liddy at the meeting. After attending one more meeting, Dean informed Haldeman of Liddy's schemes. Dean suggested that the White House not get involved. Haldeman seemed to agree. Dean did not attend any more CRP meetings. The president's counsel was getting nervous. He was beginning to enter the inner circle of big-time power politics. Though he wanted to serve the president, he began to worry about what such service would require.

In June, as he returned from a trip to the Far East, Dean learned of the Watergate break-in. John Ehrlichman told Dean to find out exactly what had happened. Dean was dismayed with what he discovered.

He learned that E. Howard Hunt and G. Gordon Liddy had been involved in the break-in. He knew that Liddy had worked for the CRP and Hunt for the White House. Dean wondered if top officials had advance knowledge of or had approved the break-in. He hoped not. If the public discovered that top presidential advisors were involved in the crime, the president's chances for reelection would suffer.

As Dean learned more about Watergate, he realized that high officials had probably approved of the break-in. Others were coming to a similar conclusion. Newspaper reporters were writing stories suggesting that the burglars were acting on the orders of top Republican officials. Neither Dean nor the reporters could determine if the president had been involved. Dean knew it was vital that the president and his advisors appear to have no connection to the Watergate episode. The president must be protected.

A strategy for protecting the president and his men began to emerge. Dean, Ehrlichman, and others met to discuss ways to prevent investigators from discovering a connection between the burglars and the White House or the CRP. They set about to cover up the truth and to "stonewall" the official FBI investigation and the investigations of news reporters.

Hunt, Liddy, and the other burglars were about to face trial for the Watergate break-in. Dean and others feared that, under pressure, the burglars might reveal that high-ranking officials had ordered the break-in. One pressure faced by the burglars was their need for money to pay legal and family expenses. Unless the burglars received money, they might start talking. Dean helped secretly arrange for money to be raised from wealthy Nixon supporters. Cash was delivered to the burglars in hopes they would continue to remain silent.

Dean was also involved in trying to block the official FBI investigation. He arranged for Hunt's White House safe to be opened. It contained evidence that would link Watergate to the White House. Dean helped destroy the evidence.

As the president's chief legal advisor, Dean liked to think he was simply trying to protect his client. After all, wasn't that what lawyers were supposed to do? In fact, however, as Dean increasingly realized, he was engaging in illegal actions by hindering the investigation.

The president and Dean rarely met, but Dean knew that his work was appreciated. At an August 29 press conference, President Nixon was questioned about possible White House involvement in Watergate. The president said that his counsel, John Dean, had conducted a complete investigation of the break-in and found no present members of the administration had been involved. He went on to say, "What really hurts in matters of this sort is not the fact that they occur, because overzealous people in campaigns do things that are wrong. What really hurts is if you try to cover it up."

Dean was both shocked and pleased. He was shocked because he had carried out no such investigation. In fact, Dean had not discussed Watergate with the president up to that time. He was pleased because the president was talking about him on national television. Dean later wrote: "The fact that I never heard of a 'Dean investigation,' much less conducted one, did not seem important then. I was basking in the glory of being publicly perceived as the man the President had turned to with a nasty problem like Watergate."

The cover-up seemed to be working. Polls showed the general public was losing interest in the Watergate affair. The election in November seemed to show the same thing. President Nixon easily defeated his Democratic opponent, George McGovern. The president received more votes than any other president in history.

After the landslide election, Dean considered resigning and seeking other work. H. R. Haldeman urged him to stay on. The Watergate investigations were continuing and needed to be put to rest. Dean decided, "I'm going to stay on until we put Watergate to bed." Unfortunately for Dean, the Watergate scandal would neither die nor go to sleep.

In January 1973, the trial of Hunt, Liddy, and the other burglars began. Although news stories still claimed White House connections to the criminals, the burglars denied any such connections. It appeared they were acting on their own. All the men were found guilty and sent to jail.

After the trial, one of the burglars, James McCord, began telling some of the truth about the break-in. In a letter to John Sirica, the trial judge, McCord said that higher-ups had approved the break-in. In talks with investigators, McCord claimed that John Dean was involved. Dean's name was also mentioned in the Senate. A Senate committee was examining the FBI's handling of the Watergate investigation. The testimony of one witness hinted that Dean may have been trying to limit the FBI in its investigation. John Dean's name began making headlines in newspapers.

In the meantime, Dean had been meeting frequently with the president. He had never been closer to President Nixon. As he wrote later, "I felt tall for having made it so close to the shadow of the Presidency." He was also beginning to feel panic and fear. Holes in the cover-up were beginning to show. Reporters kept digging for the truth and were getting closer to finding it.

On March 21, 1973, Dean met privately with President Nixon. He was uneasy. He did not know how much the president knew about the cover-up. Dean intended to tell about the serious problems developing. He said, "We have a cancer within, close to the Presidency, that is growing."

Dean told the president that investigators might soon be able to connect the break-in and the cover-up to the White House and the CRP. Mitchell, Ehrlichman, Haldeman, and Dean, among others, had been involved in various ways. In addition, the convicted burglars were demanding more money. Without it they might begin telling all they knew.

One way of possibly stopping the cancer would be for one or more of the top advisors to confess to ordering the break-in. Whoever confessed would claim that the president knew nothing about it. Such a high-level admission of guilt, and the following jail terms, might make the investigators and the public believe that the Watergate mystery had finally been solved.

The president preferred to continue with the cover-up. He said that money could be raised to pay the demands of the burglars. In addition, he wanted Dean to write a report showing that White House advisors had not been involved in wrongdoing. He wanted Dean to write the report that had been announced in the president's press conference months earlier; the report that had never been made.

Dean thought about the report. It was possible the president might use such a report against him. If investigators discovered a White House connection to Watergate, the president could say that his trusted lawyer had deceived him. It would appear that the president was acting in good faith but that he had been misled by John Dean.

Dean was in deep distress. He was torn by his desire to be loyal to the president and a growing belief that the truth should be told. He was also fearful that the president might try to blame him for the Watergate break-in and cover-up.

Slowly Dean made his crucial decision. He would not write the report. Instead he hired a top criminal lawyer, told him what had been happening, and asked for his advice.

The lawyer said that John Dean was in big trouble. Dean had clearly been involved in the serious crime of *obstruction of justice*.

Anyone who tried to interfere with a criminal investigation could be found guilty of obstructing justice, fined, and sentenced to jail. All those directly involved in the cover-up were committing criminal actions.

Following his lawyer's advice, Dean began meeting privately with the Watergate prosecutors. The prosecutors were Justice Department lawyers working on bringing charges against people believed to be involved in Watergate. In part because of McCord, the prosecutors were investigating Dean's involvement in the break-in. Dean knew of his own involvement in the cover-up and that virtually all of the president's close advisors had some connection to either the break-in or the cover-up. If Dean told all he knew, he, top advisors, and even the president would be in trouble.

It was a terrible time for John Dean. The strain of the cover-up was creating tension between him and his new wife. Fears of going to jail haunted him. He wanted to be loyal to the president, and he personally liked Haldeman and Mitchell. If he told the truth, these and other men's lives would be ruined. But would anyone believe him? It would be his word against that of the president of the United States and his powerful advisors.

At his first meeting with the prosecutors, the strain on Dean increased. The prosecutors told Dean that Liddy had been talking to them about Watergate. They said they would check Dean's version of Watergate with that of Liddy. They warned Dean that he had better be telling the truth. Dean was astonished. He knew how tough Gordon Liddy was and could not believe that he would be one to begin talking about Watergate. Still, the stress of the entire affair did strange things to people. In fact, Liddy had not been talking. The prosecutors had said that in order to pressure Dean to tell the truth. Over a series of meetings, Dean gradually began revealing what he knew.

In mid-April, Dean met with the president. He explained that he was meeting with the prosecutors and that the Watergate involvement of Mitchell, Ehrlichman, Haldeman, and others was going to be discussed. He said he hoped the Watergate problems would be settled once and for all. Dean said he was still loyal to the president and suggested that if all of his involved advisors were asked to resign, the president might still be able to protect himself. The resignations would make it appear that the president was getting rid of people who had acted wrongfully. Perhaps the public would believe the president's men were guilty, and that he had removed them when he discovered their involvement.

The president wanted to protect his top advisors. He wanted John Dean to sign a letter of resignation. Dean's letter would say he was resigning because of his involvement in Watergate. Dean would, in effect, be taking the blame for Watergate. He refused to sign alone. He said he would resign if Haldeman and Ehrlichman did so at the same time. He would not take the blame alone. The meeting with the president ended.

By the summer of 1973, Dean became nationally known. In May he began a series of appearances before a Senate investigating committee. The appearances were televised across the country. He was the star witness. His statements about the role of the president and his advisors in the Watergate scandal shocked the nation and made headline news.

No one could be certain that Dean was telling the truth. Many believed he was, in a cowardly way, trying to spread the blame for his wrongdoings onto the president and his close advisors. One news reporter called him a "bottom dwelling slug."

Other witnesses were called before the committee. In July, the testimony of one witness made news around the world. He said that the president had a secret tape recording system in the White House. Virtually all conversations in the president's office had been tape recorded. After lengthy legal proceedings, authorities obtained the tapes. The recordings showed that the major points of John Dean's testimony were true.

Further investigations eventually found that the Watergate break-in was but part of a number of illegal actions approved by top White House officials. There had been other break-ins, wiretappings, and a variety of additional wrongdoings.

The Watergate affair was a disaster for the president's men. Mitchell, Haldeman, Ehrlichman, and others faced jury trials, were found guilty, and sentenced to jail. John Dean was also sent to jail. Eventually all were released.

There was another casualty of the Watergate affair—the president of the United States. Under the Constitution of the United States, a president can be removed from office through a process known as *impeachment*. No president had ever been removed in that way. It became clear, however, that President Nixon was going to be the first. On August 8, 1974, the president announced that he was resigning from office. In 1972 he had received more votes for president than any other candidate in history. Two years later he became the first president to resign from office.

The president did not face a jury trial or serve any time in jail. The new president, Gerald Ford, pardoned Nixon for any crimes he may have committed while president.

The major sources for this story were:

Bernstein, Carl, and Woodward, Bob. *All the President's Men.* New York: Simon and Schuster, 1974.

Dean, John W., III. *Blind Ambition.* New York: Simon and Schuster, 1976.

Nixon, Richard M. *The Memoirs of Richard Nixon.* New York: Grosset and Dunlap, 1978.

The Washington Post. *The Presidential Transcripts.* New York: Dell, 1974.

ACTIVITIES FOR "COVER-UP UNCOVERED"

Write all answers on a separate sheet of paper.

Historical Understanding

Answer briefly:

1. Identify three important foreign policy problems facing President Richard Nixon in the early 1970s.

2. What was unusual about the number of votes President Nixon received in 1972?

3. What is *obstruction of justice?*

Reviewing the Facts of the Case

Answer briefly:

1. What was the CRP? Who was John Mitchell?

2. Immediately after the break-in, why did people suspect the burglars might be connected to the White House or the CRP?

3. What job did H. R. Haldeman offer John Dean? What were two things that Dean realized he would have to do in order to get ahead?

4. Why would the president's chances for re-election be hurt if the truth of Watergate came out?

5. What were two ways John Dean was involved in the cover-up?

6. In his August 1972 press conference, what did the president say about Dean?

7. Who was James McCord? In what way did he expose the cover-up?

8. Why did Dean meet with the president on March 21, 1973? What were two things that were discussed?

Analyzing Ethical Issues

This story involves the following values of truth and loyalty:

TRUTH: a value concerning the expression, distortion, or withholding of accurate information

LOYALTY: a value concerning obligations to the people, traditions, ideas, and organizations of importance in one's life

A number of ethical questions involving these values are raised by the story. An ethical question asks whether an action is right or wrong, fair or unfair. Identify two ethical questions raised by the story involving the values of truth or loyalty. Explain how the value(s) is (are) involved in each question. For example:

Would it have been right for Dean to have written the false report requested by the president?

The value of truth is involved in this question because Dean would have had to decide how much accurate information to include in the report. The value of loyalty is also involved because Dean had to decide if he had an obligation to protect the president and his advisors.

Expressing Your Reasoning

1. Should John Dean have told the truth about the Watergate affair? State reasons for your position.

2. The president wanted John Dean to resign and, in effect, take the blame for Watergate. Should Dean have resigned? Why or why not?

3. When Dean first met with the prosecutors they told him that Watergate burglar Gordon Liddy had been talking with them.

Liddy had not been, but they misled Dean in order to pressure him into telling all the truth. Were the prosecutors right in doing that? Why or why not?

4. President Ford pardoned Richard Nixon for any crimes he may have committed. Because of the pardon, President Nixon did not have to face a jury trial and possible jail sentence. Was Ford right in what he did? Write a paragraph explaining your position.

5. *Seeking Additional Information.* In making decisions about such questions as those above, we often feel we need more information before we are satisfied with our judgments. Choose one of the above questions about which you would want more information than is presented in the story. What additional information would you like? Why would that information help you make a more satisfactory decision?

Buying Your Pardon

MARIE RAGGHIANTI

(Courtesy of Marie Ragghianti)

Marie Ragghianti, Her Daughter, and Tennessee Governor Blanton
the Day Marie Took Her Oath of Office

Before Marie Ragghianti's government career ended, the political power structure of Tennessee would be a shambles. Scandals would erupt throughout the state. Reputations would be ruined. Jail sentences would be handed down. There would even be murder and suicide.

Nothing in Marie's childhood foretold that she would become the eye of Tennessee's biggest political storm. The first of five children, she was born in 1942 in Chattanooga, Tennessee. Her mother was descended from Tennessee Scotch-Irish stone masons and blacksmiths. Her Cuban-born father was a political reporter, first in Knoxville and later in Nashville. When Marie was 15 her father became a motel chain executive and moved the family to Daytona Beach, Florida.

Leaving friends in Nashville had been hard for Marie, but she adapted quickly to life in the sunshine. Pretty, vivacious, and popular, she was elected Miss Daytona Beach and beauty queen of Seabreeze High School. Many of her afternoons were spent lying in the sun at the beach. Boys swarmed around her. Modeling jobs rolled in. Sugar packets in restaurants all over Florida featured a picture of Marie posing in a bathing suit on a sand dune.

Her father warned that she was becoming self-centered, vain, and spoiled. When she graduated from high school, there was an argument over where she would go to college. Her parents urged her to attend a Catholic university. Seeking more sun and fun, the golden beach girl preferred the University of Miami. Her parents refused to send her there, so she went instead to Daytona Beach Junior College. It was much like high school. A convertible filled with boys picked her up every morning for class.

Marie's mother still wanted her daughter to attend Siena College in Memphis. Many of the Dominican sisters who had been her mother's teachers were still there. Siena College would eliminate the temptations of Daytona's resort atmosphere. To please her mother, Marie enrolled there. Her mother was comforted to learn that Marie attended daily mass on campus.

Early in the semester, the Siena girls were invited to a dance at nearby Christian Brothers College. There Marie met David Ragghianti. The two were immediately attracted to each other. At one point during the evening, David knocked another boy out cold on the floor because he gave Marie an admiring look. Even though she disapproved, she thought it was romantic. Marie and David were married in 1962. She was 19; he was 18. She dropped out of college with hopes of putting her husband through school.

One night soon after their marriage, David became enraged with Marie and began hitting her. Friends who were nearby dragged him off her. Her eye was nearly shut, and her lower lip was puffed and cut. He apologized, but a pattern was setting in—violence followed by remorse. Eventually he stabbed her in the hand.

When she was 25, Marie took the couple's three children and fled. She got a divorce (later the marriage was annulled) and moved into a roach- and rat-infested apartment in a poor section of Nashville. She had little money and survived at first on handouts.

Her youngest child, Ricky, suffered from a lung ailment. Frequently his mother would have to rush him to a hospital emergency room because he began gasping for breath and choking. Marie lived in terror of those moments. A devout Catholic, she derived strength from her religious faith during the ordeals of her son's suffering.

One of Ricky's attacks was nearly fatal. A tracheotomy was performed. During the surgery a sterling silver tube was inserted into the boy's throat through his neck. Several times each night Marie used the tube to suction the mucus from her young son's lungs. The lung ailment lasted for years. Eventually, its cause was discovered, and the boy's health became normal.

Marie earned enough money to move the family to a better apartment. On Friday and Saturday nights, she worked as a cocktail waitress in a Nashville club. On Sundays, after mass, she worked as a librarian at church. When all three children were in school, Marie enrolled at Vanderbilt University for the 1972 fall term. To pay for her schooling, she typed papers for other students. Her life was a difficult struggle, but she held her family together and dreamed of better days ahead.

Marie's grades at Vanderbilt were high. She received a scholarship. During her senior year at the university she covered politics for the campus newspaper. She also joined the Young Democrats. The political excitement of party meetings, voter registration drives, and rallies appealed to Marie. At these events she met a politically active lawyer named Eddie Sisk. Sisk was to become a key figure in her life.

As an active Democrat, Marie was involved in the campaign for governor of Ray Blanton. The election in the fall of 1974 attracted national attention. The National Republican party had been damaged by a scandal dubbed "Watergate," which culminated in the resignation of President Richard Nixon and the imprisonment of members of his administration. The Tennessee election for governor would be an indication of how much damage had been done to the Republicans by Watergate.

During the campaign, Blanton, a former Congressman, frequently reminded the voters of the Watergate scandal. "We are entitled," he said, "to see justice done whether crimes are committed in the streets or in the White House." His Republican rival had been an aide in the Nixon White House. One of Blanton's favorite lines was that when he went back to Washington to visit old friends, he saw them in their homes and offices. He said his opponent had to visit his former friends at a federal prison. Winning almost 60 percent of the vote, Blanton was elected governor of Tennessee. He pledged to carry on a clean, honest administration.

Marie Ragghianti was attracted to the new governor's promise of equal employment opportunities for women and minorities. Eddie Sisk was made legal counsel to the governor. Marie made an appointment to congratulate him. They met in the governor's office, where he asked, "Marie, how would you like to be an extradition officer for the State of Tennessee?" She accepted the job.

As state *extradition* officer, Marie coordinated transfer of criminal suspects to and from other states. Her thorough work and dedication drew praise from prosecuting attorneys throughout Tennessee.

Marie found that her job did not provide enough work to keep her occupied. When she confessed that fact to Eddie Sisk, he assigned her an additional task: liaison with the pardons and paroles board. The new assignment, said Eddie, could lead to other things.

Marie was intrigued by the new work. In Tennessee a *felon* (someone convicted of a serious crime) was not eligible for *parole* (release before a prisoner's term expires) until half of a sentence was served. The only other way for a prisoner to get released was to be granted *executive clemency* (reduction of sentence by the governor).

The state pardons and paroles board received requests for clemency from prisoners and recommended to the governor that he grant or deny the requests. Only the governor had authority to grant clemency. Communications between the governor's office and the parole board were now made through Marie.

The first letter requesting clemency that Marie read began, "Dear Governor Blanton, I pray to God that you will find the compassion within you to hear a mother's plea." Such letters absorbed Marie. Some moved her deeply.

One day, Marie was asked by Eddie Sisk to look into a case. Eddie told her the prisoner was a "real deserving" first offender. Marie checked into the case and informed Eddie that the parole board had told her the prisoner appeared to be worthy of special treatment. "Good, I thought so," said Eddie. "That boy's daddy was a big contributor." "I thought it was because he was so deserving," said Marie. Eddie replied, "Of course he is. Just because his daddy contributed doesn't make him less deserving, does it?" Marie suspected that Eddie wanted the prisoner released because his father had contributed money to Blanton's political campaign.

One day, Marie received a call at work telling her that her son Ricky had stolen money from a purse. She prepared to go home immediately and stopped in to tell Eddie why she was leaving. "Take it easy," he said. "I'll bet there isn't a boy in America who hasn't gone into a pocketbook at one time or another. . . . If he goes to prison, at least we can get him executive clemency." To Marie at the time it seemed like a harmless joke.

In May 1976, Marie received a promotion. Governor Blanton appointed her chair of the Tennessee Board of Pardons and Paroles. In less than a year and a half she had risen to a prestigious government job. She was the first female in Tennessee history to hold the high position. It paid an annual salary of $26,400 and provided a $400 monthly expense account. It seemed that the hard days of raising three children, being divorced, and putting herself through school were finally behind her. Marie was elated with her new appointment. It was an achievement beyond anything she had imagined.

News of her appointment had come from a friend of the governor. He told Marie that her troubles were over, that she'd be on easy street from now on. Marie didn't quite understand what he meant. He explained: "There'll be little side benefits and opportunities, and you'll be smart enough to see them and take advantage of them. Nobody has to know." The meaning of his words puzzled Marie.

Marie soon began to get some idea of what the governor's friend had meant. There was an extradition to Georgia that was being blocked by Eddie Sisk's office. Marie couldn't get Sisk to send the prisoners to Georgia even though all the requirements for extradition had been met. There was also a report linking Sisk to *extortion* (using an official position to obtain money) in a clemency case.

Marie discussed her suspicions with the state commissioner of corrections. She told him she suspected that Eddie Sisk, and perhaps others close to Governor Blanton, were taking money to block extraditions and selling pardons. The commissioner brushed off her concerns.

Still troubled, Marie confided in a friend. He told her to forget it. He reminded her of her three children and how hard she had worked to support them. She at least had a good job, he reminded her, one that enabled her to care for herself and her children. He assured her that it was an opportunity for her to begin to enjoy life. "Don't blow it," he said. "Don't try to fight it. You can't change the system."

It was to the governor himself that Marie next voiced her concerns about the Georgia extraditions. "What's holding them up?" he asked. Marie replied that Eddie Sisk was delaying them. The governor seemed noncommittal. "Use your best judgment," he said. "That's why I put you there. That's what I expect."

After her meeting with Blanton, Marie received a phone call from Eddie. He was furious with her for complaining to the governor. Marie wondered how Eddie had found out about her meeting with the governor.

Pangs of guilt haunted her. She felt disloyal, like an informer. After all, she thought, Eddie Sisk was her friend. He had hired her. She pondered where her loyalty lay. Was it to Eddie, to the people of Tennessee, or to prisoners who knew others were buying their way out of jail? Also, there was the possibility of harming the entire Blanton administration by exposing a scandal within it. Marie was tormented.

Gradually, evidence accumulated to convince Marie that the governor's office was involved in a conspiracy to sell pardons and paroles. Sisk and others, perhaps Blanton himself, she believed, were accepting money in exchange for pardons and paroles. It seemed that murderers, drug dealers, and rapists were buying their way out of prison.

Marie decided to take her information to the FBI. She was flirting with grave personal danger. In the course of her work, she spent time in the state prison. If word got around the prison population that she was trying to block deals to get convicts out, she would be in jeopardy. There was also danger beyond the prison walls. Prisoners hoping to buy their release apparently had friends in high places.

On the basis of Marie's information, FBI agents raided the offices of the governor's legal counsel and the Board of Pardons and Paroles. Records were seized. *Subpoenas* (orders to appear in court) were given to Sisk, his assistant, members of the board, and the corrections commissioner. The fact that Marie was an FBI informant was kept secret to protect her. To avoid suspicion, she was given a subpoena with the others.

Nashville's newspapers headlined the story on October 23, 1976. The front page of the *Tennessean* said, "FEDS SEIZE STATE FILES ON CLEMENCY, PARDONS." *The Nashville Banner* read, "FBI PROBING PAROLE PAYOFFS." The governor's legal counsel, Eddie Sisk, denied that payoffs had been involved in the granting of clemencies.

Not enough information was obtained from the FBI raid to bring criminal charges against the suspects. Making a case against them was not going to be easy. There had to be hard evidence that money had been exchanged, that there had been criminal influence peddling. Marie continued to cooperate with the FBI investigation. She testified in secret sessions of a federal *grand jury* (a group of citizens who decide whether there is sufficient evidence for a trial). Her testimony alone, though important, wouldn't be enough for a conviction in a criminal trial.

Meanwhile, Eddie Sisk came to the conclusion that Marie was somehow behind the FBI investigation. He accused her of being ungrateful. He'd provided one of the best jobs in state government for her, he complained, and she'd stabbed him in the back. Marie denied turning against him.

The Blanton administration took the offensive. The governor went to see the attorney general of the United States to complain about FBI harassment. A fellow southern Democrat was in the White House at the time, and Tennessee would be an important state in his bid for reelection. Next, Blanton fired Marie Ragghianti from her job as head of the Pardons and Paroles Board. He charged her with misconduct in office, claiming, among other things, that she had used public money for private expenses.

Marie was followed by agents of the Tennessee Bureau of Criminal Investigation. Twice she was arrested by Nashville police for drunk driving. The first time she was taken to jail even though the breath test showed her to be sober. The second time the test showed her to be slightly over the legal limit for alcohol in the bloodstream.

Marie's firing and reports of her arrest for drunken driving took some of the pressure off the governor's office. That the federal government still had brought no charges since the FBI raid almost a year earlier further eased pressure on the Blanton administration. Public suspicion was shifting from the governor's office to Marie.

Some peculiar events soon occurred. A key witness in the FBI case was found dead, an apparent suicide. Next, an employee of the Corrections Department who was going to testify about pressure exerted on Marie to ease pardons was found murdered. Marie was shaken by the murder of her friend, and she thought her cause was lost. Nonetheless, she pursued a lawsuit she had filed to regain her job.

A decisive breakthrough occurred when the FBI finally found its key evidence. A witness linked Eddie Sisk directly to a payoff. The witness testified before a grand jury that he had given Sisk an envelope containing $2,000 in one-hundred dollar bills to keep from being extradited to Georgia. Soon afterward, the FBI arrested Sisk, his wallet filled with $1,200 in bills that could be traced to another payoff.

In July 1978, Marie won her lawsuit to get her job back. The jury had not been persuaded by Governor Blanton's charges against her. The judge ruled that Marie was to be reinstated and receive a year's back pay.

There was no direct evidence linking the governor to the scandal. The voters, however, defeated Blanton by a large margin in November. The new governor was not scheduled to be sworn into office until January. Blanton lost no time in granting a sudden flurry of clemencies. One day in January he signed 52 executive clemencies. Among those released were 24 murderers. Alarmed at the prospect of even more clemencies, the Tennessee Supreme Court swore in the new governor three days ahead of schedule.

Indictments (formal accusations of committing a crime) were brought against several members of Blanton's administration, including Eddie Sisk, in March 1979. Sisk confessed to criminal conspiracy to sell clemencies to state inmates. He was sentenced to five years in prison. No charges of selling clemencies were brought against Blanton. As an outgrowth of the FBI investigation, however, direct evidence was discovered that the governor had been taking bribes for granting liquor-store licenses. He was convicted, sentenced to three years in prison, and fined $11,000.

The new administration in Nashville wanted to begin with a clean slate. Marie was not reappointed to the Pardons and Paroles Board. Democrats in the legislature opposed her. They blamed her for losing the executive branch to the Republicans. Marie Ragghianti left the scandal in Nashville and moved with her children to Daytona Beach.

The major sources for this story were:

Maas, Peter. *Marie: A True Story.* New York: Random House, 1983.

Steinem, Gloria. "What Happens When an Ordinary Woman Blows the Whistle on Her Boss." *Ms.* (June 1983), pp. 43 77.

ACTIVITIES FOR "BUYING YOUR PARDON"

Write all answers on a separate sheet of paper.

Historical Understanding

Answer briefly:

1. What connection was there between the Watergate scandal and Ray Blanton's campaign for governor of Tennessee?

2. Explain the meaning of the following: *extradition, grand jury, indictment, executive clemency,* and *extortion.*

Reviewing the Facts of the Case

Answer briefly:

1. How did Marie Ragghianti come to be appointed state extradition officer?

2. What was Eddie Sisk's official position in the Blanton administration?

3. What hardships were eased for Ragghianti when she received her first state job?

4. What was the function of the Tennessee Board of Pardons and Paroles?

5. What steps did Ragghianti take once she suspected corruption in the state corrections system?

6. Why did Ragghianti feel guilty after reporting her suspicions of Sisk to the state commissioner of corrections and to the governor?

7. What key evidence was finally turned up by the FBI?

Analyzing Ethical Issues

There is agreement about the answer to some questions. For other questions there is disagreement about the answer. We call these questions issues. Issues can be categorized as factual or ethical. A factual issue asks whether something is true or false, accurate or inaccurate. An ethical issue asks whether something is right or wrong, fair or unfair. Factual issues ask what *is*; ethical issues ask what *ought to be*. Both types of issues are raised in this story. For example:

FACTUAL ISSUE: *Was Marie Ragghianti's friend murdered because of the testimony expected from him in court?*

ETHICAL ISSUE: *Was it right of Ragghianti to lie to Eddie Sisk about her becoming an FBI informant?*

Identify another example of both a factual issue and an ethical issue raised in the story and state each as a question, as illustrated above.

Expressing Your Reasoning

1. Should Marie Ragghianti have gone to the FBI with evidence that convicts were buying clemencies from the governor's office? Why or why not?

2. Eddie Sisk suspected that Ragghianti may have been the one who triggered the FBI raid on his office. When he questioned her about it, she denied it. Was it right for her to lie to him? Why or why not?

3. In order to obtain testimony against a major suspect in the case, the FBI offered immunity to another suspect. It was agreed that in exchange for direct evidence against the friend and accomplice, the suspect would escape prosecution. Write a paragraph expressing your opinion of whether law-enforcement officials should make such deals to get convictions in court. State reasons for your position.

4. Marie Ragghianti came to believe that she had been hired by Sisk because he thought she was pretty and naive. Her experience raises the issue of whether someone should consider the reasons a job is being offered in deciding whether or not to accept it. For each example below, decide whether the person being offered the job ought to accept it. Explain your thinking.
   a. A man is hired as a teacher because he is a member of a minority group.
   b. A woman is hired as a waitress because she has a shapely figure.
   c. Someone is appointed to a vacancy in a legislature because his father was famous.
   d. A job is offered to someone because of the applicant's political views.

5. *Seeking Additional Information.* In making decisions about such questions as those above, we often feel we need more information before we are satisfied with our judgments. Choose one of the above questions about which you would want more information than is presented in the story. What additional information would you like? Why would that information help you make a more satisfactory decision?

Affirmative or Negative

BAKKE DECISION

(*Courtesy of AP/Wide World Photos*)

Allan Bakke

In 1973 Allan Bakke applied to the medical school of the University of California at Davis and was rejected. He decided to try again the following year. He had no idea that his ambition to become a doctor would divide the nation and make his name a household word.

Bakke had attended the University of Minnesota, where he majored in mechanical engineering and earned just under an A average. To help pay the costs of his college education, he joined the Naval Reserve Officers Training Corps. After graduation he fought as a marine captain in Vietnam.

Upon returning to the United States in 1967, Bakke earned a masters degree in engineering at Stanford University. He then took a job as an aerospace engineer at a National Aeronautics and Space Administration (NASA) research center in California. "I don't know anyone brighter or more capable," said his boss at NASA. Married, father of three children, and well paid, he seemed comfortably set in life.

What he really wanted, however, was to become a doctor. So determined was he that he took biology and chemistry courses required for medical school while working as an engineer. To make up the time missed from his job, he worked early mornings and evenings. Bakke also worked off-hours as a hospital emergency room volunteer. He took tough assignments working with battered victims of car accidents and fights.

He was 33 years old when he finally applied to medical school. All 12 of the schools he applied to, including the University of California at Davis, turned him down. He thought it was because of his age. Some of the schools said he was too old. Davis had been his first choice, because it was near his suburban San Francisco home. He soon learned that it was not because of his age that his application to Davis had been rejected.

Davis had a special admissions program that reserved 16 of 100 places in its entering class for disadvantaged minority students, principally blacks, Chicanos, and Native Americans. Students accepted under the special admissions program had lower grade-point averages (GPA) and admissions test scores than the 84 students accepted under the regular admissions program. In 1973 the average GPA of special admissions students was 2.88 compared with 3.49 for regular students. On the Medical College Admissions Test (MCAT) the average ranking of special admissions students was the thirty-fifth percentile, whereas regular students averaged in the eighty-third percentile. GPA and MCAT scores, though not the only factors, were the major ones considered in screening applications under the regular admissions program.

Because Bakke was white, he was prevented from competing for the 16 places set aside under the special admissions program. His GPA and MCAT scores were higher than those of the students accepted under the special program. On the MCAT he scored in the ninetieth percentile, and his GPA was 3.51. Bakke believed that the special admissions program had kept him out of medical school.

In a letter to the chairman of the Davis admissions committee, Bakke expressed his frustration:

> I am convinced that a significant fraction of medical school applicants is judged by a separate criteria. I am referring to quotas, open or covert, for racial minorities. I realize that the rationale for these quotas is that they attempt to atone for past racial discrimination, but insisting on a new racial bias in favor of minorities is not a just situation.

After being rejected a second time, Bakke filed suit in California court claiming the university had unlawfully discriminated against him on the basis of race. He asked the court to order the university to admit him.

The clash between Allan Bakke and the University of California over racial equality had deep roots. Since the birth of the nation there had been disparity between the American promise of equality and the treatment of black people. Thomas Jefferson's claim that "all men are created equal" had been an unfulfilled promise until the Civil War.

During Reconstruction (1865–1876) there was hope that the promise would be realized. Three amendments designed to grant political rights to former slaves were added to the Constitution (Thirteenth, Fourteenth, and Fifteenth). Also, a sweeping Civil Rights Act prohibiting racial discrimination was passed by Congress in 1875. Hope was short-lived however. Court interpretations of the new laws soon made them ineffective.

By the end of the century the color line was deeply etched in the United States. In the South, state laws were enacted to deny blacks the rights of citizenship. They could not vote, hold office, serve on juries, or testify against whites. Blacks were also *segregated* (kept separate) from whites. By law, blacks attended separate schools, traveled in separate cars on trains, ate in separate restaurants, attended separate churches, played in separate parks, and were buried in separate cemeteries. In addition, blacks were denied opportunities to participate fully in the economic life of the nation. Most of them lived in poverty.

In 1896, the Supreme Court put the federal government on the side of racial segregation. In the case of *Plessy* v. *Ferguson* the high court endorsed state laws that separated the races. States were permitted to require separation of the races as long as both groups were treated equally. "Separate but equal" became the law of the land. For more than half a century there would be nearly total separation. Equality, however, remained little more than a promise.

The fact of racial inequality was squarely confronted in 1954. That year the Supreme Court reversed the pattern of separate but equal. In the case of *Brown* v. *Board of Education* the justices unanimously struck down segregation in public schools. Segregation of school children on the basis of race, said the court, was "inherently unequal." According to the justices, school segregation was a violation of equal protection of the law guaranteed by the Fourteenth Amendment. The 17 states with legally segregated schools, mostly in the South, were ordered by the court to desegregate.

The *Brown* case marked the beginning of what some call the Second Reconstruction. The color line, at least the one drawn by government, was finally being erased.

Progress toward desegregation was slow. The *Brown* decision, and others based on it, were met with token compliance, obstruction, and even defiance. By 1962, not a single black child attended a white school in Mississippi, Alabama, or South Carolina. One decade after the decision, only 2.3 percent of southern blacks were enrolled in desegregated schools.

The *Brown* case spawned a mass movement for racial equality. Less than a year after the decision, Rosa Parks, a 43-year-old seamstress in Montgomery, Alabama, refused to give up her seat on a bus to a white man as required by law. She sparked a year-long black *boycott* (refusal to use or buy) of public transportation led by Martin Luther King, Jr. The Montgomery bus boycott succeeded in changing the law and triggered other successful boycotts throughout the South.

Although the Supreme Court had outlawed segregation in publicly owned facilities, private individuals were still allowed to discriminate on the basis of race. Privately owned facilities such as lunch counters, hotels, barbershops, movie theaters, and restaurants continued to exclude blacks. In 1960, college students launched a second stage of the movement with sit-ins at segregated lunch counters in North Carolina. A full-scale, nonviolent campaign for civil rights had begun. In some places, however, demonstrators were greeted by violent reactions.

The civil rights movement culminated with the most comprehensive civil rights law ever proposed. Just before President John Kennedy sent the bill to Congress, he spoke to the nation on television. He challenged the United States to fulfill its promise of equality. The president said,

> We are confronted primarily with a moral issue. It is as old as the Scriptures and is as clear as the Constitution. If an American, because his skin is dark, cannot eat lunch in a restaurant open to the public; if he cannot send his children to the best public schools available; if he cannot vote for the public officials who represent him; if in short, he cannot enjoy the full and free life which all of us want, then who among us would be content to have the color of his skin changed and stand in his place?

In the nation's capital a massive march took place in support of the proposed Civil Rights Act. Leading the march on Washington was a champion of nonviolence, Martin Luther King. "I still have a dream," said the civil rights leader before thousands assembled at the Lincoln Memorial.

> It is a dream deeply rooted in the American dream. I have a dream that one day this nation will rise up and live out the true meaning of its creed: "We hold these truths to be self-evident, that all men are created equal" . . . I have a dream that my four little children will one day live in a nation where they will not be judged by the color of their skin but by the content of their character.

The Civil Rights Act of 1964 was passed by Congress, in part, as a monument to a slain president. John F. Kennedy was assassinated in November 1963. Provisions of the act were sweeping. It outlawed discrimination in all public accommodations, including restaurants and lunch counters, motels and hotels, gas stations, theaters, and sports arenas. The act also put Congress and the executive on the side of school desegregation. It authorized the Justice Department to sue school districts that were not desegregating.

Other civil rights laws followed. In 1965 the Voting Rights Act was passed. It removed obstacles to voting by blacks. Three years later, the Fair Housing Act prohibited discrimination in the rental or sale of housing.

In the area of school desegregation there had been modest progress. By 1966, 12.5 percent of southern black children attended desegregated schools. To remedy the widespread school segregation still in effect, north and south, federal courts began to order busing. Where intent to segregate in the past could be shown, school districts were ordered to transport students on buses to create racial integration.

During the early 1970s, busing was a flash point of domestic politics. In northern cities "No Forced Busing" became a popular political slogan. There was a fierce and somewhat violent backlash to court-ordered busing. Many whites enrolled their children in private schools or moved to avoid busing. A Gallup poll in 1973 reported only 5 percent of the nation favored busing to achieve racial integration of the schools.

Urban school systems became increasingly black as whites moved to the suburbs. The prediction of a commission that studied a rash of urban race riots in the late 1960s seemed to be coming true. The commission warned that the United States was becoming two societies, "a white society principally located in suburbs . . . and a Negro society largely concentrated within central cities."

By the middle of the 1970s the nation was divided over what to do about the effects of its history of racial discrimination. Many argued that the legal barriers to integration had been lifted. Given time, they believed, the problem would now cure itself. Others were not convinced that racial equality was inevitable. In their opinion, affirmative steps would have to be taken to overcome the past.

Those favoring *affirmative action* pointed out gaps between whites and blacks. For example, average income for a black family in 1975 was $15,000 compared with $24,000 for a white family. Also, the unemployment rate for blacks was twice as high as for whites. The National Urban League, a civil rights organization, conceded that much progress had been made but ended its 1978 annual report on a somber note: "Still the harsh truth remains . . . that the majority of blacks have not seen their status materially improved over the past decade, and that for many, their lives are still lived out in despair and deprivation."

To those who supported affirmative action, it meant compensation to minority groups for the historic discrimination against them. This was to be accomplished by restoring minorities to the positions in society they would have held had there been no discrimination. According to advocates of affirmative action, that point would be reached when the percentage of minorities in favored positions was roughly equal to their percentage in the population. For example, because blacks were 12 percent of the population, approximately 12 percent of U.S. doctors should be black. In fact, only 2 percent of the nation's medical students were black in 1970.

Founded in 1968, the University of California at Davis Medical School had no intent to discriminate against minority applicants. Among the 50 students in its first class however, none was black, Hispanic, or Native American. To ensure minority representation in future classes, Davis instituted an affirmative action plan. Under the plan, 16 of the 100 places in the entering class were reserved for disadvantaged minorities. It was this plan that Allan Bakke challenged in court in June 1974.

Bakke claimed that the Davis special admissions plan was *reverse discrimination*. His complaint charged that he was fully qualified for admission and that his application was rejected because of his race. He maintained that the university, as a result of its racial quotas, had denied him equal protection of the law as guaranteed by the Fourteenth Amendment to the Constitution.

In response, the university's lawyers argued that the racial classification in this case was permitted by law. Unlike illegal classifications of the past that were designed to *exclude* minorities, the Davis plan, it was claimed, placed minorities in a special category in order to *include* them. According to the university, this was a necessary corrective action to remedy the effects of past discrimination. More specifically, the university presented four reasons to justify its special admissions program:

1. To improve medical education by including men and women from diverse segments of society in medical school;
2. To reduce separation of minorities from the mainstream of American life by drawing them into the medical profession;

3. To provide role models for minority children to demonstrate that there were now opportunities open to them;
4. To improve medical care in seriously underserved minority communities.

The California court concluded that the program at Davis, by granting preference to minority students, violated the equal protection clause of the Fourteenth Amendment. The program was declared illegal.

Fearing that the ruling would invalidate all of its affirmative action programs, the university appealed the lower court decision to the California Supreme Court. The state's highest court upheld the lower court. It ruled that the Davis program violated the constitutional rights of nonminority applicants by granting preference on the basis of race. The Constitution, claimed the majority of the court, should be color-blind. One member of the court disagreed with the majority decision. He argued that it was a sad irony to find the Fourteenth Amendment aimed against blacks when its original purpose was to provide opportunities for former slaves.

Because a federal constitutional issue was involved in the case, the university could appeal to the U.S. Supreme Court. In September 1976, a final appeal was made to the nation's highest tribunal. Few Supreme Court cases in U.S. history stirred as much debate as *Regents of the University of California* v. *Allan Bakke*. The main issue to be decided was whether any government agency should be allowed to consider who was black and who was white in an attempt to overcome past discrimination.

On a crisp October morning in 1977, a huge crowd gathered on the Supreme Court plaza in Washington. The inscription above the monumental columns of the building read, "Equal Justice Under Law." There were differing opinions in the crowd about just what equal justice required in the case to be heard that morning.

At precisely ten o'clock, nine black-robed justices appeared from behind red velvet curtains and took their seats at the elevated bench. They were about to hear arguments in what was considered the most important civil rights case in a generation.

The justices would hear from the University of California's lawyer, Allan Bakke's lawyer, and the *solicitor general* of the United States. The solicitor general is the one who argues the position of the United

States government in cases where the federal government has a special interest.

First came the university's case. The 16 minority places at Davis, argued its lawyer, should not be considered a traditional quota. In the past, quotas had been used to limit minority participation, but here they were used to increase it.

The university's argument included other points. Color-conscious admissions policies, its lawyer said, were necessary to bring minorities fully into the American mainstream. Without affirmative action plans, no more than a trickle of minority students would be admitted to professional schools. In addition, argued the university, society benefits from special admissions. Whites and minorities learn from each other, and minority graduates are more likely to practice in minority communities where there is a greater need for medical doctors.

Furthermore, merit alone—as reflected by grades and test scores—has never been the sole basis of selection for schools. If colleges and universities can select students on the basis of geography and athletic ability, why not add racial diversity as a criterion for selection, asked the university.

Next came the lawyer on behalf of Allan Bakke. He began by attacking quotas. He said the Davis program used a racial quota that allowed minority students to satisfy lower standards than white students. Racial quotas, he claimed, should not be permitted under the Constitution because they grant rights on the basis of ancestry and not on the basis of individual achievement.

Bakke's lawyer asked the justices whether there would be any limit on how high the quota could go. Could it be set, he wondered, at 32, 64, or even 100? Emphasizing the color-blindness of the Constitution, he argued that quotas should be unconstitutional even when minorities benefit from them. "The equal protection clause does not expand and contract depending upon the purpose behind racial discrimination." It was not fair, according to this argument, for Bakke to be moved to the back of the line because he was white.

Bakke's lawyer also pointed out that not all minority students are disadvantaged. There could be affirmative action programs that considered hardships faced by applicants, without using race itself as the measure for admissions.

The U.S. government's position was presented last to the justices. The solicitor general pointed out that Congress and the executive have permitted race to be taken into account in other matters. For example, special scholarships were offered for minorities, loans were reserved for minority-owned businesses, and companies with government contracts were required to hire minorities. These were temporary but necessary steps, he argued, to achieve racial equality.

Next, he maintained that the Fourteenth Amendment protects all persons without regard to race, but the lingering consequences of past discrimination must be addressed. As he put it: "The Fourteenth Amendment should not only require equality of treatment, but should also permit persons who were held back to be brought up to the starting line where the opportunity for equality will be meaningful."

Finally, the government's lawyer maintained that color-sensitive programs were fair. Minority students with lower test scores and grade-point averages, he said, may have as much potential to be physicians as whites with higher scores. The minority students have demonstrated the determination and ability to overcome hurdles not faced by whites.

The justices listened and questioned for two hours. Then they retired for months to reach a decision. Unable to reach agreement, they presented sharply divided opinions. It took 154 pages to express them.

Four of the justices decided the case on narrow grounds. They did not think the case required a decision based on the Constitution. For them, the laws passed by Congress were sufficient basis for deciding the Bakke case. In the opinion of these four justices, the university as a recipient of federal funds had violated the Civil Rights Act of 1964. That law prohibited programs receiving federal funds from excluding anyone on account of race. As one justice stated, "Race cannot be the basis of excluding anyone from participation in a federally funded program." They believed that the special admissions program was unlawful and they wanted Bakke admitted to the medical school at Davis.

Another four justices voted to uphold the Davis admissions program. They concluded that it violated neither the 1964 Civil Rights Act nor the Fourteenth Amendment to the Constitution. In their opinion, the California Supreme Court should be reversed. To support this view, one of the justices said: "In order to get beyond racism, we must first take account of race. There is no other way. In order to treat some persons equally, we must treat them differently. We cannot—we dare not—let the Equal Protection Clause perpetrate racial supremacy."

Four justices do not make a majority on the Supreme Court. A majority of justices is required for the Court to render a decision in a case. The ninth justice, Lewis Powell, broke the deadlock. On the issue of Bakke's admission, he voted with the first four justices. On the issue of race-conscious affirmative action he voted with the second four justices. The compromise decision ordered Bakke admitted to the Davis medical school but allowed the university to consider race as a factor for admissions.

According to the decision, colleges and universities were permitted to take an applicant's race into account as long as they did not establish a rigid racial quota. What justified the use of race in college admissions, according to Justice Powell, was educational diversity. He claimed that minorities had something to contribute to higher education. Said the justice, "It is not too much to say that the nation's future depends upon leaders trained through wide exposure to the ideas and mores of students as diverse as this nation of many peoples."

Six years after first applying to the University of California Medical School at Davis, Allan Bakke was admitted. He graduated and became a physician.

The major sources for this story were:

Dreyfuss, Joel. *The Bakke Case: The Politics of Inequality*. New York: Harcourt Brace Jovanovich, 1979.

Eastland, Terry. *Counting by Race: Equality from the Founding Fathers to Bakke and Weber*. New York: Basic Books, 1979.

Regents of the University of California v. *Allan Bakke*. 438 U.S. 265 (1978).

Wilkinson, J. Harvie, III. *From Brown to Bakke*. New York: Oxford University Press, 1979.

ACTIVITIES FOR "AFFIRMATIVE OR NEGATIVE"

Write all answers on a separate sheet of paper.

Historical Understanding

Answer briefly:

1. What purpose did the post–Civil War amendments to the Constitution have in common?

2. At the turn of the century, what were two kinds of discrimination against blacks in the South?

3. How was the U.S. Supreme Court precedent in *Plessy* v. *Ferguson* (1896) changed by its decision in *Brown* v. *Board of Education* (1954)?

4. What were two events during the civil rights movement in which Martin Luther King was a leader?

5. What were three provisions of civil rights laws passed by Congress during the 1960s?

6. What is the aim of *affirmative action*?

Reviewing the Facts of the Case

Answer briefly:

1. Briefly describe the special admissions program at the medical school of the University of California at Davis.

2. What were Allan Bakke's main arguments against the Davis special admissions program?

3. What were the major arguments of the university in defense of its special admissions program?

4. What were two points made before the Supreme Court by the solicitor general of the United States in the Bakke case?

5. How did Justice Powell strike a compromise in the Bakke decision?

Analyzing Ethical Issues

Many discrimination cases came before the courts as a result of the civil rights laws of the 1960s. These cases involved discrimination on account of age, sex, national origin, race, and religion. Some of these cases presented situations in schools, neighborhoods, or work places in which there were few or no minorities. The courts had to determine if minorities had been excluded intentionally. In other words, was there *intent to discriminate*? Such intent was sometimes not found. At the medical school of the University of California at Davis, for example, there were few minority students but no intent to exclude them.

Could each situation listed below have occurred if there had been no intent to discriminate? Why or why not? What evidence would establish an intent to discriminate? Answer these questions for each of the situations. For example:

A college basketball team is all black.

Yes, the team could have been all black if blacks were the only or best players who tried out.

Evidence of an outstanding white player who tried out but did not make the team would probably establish intent to discriminate.

1. An elementary school is all white.

2. Only Jewish people live in a large apartment building.

3. All flight attendants working for an airline are female.

4. A trade union has no Hispanic members.

5. A public transportation system has no handicapped riders.

6. A fast-food restaurant has only teenage employees.

Expressing Your Reasoning

1. Should the medical school at the University of California–Davis have established a special admissions program for disadvantaged minority applicants? Why or why not?

2. Affirmative action programs have been adopted in a variety of places. State whether or not you think each of the following plans is fair. Present reasons for your positions.

   a. To correct admitted past discrimination against blacks, the Detroit Police Department adopted a plan to promote equal numbers of black and white officers. The plan involves two separate lists, one for black officers and the other for white. Promotions to lieutenant are made alternately from the two lists. The plan will continue until one-half of the police lieutenants are black. Blacks make up 63 percent of Detroit residents.

   b. Dade County, Florida, set aside 10 percent of its public works contracts for minority-owned firms. Blacks make up 17 percent of the Dade County population. At the time the new plan took effect, less than 1 percent of county construction contracts were with black-owned firms.

c. In 1974, the Kaiser Aluminum Company and the United Steelworkers of America voluntarily agreed to a plan. It was designed to increase the number of black workers in skilled positions at the Kaiser plant in Gramercy, Louisiana. Kaiser had recruited minority applicants for skilled jobs since the plant opened, but few applied. Under the plan there was a training program for unskilled Kaiser workers. Fifty percent of the training positions went to blacks and 50 percent to whites. Some of the black workers selected had less seniority (years of experience) than some of the whites rejected. The plan was to continue until the percentage of blacks in the skilled work force was roughly equal to the percentage of blacks in the work force of the surrounding area.

3. Allan Bakke was rejected by some medical schools because of his age. Was this fair? Write a short essay stating your position. In your essay, explain your view of when, if ever, it would be fair to treat people differently because of their age. Cite specific examples, and present reasons for your position.

4. *Seeking Additional Information.* In making decisions about such questions as those above, we often feel we need more information before we are satisfied with our judgments. Choose one of the above questions about which you would want more information than is presented in the story. What additional information would you want? Why would that information help you make a more satisfactory decision?

King to Pawn

IRANIAN HOSTAGE CRISIS

President Carter (left) Toasting the Shah of Iran

"Death to Carter!" "Death to the Shah!" "Death to America!"

It was 1979 in Tehran, the capital city of Iran. Day after day tens of thousands of frenzied Iranians marched past the U.S. embassy chanting slogans of hatred. The daily demonstrations of Iranian loathing of the United States were dramatic evidence of the emotional intensity surrounding one of the most complicated problems faced by the United States in this century.

On a drizzly Sunday morning, November 4, 1979, the words of hatred turned into action. Hundreds of young Iranians, many of them university students, scaled the walls encircling the sprawling U.S. embassy. The 66 Americans working there were captured, blindfolded, and tied up. Some were beaten. The militant Iranians announced that they would hold the Americans hostage until the United States met their demands. These demands would cause Jimmy Carter the most anguishing times of his presidency.

The forces that led to the hostage crisis had been building for decades. They were forces that resulted in a bloody revolution overthrowing the shah of Iran, a man who had held power for 37 years. They were also forces that most Americans, including top government officials, could not understand.

It is especially difficult for Americans, and most citizens of Western nations, to understand the power of religion in Iranian life and politics. There are many different religions in Iran, but the vast majority of the people, about 90 percent of the population, are Shiite Moslems, members of a branch of the Islamic faith. Speaking from their mosques, religious leaders have a strong hold over the lives of their followers. One of the most powerful religious leaders, the Ayatollah Khomeini, played a key role in the Iranian revolution and the hostage crisis.

Another key actor in mid-century Iranian history was Shah Reza Pahlavi, the "King of Kings," who ruled Iran from the Peacock throne. Early during World War II, the Iranian government was developing close relations with Nazi Germany. Fearing that Iran would allow Germany to control the strategically vital Persian Gulf, England and the Soviet Union invaded. The Iranian government was overthrown and the shah placed in power. After the war, the British withdrew, but the Russians seemed determined to remain. Finally, after intense pressure from the United States, the Soviet troops were withdrawn. Thereafter, the shah intended to develop close relations with the United States.

As the years passed, the shah became one of the most powerful rulers in the world and one of America's most important allies. The United States wanted friendly relations with Iran. Iran, a major oil-producing country, borders the Persian Gulf. Much of the world's oil supply passes through the gulf. If Iran interfered with the flow of oil, it would cause major problems in the industrial nations of the world. U.S. leaders have long feared what might happen if the Soviets were in a position to control the gulf. Since Iran stands between the Soviet Union and the gulf, a strong, friendly Iran would help keep the Soviets from gaining control. In addition to its strategic location, Iran was also economically important to the United States as a major trading partner. Billions of dollars of U.S. goods and military equipment were sold to the shah. Iranian oil was exported to the United States.

Many groups in Iran opposed the shah, and his grasp on power was not always secure. In the early 1950s he was driven from power and replaced by a new leader. U.S. officials were convinced the new leader planned to develop friendly relations with the Soviet Union and to disrupt the oil trade. In 1953, the Central Intelligence Agency (CIA) aided pro-shah forces in Iran, and the shah was returned to power. It is possible that the shah might have recovered his throne without CIA help, but many Iranians became convinced that the shah regained power only because of U.S. intervention. Many of those who hated the shah also hated the United States.

Having regained power, the shah was determined to hold it. In 1957 he created SAVAK, a type of secret police force. SAVAK worked to eliminate political opposition to the shah. Its tactics could be brutal. Real and suspected enemies of the shah were often tortured and killed. Many Iranians have reported that members of their families disappeared, presumably eliminated by SAVAK. It was claimed that the CIA helped train the members of SAVAK.

The shah was interested in more than simply holding power. He had many ideas of ways to improve life in Iran. He wanted his nation to become more like Western industrial nations. Factories were built, highways constructed, television and other forms of electronic communications were established. In 1963 he began what is known as the "White Revolution." Among the changes brought by the revolution was an effort to break up large landholdings so that more people could own property. He also ruled that women could have the right to vote.

The shah's efforts to change Iran were vigorously opposed by many religious leaders. They condemned his policies on women's rights. They were disgusted with the influx of foreigners and with the night-clubs and gambling casinos the shah permitted to operate.

Major riots in opposition to the shah and his White Revolution occurred in the streets of Tehran and elsewhere. The ayatollah was a major leader of the religious opposition to the shah and active in encouraging the rioting. Khomeini was arrested and sent out of the country. Years later he would return in triumph.

The shah's efforts to change Iranian life brought continuing controversy. Anti-shah demonstrations and riots became more frequent, as did bloody clashes with the police. From outside the country, the Ayatollah Khomeini called for the overthrow of the shah and a return to traditional Islamic ways. Tape recordings of the ayatollah's speeches were smuggled into Iran, and his followers listened intently to his messages.

U.S. leaders continued to support the shah. They did not understand the degree to which his reign was threatened. They also did not realize how much hatred there was for the United States among the anti-shah forces.

In December 1977, President Jimmy Carter visited the shah. At an elegant New Year's Eve dinner he toasted the monarch. He praised the shah as a great leader who was loved and respected by his people. In closing the president said, "There is no leader with whom I have a deeper sense of personal gratitude and personal friendship." The president's speech reinforced the belief that the United States would be unwavering in its support of the shah.

Neither the shah nor SAVAK could restrain the revolutionary feelings sweeping Iran. Demonstrations and riots continued even though hundreds of people were killed by the police. The lives of Americans and other foreigners were threatened. Mobs attacked banks, night clubs, and other symbols of foreign influence in Iran. Police stations were overrun. Workers went on strike. Through it all came messages from the ayatollah encouraging the revolution. He spoke of the evil influence of the United States. He called the United States the "great satan" of the world. He said proper religious authority must be established in Iran.

It became clear that the shah could no longer rule. On January 16, 1979, the shah and his family left Iran. He claimed he was taking a vacation, but he would never return. Now, who would govern Iran?

The shah had appointed a new government before he left, but it was unable to establish firm control. On February 1, the Ayatollah Khomeini returned to Iran. Hundreds of thousands cheered his arrival. An intense power struggle began.

The revolutionary forces had been united in their opposition to the shah and their hatred of the United States. They were not united, however, in their opinions about how Iran should be ruled once the shah was gone. The ayatollah had a devoted following, but not all revolutionary groups wanted a government based on his strict religious beliefs.

The 78-year-old ayatollah formed his own government. For a time there were two governments claiming the right to control Iran. It was not clear who had the right or the power to govern. Various groups continued to compete for power and street violence was common in Iran.

The United States had ordered most of its employees home, but a small staff remained at the embassy in Tehran. In February the embassy was attacked, and the workers taken prisoner. Representatives of the ayatollah persuaded the mob to release the prisoners and to leave the embassy. The brief but frightening incident was a preview of what was to come in November.

The ayatollah's government worked to establish control. Hundreds of people were executed without fair trials. Many had been members of SAVAK, others were charged with vague crimes such as "war against God," or "corruption on earth." The ayatollah, convinced that he spoke for God, gave many orders. Music and dancing were forbidden. Nightclubs were closed. Women were ordered to wear the *chador*, a full-length traditional Islamic garment. Strict censorship was placed on newspapers and other forms of mass communication. In his speeches the ayatollah continued to condemn the shah and the United States—"the moral corrupter of the world."

The shah was a man without a country. The king became a pawn in a diplomatic chess game. Many nations, once friendly with the shah, refused to admit him. They feared their citizens in Iran might be attacked or that vital oil supplies would be shut off. In addition, citizens in many countries believed the shah to be a brutal dictator and did not want their governments to offer him refuge. For a time the shah stayed in Egypt, Mexico, and elsewhere. He knew that many in the United States would not welcome him. There had been many anti-shah demonstrations in the United States.

For years the shah had been suffering from cancer, but he kept his illness secret from the public. While in Mexico his condition worsened. Some medical experts said the shah's disease could only be properly treated in the United States. Would the U.S. government allow the shah to enter the country?

President Carter discussed the shah's difficulties with his advisors. Some prominent Americans had urged the president to admit the shah for treatment. They argued that the shah had long been a faithful ally of the United States and deserved to be well treated. The president initially opposed allowing the shah to enter but changed his mind after being convinced of the seriousness of the shah's illness. The president feared trouble. He asked his advisors who had recommended admitting the shah, "What are you guys going to advise me to do if they overrun our embassy and take our people hostage?"

On October 22, 1979, the shah was flown to New York City for treatment. On November 4, the U.S. embassy in Tehran was overrun and its occupants taken hostage. The captors announced that the hostages would not be released unless the shah was returned to Iran to stand trial for his alleged crimes.

The embassy takeover, a major violation of diplomatic law, was condemned by virtually every nation in the world. In effect Iran had become an international outlaw. In Iran, however, the takeover was a cause for great celebration. Hundreds of thousands marched past the embassy chanting their support for the radicals who had seized it. The ayatollah praised the radicals. The embassy was called a "nest of spies," and the hostages were to be placed on trial as spies. The United States was told that the hostages would be immediately killed if an effort was made to rescue them by force.

President Carter and most of the American people were outraged by the takeover. A majority of Americans favored military action against Iran if any of the hostages were hurt. Polls also showed that people favored the admittance of the shah for medical treatment but opposed allowing him to remain permanently. A majority of Americans rejected the idea of returning the shah to Iran in exchange for the hostages, although about 30 percent favored the idea. The president would not trade the shah for the hostages, but he did not want him to remain in the United States. It was arranged for the shah to move to Panama.

Some Iranians living in the United States supported the ayatollah. A group of them requested a permit to hold a pro-Khomeini demonstration in front of the White House. Many groups were routinely given permits to demonstrate. This time, however, the president ordered that no permit be given. In part he feared the demonstrators would be attacked by angry Americans. If such an attack occurred, the president feared the hostages might be hurt or killed in retaliation.

The president began what would be a long, painful, and frustrating process of trying to gain release of the hostages. The ayatollah had ordered that no Iranian officials speak to Americans. Behind the scenes, however, third parties attempted to negotiate with some Iranian officials. Time and time again the secret negotiations led to arrangements for the hostages' release, but time and time again the deals fell through at the last moment.

The United Nations condemned Iran, but still the hostages were held. The International Court ordered the hostages to be released, but still they were held. No one could persuade the ayatollah or the radicals to release the hostages.

President Carter ordered an end to oil imports from Iran. He ordered that military supplies scheduled for delivery to Iran not be sent. He ordered that all Iranian money in U.S. banks be frozen. This meant that Iran could not withdraw any of its billions of dollars deposited in U.S. banks. Still the hostages remained captive.

Months passed. Secret negotiations continued to fail. Political and economic pressure, although hurting Iran, could not secure the hostages' release. Finally the president made a fateful decision. Since the beginning of the hostage crisis, military experts had been developing a plan for the rescue of the hostages. From a secret base in the Iranian desert, helicopters would be flown to the embassy. Specially trained troops would storm the embassy, surprise the captors, and release the hostages. It was a risky plan. It was possible that hostages would be killed. The president became convinced that all efforts to free the hostages had been made and failed. He ordered the rescue mission to be attempted.

Late in April 1980, the rescue raid was attempted. It failed. Sandstorms in the desert disabled some of the helicopters and, in a fiery crash, eight American servicemen were killed. A deeply saddened President Carter announced the failure of the secret mission.

Many feared the hostages might be killed because of the attempted military rescue, but they were not. Instead the hostages were removed from the embassy to secret locations throughout Iran.

The hostage crisis dragged on. Various factors led to its final resolution. In July the shah died. Demands for his return were now pointless. In September, Iran went to war with its neighbor Iraq. Money was needed to fight the war. The release of the approximately $8 billion frozen in U.S. banks could help pay the costs of war. The delicate secret negotiations succeeded at last.

On January 20, 1981, 444 days after their capture, the hostages were released in exchange for the frozen Iranian dollars. It was the day of Ronald Reagan's inauguration as president. In part because of his inability to solve the hostage crisis sooner, Jimmy Carter had failed in his attempt to be reelected.

The major sources for this story were:

Jordan, Hamilton. *Crisis: The Last Year of the Carter Presidency.* New York: G. P. Putnam's Sons, 1982.

McFadden, Robert D., Treaster, Joseph B., Carroll, Maurice. *No Hiding Place.* New York: Times Books, 1981.

Salinger, Pierre. *America Held Hostage: The Secret Negotiations.* Garden City, N.Y.: Doubleday, 1981.

Stempel, John D. *Inside the Iranian Revolution.* Bloomington, Ind.: Indiana University Press, 1981.

Time (January 7, 1980).

ACTIVITIES FOR "KING TO PAWN"

Write all answers on a separate sheet of paper.

Historical Understanding

Answer briefly:

1. How did Shah Reza Pahlavi originally come to power in Iran?

2. What were two reasons that a stable, friendly Iran was believed important for U.S. interests?

3. How did the United Nations, the International Court, and most nations of the world react to the embassy takeover?

4. Why were many nations unwilling to admit the shah after he left Iran?

Reviewing the Facts of the Case

Answer briefly:

1. What did the militant Iranians demand before they would release the hostages?

2. Why did many Iranians despise the United States?

3. Why did Iranian religious leaders oppose the shah's attempts to change Iran?

4. How did Ayatollah Khomeini continue to influence events in Iran after he was expelled from the country?

5. What were three policies enacted by the ayatollah when he gained power in Iran?

6. How did President Jimmy Carter respond to the pro-Khomeini Iranians' request for a permit to demonstrate in front of the White House?

7. What were three things President Carter did to try to gain the release of the hostages?

Analyzing Ethical Issues

The following values are involved in this story:

AUTHORITY: a value concerning what rules or people should be obeyed and the consequences for disobedience

PROPERTY: a value concerning what people should be allowed to own and how they should be allowed to use it

LIBERTY: a value concerning what freedoms people should have and the limits that may be justifiably placed upon those freedoms

LIFE: a value concerning when, if ever, it is justifiable to threaten or take the life of another

LOYALTY: a value concerning obligations to the people, traditions, ideas, and organizations of importance in one's own life

The story describes incidents or problems in which these values are involved. Select *two* of the above values, describe an incident or problem from the story in which the value is involved, and then explain your answer. For example:

The value of authority was involved when for a time there were two governments claiming the right to rule Iran. The people had to decide which government to obey.

Expressing Your Reasoning

1. Should President Jimmy Carter have allowed Shah Reza Pahlavi into the United States for medical treatment? Why or why not?

2. While the shah was in the United States, the hostages were taken. Their captors said they would not release the hostages unless the shah was returned to Iran. Should the president have traded the shah for the hostages? Why or why not?

3. The president finally ordered that a military rescue attempt be made. Should the president have done that? Write a paragraph explaining your answer.

4. *Seeking Additional Information.* In making decisions about such questions as those above, we often feel we need more information before we are satisfied with our judgments. Choose one of the above questions about which you would want more information than is presented in the story. What additional information would you like? Why would that information help you make a more satisfactory decision?